A SHORT HISTORY
OF ROMAN LAW

A SHORT HISTORY
OF ROMAN LAW

Olga Tellegen-Couperus

London and New York

First published in Dutch in 1990 by Kluwer

Revised English language edition first published 1993
by Routledge
11 New Fetter Lane, London EC4P 4EE

Simultaneously published in the USA and Canada
by Routledge
29 West 35th Street, New York, NY 10001

Phototypeset by Intype, London

Printed in Great Britain by Clays Ltd, St. Ives plc.

British Library Cataloguing in Publication Data
Tellegen-Couperus, Olga
Short History of Roman Law
I. Title   II. McNab, Sheila
343.7

Library of Congress Cataloging in Publication Data
Tellegen-Couperus, O. E. (Olga Eveline)
[Korte geschiedenis van het Romeinse recht. English]
A short history of Roman law / Olga Tellegen-Couperus.
p.   cm.
Includes bibliographical references and index.
1. Roman law—History. I. Title.
KJA147.T4513   1993
340.5'4—dc20   92–21949

ISBN 0–415–7250–6 ISBN 0–415–07251–4 (pbk)

CONTENTS

MAPS

PREFACE

This historical introduction to Roman law is written primarily for law students whose course includes legal history. It may also be useful to classicists and historians. Nowadays no lecturer dare assume that law students have a thorough knowledge of classical antiquity. I have therefore given considerable attention to the socio-economic and political factors that influenced the development of the law.

This book was written originally as a textbook for Dutch law students and has been used successfully for a number of years now. Professor P. B. H. Birks (All Souls, Oxford) suggested that an English version of the text might be useful in law courses at universities in the English-speaking world.

As I read through the English translation I became more critical of the original text and decided that certain points needed to be clarified and adapted. In particular the section on the formulary procedure seemed to require more detailed treatment since it played a crucial role in the development of Roman law. I have also compiled some explanatory notes for the English version and I refer to sources and background literature. Because the text is now intended for English-speaking countries I have referred mainly to literature written in English. As a basis for ancient history I have used *A History of Rome* by M. Cary and H.H. Scullard (Macmillan, 1975); for more detailed information about the juridical elements I always refer to *A Historical Introduction to the Study of Roman Law* by H. Jolowicz and B. Nicholas (Cambridge University Press, 1972), but the information given in these books has been supplemented by references to more recent literature.

This work could not have been completed without the help of

a number of people. In particular I should like to thank Peter Birks for encouraging me to publish an English version and Sheila McNab (Utrecht University) for actually producing it. I think she has succeeded in giving an accurate and readable English rendering, while preserving the character of the original text. As a result of our discussions some of the English text is no doubt clearer than the Dutch original. I am indebted to the Law Faculty and the Department of Legal History of Tilburg University for providing the facilities for the preparation of the final version; Marianne Stolp, secretary to the Department of Legal History, meticulously computerised most of the manuscript. Last but not least I am very grateful to my husband, Jan Willem, who lectures in law at Utrecht University. Due to his detailed knowledge and thorough understanding of the subject matter he was able to give me many valuable suggestions.

ABBREVIATIONS

ANRW   *Aufstieg und Niedergang der römischen Welt.* Geschichte und Kultur Roms im Spiegel der neueren Forschung, Berlin and New York, de Gruyter, 1972.

C.   Codex Iustiniani.

C.Th.   Codex Theodosianus.

D.   Digesta.

F.V.   Fragmenta Vaticana, in: *FIRA* II, pp. 461–540.

FIRA   *Fontes iuris romani anteiustiniani* I, *Leges*, ed. S. Riccobono, Florence, Barbèra, 1941 (reprinted 1968); II, *Auctores*, I. Baviera and I. Furlani (eds), Florence, Barbèra, 1940 (reprinted 1964); III, *Negotia*, ed. V. Arangio-Ruiz, Florence, Barbèra, 1943 (reprinted with appendix 1968).

G.E.   Gai Institutionum Epitome, in: *FIRA* II, pp. 229–57.

Inst.   *Gai Institutiones*, M. David and H.L.W. Nelson (eds), Leiden, Brill, 1948.

RIDA   *Revue Internationale des Droits de l'Antiquité*, Brussels. 1st series since 1948, now 3rd series (since 1954).

SZ   *Zeitschrift der Savigny Stiftung für Rechtsgeschichte*, romanistische Abteilung, Weimar.

U.E.   Tituli ex corpore Ulpiani, in: *FIRA* II, pp. 261–301.

INTRODUCTION

The history of Roman law falls into two distinct periods. Roman law originated and developed in classical antiquity and culminated with the legislation of Justinian in the sixth century. The second period, although beginning in the sixth century, did not really become important until the end of the eleventh century. Then it was 'rediscovered' and began to be studied in the whole of western Europe.

This book concentrates on Roman law in classical Antiquity and covers a period of more than a thousand years. Since this period is really too long to deal with as a whole, it has been divided into a number of shorter periods. However, although Roman law went through many stages of development the stages cannot always be clearly distinguished. The reason is that law generally develops very gradually. In this survey emphasis is on the political structure of the Roman empire. This is the field that scholars have studied the most thoroughly and therefore it provides a suitable framework for the history of law as presented in this book. For each period there is first a brief survey of the sources of our knowledge, of the territory under Roman rule and of the socio-economic situation at the time. Then the political development is discussed. Nearly all these factors influence the way in which law is formed. The last chapter of each part deals with the development of the law during the period in question.

Part I

FROM MONARCHY TO EARLY REPUBLIC (–367 BC)

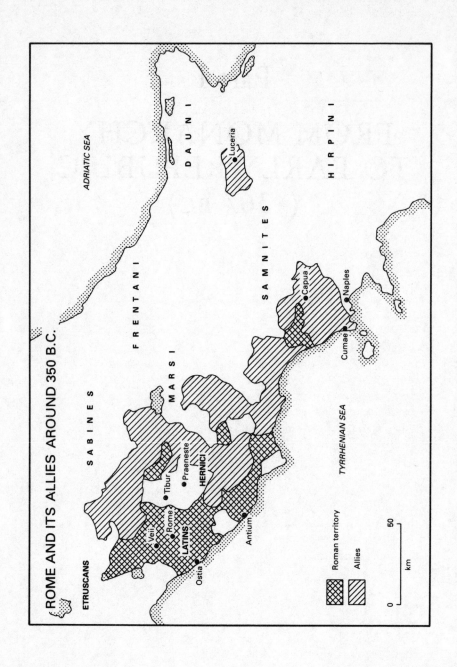

ROME AND ITS ALLIES AROUND 350 B.C.

ETRUSCANS

SABINES

ADRIATIC SEA

DAUNI

• Luceria

FRENTANI

MARSI

HIRPINI

SAMNITES

• Veii
Tibur •
Praeneste •
HERNICI
• Rome
LATINS
Ostia •
• Antium

Capua •
• Naples
Cumae •

TYRRHENIAN SEA

Roman territory

Allies

0   50
km

1

FROM MONARCHY TO EARLY REPUBLIC: GENERAL OUTLINE

1.1. THE SOURCES

Very little factual information is available about the earliest period of Roman history. The oldest historical studies that have survived date from the beginning of the first century AD. The authors of these studies, e.g. Livy, Plutarch and Dionysius of Halicarnassus, made use of the works of older historians who lived in the third to the first centuries BC and described the history of Rome year by year (the so-called annalists). However, the sections of their works relating to the early period of Rome's history were far from reliable. Although the annalists had access to a wealth of source material for the period dating from 387 BC up to their own day, there were practically no written documents left for the period before that year. These documents were lost in 387 BC when Rome was conquered and set on fire by the Celts. In order to fill the gaps in the source material the annalists made use of legends; although these legends may have been based partly on history they were certainly not historically reliable. The annalists elaborated these legends using their imagination and sometimes altered the chronological order of the events. Information about the founding of Rome and its early history therefore has always to be checked against information obtained with the help of other disciplines such as archaeology and linguistics.

Our knowledge of the oldest form of Roman law is also based on sources of later date. These sources include some of the literary sources mentioned above as well as some juridical sources such as the Enchiridion of Pomponius and the Institutes of Gaius, both dating from the second century AD; legal historians have doubts about the reliability of these sources as well, but nowadays there

3

is a tendency for some Romanists to regard them as useful nevertheless.

1.2. THE TERRITORY

As from 1000 BC various tribes came from the Danube basin and began to settle on the Italian peninsula. Some of them were to have a special influence on the founding and development of Rome. They were Indo-European tribes who were known collectively as Italians; two of these Italian tribes, the Latins and the Sabines, settled in Latium on the left bank of the Tiber[1]. They lived in a number of small settlements and engaged in agriculture and cattle-rearing. Some of these settlements were on the hills in the area where Rome was built later on. In the course of the seventh century BC the inhabitants of these hill-settlements formed an alliance and they gradually obtained a powerful position in Latium. It was easy to cross the Tiber at this spot, so the alliance was able to control the trade between the left bank of the Tiber and the Etruscans on the right bank. It was the Etruscans who ultimately founded Rome.

Until recently it was assumed that the Etruscans came to Italy from Asia Minor about 900–800 BC and settled initially on the coast of modern Tuscany. The latest view, however, is that they settled in Italy much earlier than this and that they formed a complex of eastern, continental and indigenous elements[2]. The Etruscans differed from the Italians in many respects. Unlike Latin, Greek and Celtic, their language, Etruscan, did not belong to the Indo-European group. As a result the Etruscans were long regarded as a mysterious people, but now much more is known about them. Because the Etruscans adopted the Greek alphabet and made only slight changes, Etruscan inscriptions are easy to read. We have known the exact meaning of most of their words for several decades now. Our information about the Etruscans is therefore no longer based solely on the work of Greek and Roman historians and archaeological finds (e.g. the wall-paintings on the graves in Tarquinia and Chiusi). Recently we have also been able to consult about 10,000 inscriptions that have survived. As a result, we know that the Etruscans, unlike the Latins and the Sabines, did not live in small scattered settlements. They lived in independent city-states which formed the centre of local trade and politics. Until the fifth century BC the city-state was ruled by a king

4

and thereafter by a magistrate. Private law of the Etruscans, and particularly the law of persons, was very different from, for example, Roman private law.³ Their culture was more highly developed than that of the Latins and the Sabines. We know from archaeological finds that the Etruscans had considerable knowledge of architecture and mining and were able to install a drainage system. Like the Italian tribes the Etruscans made their living from agriculture and cattle-rearing, but they also engaged in trade; because of their superior technical knowledge they were able to develop some sort of industry which produced ceramics, materials, implements and utensils, jewellery and ornaments. The Etruscans were also fearsome pirates who plundered ships in the coastal waters of the Mediterranean. In the course of the seventh century BC the Etruscans extended their power in a south-easterly direction, to Latium and Campania, and introduced their way of life to those areas.

According to legend Rome was founded by Romulus in 753 BC; on the basis of archaeological evidence, however, it seems much more likely that Rome was founded by the Etruscans in the seventh century BC. The territory of the Latins and Sabines was of great strategic importance for the Etruscans. This was why they founded the city-state of Rome on that site. They did this in accordance with their own customs: they built temples and reservoirs, cisterns and a city wall; they drained the swamps between the hills, they organised the people into political and military units and let the city-state be governed by a king who was generally of Etruscan origin. Tradition has it that the last Etruscan king was overthrown and driven out of Rome in 509 BC. This event marked the beginning of a new era for Rome. The expansion of the Etruscans towards the south ceased and they even had to withdraw from Campania and Latium. Rome became a republic governed by a senate and magistrates.

The young republic, however, was surrounded by a number of powerful neighbours: the south of Italy was in the hands of some Greek colonies and the Etruscans still constituted a formidable force in the north. In Latium there were some other city-states besides Rome which had joined to form the Latin alliance. In 493 BC Rome came into this alliance too, as an equal partner rather than as a member. As from the end of the fifth century BC the Romans began to extend their territory. First of all they moved northwards. As a result of a war against the Etruscans (406–396

BC) Rome acquired part of Tuscany; from then onwards the Tiber no longer formed Rome's northern frontier. About this time Celtic tribes settled in the Po valley. They soon decided to extend their territory southwards; they managed to defeat the Romans, capture Rome and set it on fire (387 BC); the citadel, the Capitol, was probably the only building left standing. Finally the Celts were repulsed and they retreated northwards. Throughout the fourth century and at the beginning of the third century BC the Romans fought battles: against the Samnites (a tribe from the Apennine area), against the Latin alliance which rose in revolt, against the Etruscans and the Celts and finally against the Greek colonies in the south of Italy.

By the time these battles were over, the Romans had subjugated the tribes in central and southern Italy. This did not mean that these tribes were governed from Rome: the various tribes were more or less allowed to rule their own areas but they were made subordinate to Rome in very different ways.

1.3. THE POPULATION

1.3.1. *Familia* and *gens*

Roman society was made up of two elements, the *familia* and the *gens*. A *familia* consisted of all those persons who were in some way subject to the power of a *pater familias*.[4] This power could be based on parentage, marriage or adoption and was in principle unlimited. Religious norms imposed a certain number of constraints and the possible abuse of power by a *pater familias* was kept in check by strong social control. Within the *familia* the *pater familias* was the only person who had any rights in private law.

Being subject to the power of a *pater familias* had nothing to do with age; a person was in this position until the *pater familias* died or relinquished his power in a formal manner, e.g. by means of *emancipatio*; the person concerned was then independent and could have his own property (*sui iuris*).

Familiae with a common progenitor (even if he was a legendary figure) together founded a *gens* and had a common *gens*-name.[5] They could hold meetings and pass resolutions that were binding on the members, and they had a common cult. According to Livy (*Ab urbe condita*, 10.8.9) at first only patricians formed a *gens*, but names of old plebeian *gentes* are also mentioned in the sources. The law of the XII Tables of 449 BC contained rules on guardianship and intestate succession for the *gentes*; these rules were applied until the end of the republic. The *gentes* themselves continued to exist during the early empire, but then they no longer had any juridical function.

1.3.2. Patricians and plebeians

This early period of Roman history is characterized by the division of the population into patricians and plebeians. Nobody is quite sure how this division originated; it may have been based on ethnic differences (for instance, the plebeians were of Latin origin and the patricians were the descendants of the Sabines, or vice versa), but we have no proof and such theories can only be speculative.[6] The sources, however, do demonstrate that the plebeians were not regarded as foreigners but were Roman citizens, just like the patricians. The differences between the patricians and the plebeians were clearly visible from their respective economic and social position. The patricians formed a kind of nobility; they owned a considerable amount of land and kept cattle and slaves. They were entitled to serve as magistrates and priests and because of the voting system had a decisive influence on legislation (see section 2.2.3). The plebeians on the other hand were mainly artisans and small farmers; in times of war they had no slaves to keep their businesses running and this increased their chance of impoverishment. Furthermore, as mentioned already, they were not allowed to hold public office and, as a result of the abovementioned voting system, they had very little influence on legislation. Finally, in the law of the XII Tables it was stated that intermarriage between patricians and plebeians was forbidden.[7]

In the early years of the republic the number of impoverished plebeians increased whereas some plebeian families became wealthy and sought to have the same rights as the patricians. This gave rise to considerable tensions. In the long struggle between the orders which began about 500 BC and continued until 286 BC the differences in the rights of patricians and plebeians were gradually removed. According to tradition, in 471 BC the plebeians were granted the right to hold their own assemblies (called *concilia plebis*) and choose their own officers, called tribunes; the decisions made by these assemblies (plebiscites) applied exclusively to the plebeians. The patricians did not consider themselves bound by these decisions. The next important step was the recording of the law in writing in the XII Tables; this enabled the plebeians to become acquainted with the law and to protect themselves more effectively against patricians who, by serving as priests or magistrates, abused their power. The XII Tables will be discussed in more detail in section 3.2. Shortly after this law had come into being, a *lex Canuleia* removed the ban on intermarriage between patricians and plebeians. The *leges Liciniae Sextiae* of 367 BC opened the way for plebeians to serve in the top ranks of the magistrature and become, for instance, consuls. And finally the *lex Hortensia* of 286 BC decreed that the plebiscites were binding for all the Roman people, including patricians. The political distinction between patricians and plebeians had thus disappeared for ever; the only difference that remained was between rich and poor citizens.

1.3.3. Citizenship and *clientela*

Rome, like other city-states in antiquity, observed the personality principle: each person lived according to the law of the town to which he or she belonged. Although the Romans conquered the tribes of central and southern Italy, this did not mean that these tribes were automatically granted Roman citizenship: the various tribes retained their own form of law but were also allowed to use Roman law to a certain extent. In Rome, this situation stimulated, quite early on, a large-scale development of the phenomenon known as *clientela*.

It is not certain how the *clientela* came into being. The *clientes* may originally have been foreigners who had settled in Rome and had placed themselves under the protection of a Roman *gens*. Anyway, in the early republic it was mainly Roman citizens with a weak social and economic position (namely plebeians) who sought the protection of a Roman citizen in high office; this Roman then became their patron. In a juridical sense the *clientes* were free but they were expected to show their patron respect and loyalty and support him in his political ambitions; this meant for instance that in the *comitia* they had to vote in the same way as their patron.[8] In return a patron had to give his *clientes* the use of a piece of land or assist them in a lawsuit by giving legal advice or appearing for them in court. He was not supposed to take legal action against his *clientes* or to give evidence against them in a trial. The *clientela* phenomenon continued throughout Roman history, but from the empire onwards it played a less important role.

1.4. ECONOMY

For a long time after its foundation the city-state of Rome occupied quite a small area. About 500 BC, Rome covered an area of only 700–800 km². Agriculture and cattle-rearing were the main means of livelihood. It is not clear whether the Romans at that time were familiar with the principle of private ownership; perhaps at first only ownership of movables such as cattle and implements was possible; ownership of immovables may not have been possible until later.[9]

Because of Rome's favourable situation on the Tiber – and its proximity to the *via Salaria* – the city soon developed as a trading-centre. Until the late fourth century BC the Romans had no coinage, but instead they used pieces of bronze: prices of goods were determined by the weight of an amount of bronze. The weight was determined by a weigher (*libripens*) who weighed the bronze (*aes*) on scales (*libra*). After the introduction of coins, the procedure continued for centuries as a formality for certain legal acts such as the *emancipatio*, the making of a mancipatory will and property transfer by *mancipatio* of *res mancipi* (land in Italy, slaves and cattle); these acts were also called acts *per aes et libram*.

In this connection it should be mentioned that a written alphabet and writing were introduced in Rome about the beginning of the fifth century BC. It now became possible for the Romans to record their customs in writing (hitherto these had been handed down orally) and to draw up a deed for certain economic transactions and for last wills and testaments.

9

2

FROM MONARCHY TO EARLY REPUBLIC: THE STATE

In the period up to 367 BC Rome had two different forms of government. Until 509 BC there had been a monarchy, the political structure of which consisted of a king, a senate and an assembly. Then Rome became a republic with a political structure consisting of a senate, a magistrature and an assembly.

2.1. THE MONARCHY

It is difficult to construct an accurate picture of the period of the monarchy because it coincided with the earliest period of Roman history. The historians describing the period based their accounts largely on legends; furthermore, they were accustomed to describing the primitive institutions associated with the monarchy in terms that were appropriate for their own times but were not always applicable to the earlier periods. According to these historians the names of the first kings of Rome (Romulus, Numa Pompilius, Tullius Hostilius and Ancus Marcius) showed that they were of Latin-Sabine origin. In the historians' view the senate and the popular assembly were both involved in choosing the king. Tradition has it that the king's task was largely of a religious nature: he was the chief intermediary between the community and the gods. In the course of time he also became head of the army and was involved in settling disputes between citizens. The king performed these tasks in close conjunction with heads of the leading families.

Because Rome was so small in those days it can be assumed that the king was able to combine these various tasks and duties. It is however doubtful whether the first kings of Rome were in fact of Latin-Sabine origin. As was stated in section 1.2, Rome was not founded until the seventh century BC and the founders were Etruscans. Of the three kings of this period (Tarquinius Priscus, Servius Tullius and Tarquinius Superbus), the first and the third would seem, from their names, to be of Etruscan origin. They stimulated economic life in Rome by building large temples and by installing a drainage system in the swamps between the hills (the famous Cloaca Maxima). Servius Tullius and Tarquinius Superbus also strengthened their own positions considerably. They introduced a new kind of supreme command, the *imperium*, which gave them unlimited power over the army and some control over religious affairs and the administration of justice. According to the Roman historians it was this increase in power which made the Romans drive out Tarquinius Superbus in 509 BC and set up a republic.

Originally the senate (*senatus*, from *senes* = old) seems to have consisted of a hundred citizens who were all leading members of patrician families and were referred to as *patres*. The senators were appointed by the king. Their task was primarily to advise and support the king. If the king died the senate could wield supreme power by means of an *interregnum* until a new king was appointed. The powers of the senate were not laid down officially. The degree of influence exerted by the senate was totally dependent on how powerful a particular king was. About the time when Rome was changing over from a monarchy to a republic the number of senators was increased considerably: up to 300, it is said.

Under the monarchy the usual form of assembly was the *comitia curiata*. When the people assembled they were divided into thirty *curiae*. Originally a *curia* was based on kinship but later it was also determined by place of residence. In the assembly voting was not performed on the basis of a head-count. Voting took place in two stages: first votes were cast in the *curia*, then the votes of the *curiae* were cast in the assembly. According to the Roman historians decisions were made in the *comitia curiata* about matters of war and peace and votes were taken about laws proposed by the king; however, the information is not very reliable. The functions of the *comitia curiata* were probably mainly in the religious field and included the inauguration of the king. When two new forms of popular assembly were introduced at the end of the monarchy the *comitia curiata* continued to exist but were used for other purposes.[1]

2.2. THE REPUBLIC

It is also difficult to obtain a reliable picture of the political structure during the first few centuries of the republic; one reason is again the lack of source material; another reason is that constitutional law was based largely on customs and conventions, just as it is today. Modern legal historians have very different views on the crucial question of where power was concentrated during the early republic. Many people support the view expressed by the famous German legal historian Theodor Mommsen, namely that in 509 BC the absolute power of the king was transferred to two high-ranking magistrates and that the senate retained its advisory function.[2] However, this view is being challenged increasingly, and with good reason. It is unlikely that after overthrowing the king the leading Roman families would have wished to become dependent again on the whims of one or two persons. It is much more likely that the leading citizens, coming together in the senate, took power into their own hands and charged one or more of their fellow-senators with a specific task whenever the need arose. In the first 150 years of the republic all kinds of constructions must have been used to define these tasks; in the sources one comes across various names for magistrates, e.g. praetor, consul, *decemviri legibus scribundis* (ten men whose task was to write down the laws) and *tribuni militum consulari potestate*. The *leges Liciniae Sextiae* of 367 BC were the first to give a ruling about the magistrature, a ruling which was to remain in force for several centuries; both before and after that time supreme power was probably in the hands of the senate.[3]

2.2.1. The senate

As was stated above, according to tradition at the beginning of the republic the senate consisted of 300 citizens. They were the most highly esteemed members of society and as a symbol of their high position they were entitled to wear a tunic with a purple hem. There was no time limit for membership of the senate: senators were appointed for life. Little is known about the way in which new senators were appointed. We know from a law passed in 312 BC that one magistrate, the *censor*, usually had the task of forming the senate, but we have no idea how long the senate had been formed in this way or how it was formed earlier.

12

The senate was not only involved in legislation; it also had all kinds of administrative functions. First of all, the decisions of the assemblies concerning laws, the election of magistrates, etc., were not valid until they had been ratified by the senate. Secondly, it was customary for magistrates to consult the senate in connection with decisions that were of political significance. The senate was in charge of religious affairs in the state. In addition it supervised the *aerarium*, the treasury. Last but not least, the senate was responsible for foreign policy: the senate received envoys, could declare war and make peace. In the first centuries of the republic these activities must still have been of a fairly simple kind.

2.2.2. The magistrature

Before 367 BC there was no general ruling about the magistrature. Until then there had been various magistrates with varying degrees of power; these included the offices mentioned above, namely praetor, consul, *tribunus militum* and *decemviri*, but we know so little about these offices that they will not be considered further here. However, we do have some information about some of the other magistrates of the period.

In 443 BC two magistrates, censors, were appointed for a period of eighteen months for the purpose of performing the *census*. Their task was to estimate the wealth of individual citizens and determine the *census* class. Soldiers were recruited on the basis of the census list, which was revised every five years. The census list also provided information about how much tax each person had to pay. When it became customary to make notes on the census list about a citizen's misconduct – which could have serious consequences for the citizen (e.g. exclusion from the senate or the *comitia*) – the censor had the additional task of supervising morals. The censors were chosen by the *comitia centuriata*; for a long period it was only the patricians who were eligible for these positions. It was not until the middle of the fourth century BC that a censor was chosen from the plebeians. A censor became really important when he was involved in forming the senate; as was stated above, we do not know when this first occurred.

Two magistrates of lower rank, the quaestors, had the task of supervising the treasury. They were elected by the *comitia tributa*; up to 421 BC they were of patrician origin and after that date some were of plebeian origin. In the early days there had been only two quaestors, but from 421 BC there were four.

In connection with the magistrature, mention should also be made of the *tribuni plebis*, the tribunes of the plebeians, although originally they were not magistrates. As was mentioned above, the function came into existence during the struggle between the orders at the beginning of the fifth century BC. Via the tribunes the plebeians were able to protect themselves from patricians who abused their power. The tribunes, ten in number, were elected in the *concilium plebis*, the assembly of the plebeians; they were able to convene a meeting of the plebeians and to bring a bill before them. In the course of time they also acquired the right to veto the acts of a magistrate and the right to protect the plebeians from punishment inflicted by the (patrician) magistrates. As from 449 BC the tribunes were 'inviolable'; in other words the plebeians outlawed anyone who attacked the tribunes or hindered them in the performance of their duties. The tribunes were assisted by *aediles plebis*, who were also chosen in the *concilium plebis*. When in the course of the fourth century BC the struggle between the orders was drawing to a close the tribunes had taken part in Roman public life for such a long time that no attempt was made to abolish them. They continued to exist throughout the republic and during part of the empire, when they became one of the pillars of imperial power.

2.2.3. The assemblies of the people

As mentioned above, at the end of the monarchy the *comitia curiata* ceased to be the only form of assembly; two new forms were introduced, namely the *comitia centuriata* and the *comitia tributa*. In addition, as from 471 BC the plebeians assembled in the *concilium plebis*, a form of assembly that finally merged completely with the *comitia tributa*. A feature common to these new assemblies and the *comitia curiata* was that voting took place in two phases: first of all within the group (*curia*, *centuria* and *tribus*) and then per group in the assembly; however, these assemblies differed from each other with regard to composition, tasks and powers.

The *comitia centuriata* was originally the assembly of the Roman people in military array but they soon turned into a political assembly. The *comitia centuriata* developed after the penultimate king, Servius Tullius, had drastically reorganised the army and had adopted a new technique of waging war: in the army the emphasis was no longer on individual soldiers but on units of heavily armed foot-soldiers, known as 'hoplites'.[4] A hundred hoplites formed a century and there were 197 centuries. In order to recruit and finance these units the citizens were divided into five classes, each of which had to supply a set number of centuries: the first class consisting of the richest citizens had to supply the most; the other classes successively fewer and the citizens without any property together had to supply one century. When in the course of the fifth century BC an assembly was formed in which the centuries had a vote, the well-to-do citizens were again in the majority. Citizens therefore did not have equal political rights in the absolute sense, but, as was customary in cities in antiquity, these rights were determined by the contribution the citizens made to the defence of their city. Consequently Roman women, who were not directly involved in this task, did not have any political rights.[5]

In the *comitia centuriata* the supreme magistrates were elected and votes were cast concerning bills which the magistrates had submitted to the assembly; if the proposed law was approved, then that law (*lex*, plural: *leges*) was given the *gens*-name (or names) of the magistrate (or magistrates) who had proposed it, e.g. the *lex Valeria* was named after the *gens* of the *Valerii* and the *lex Poetelia Papiria* after the *gentes* of the *Poetelii* and the *Papirii*. From the middle of the fifth century BC the *comitia centuriata* was also involved in judging criminal cases.

The *comitia tributa* was the assembly of the citizens as residents of Rome. In this assembly votes were cast per *tribus*. The Roman people were divided into urban and rural tribes according to their place of residence. There were four urban tribes, consisting largely of people with a fairly low position in society. The twenty-one rural tribes consisted of people who owned land outside Rome and lived on it; these tribes were fairly small and most of their members enjoyed a fairly high social status. It followed therefore that in this assembly too it was the well-to-do citizens who – indirectly – swayed the vote. The tasks of the *comitia tributa* included choosing the minor magistrates, e.g. quaestors, and voting on laws that had little political importance. It is not certain whether the *comitia tributa* had always had to perform these tasks. Little is known about the origin and the history of this form of assembly either; this is partly because yet another type of assembly developed, namely the *concilium plebis*.

The *concilium plebis* was the assembly of the plebeians. Its development was one of the first results of the above-mentioned struggle between the patricians and the plebeians. Since 471 BC the Roman senate had allowed the plebeians, divided into *tribus*, to assemble to choose their leaders, the tribunes, and to discuss their own affairs. The decisions made by the *concilium plebis*, the *plebiscita*, applied only to the plebeians; the patricians were not involved in these decision-making procedures. When, during the republic, there was an extension of Roman territory and an increase in population, the number of patricians declined in relation to the number of plebeians. As a result there were fewer differences between the *concilium plebis* and the *comitia tributa* and between the decisions made by these assemblies.

3

FROM MONARCHY TO EARLY REPUBLIC: THE LAW

3.1. INTRODUCTION

The law under the monarchy and the early republic is usually referred to as archaic law because it was still in an early stage of development. In primitive Rome social life was regulated by a series of norms, the *mores maiorum*, which the Romans had inherited from their ancestors. Some of these norms were regarded as being of human origin, some as of divine origin, but there had never been any clear distinction between the two categories. Traditional Roman religion was not particularly concerned about the hereafter; it focused chiefly on the maintenance of good relations with all kinds of supernatural powers that were considered to influence human existence; for this purpose prayer meetings and sacrificial services had to be held in accordance with certain rites that were prescribed in great detail. Quite early on, however, at the end of the monarchy, the Romans began to distinguish between human and divine norms, but even then – and for the next 150 years or so – there was still some interaction between human law (*ius*) and divine law (*fas*).[1]

Any behaviour that did not violate the rules that regulated the relationship between the gods and man was considered to conform to *fas*. Any behaviour that did violate these rules was considered to be *nefas*; such behaviour could arouse the anger of the gods and the whole community could be afflicted by diseases and disasters. Behaviour that did not offend other citizens was considered to conform to *ius*; behaviour that did contravene the norms of the community was termed *iniuria*.

The link between *ius* and *fas* is evident from the fact that certain types of behaviours that were first designated as *nefas* (e.g. murder

17

or treason) were later regarded as *iniuria*, whereas certain juridical transactions which had originally come under *ius* acquired a divine dimension (e.g. *sponsio* = a solemn vow to fulfil an obligation, which had nothing to do with divine law; failure to fulfil such an obligation was regarded as particularly reprehensible because it was also interpreted as *nefas*). The concepts of *ius* and *fas* are also linked (a) by the person of the king who was the leader of the state in matters relating to both *ius* and *fas*, and (b) by the fact that during the first 150 years of the republic law-making was in the hands of the college of *pontifices* (= pontiffs). During that period the college consisted of about five patricians. For them the priesthood was not a profession; it was an honorary position which they generally held while they exercised a political function. The pontiffs have always been regarded as guardians of the law; they were primarily concerned with the application of sacral law such as the regulation of the calendar, but at the same time they supervised secular law.

Furthermore, archaic law – like the law of nearly all primitive peoples – was of a formalistic nature. To ensure that a certain transaction would have the desired result, it always had to be performed in accordance with meticulously detailed rituals, e.g. certain words had to be used or certain gestures had to be made. This formalism applied to transactions in both the sacral and the juridical field, and in the latter it applied to both legal transactions and civil procedure. A number of legal transactions which developed in this period (e.g. the *stipulatio* and the *mancipatio*) were still used in the republic and in the empire, but by then the ritual transaction had only a symbolic value.

Archaic Roman law was also called *ius Quiritium*, *Quirites* being the word by which Roman citizens were addressed in the assembly. At this time Roman law applied only to Roman citizens. This was nothing out of the ordinary: the personality principle mentioned above in section 1.3.3 prevailed in antiquity. The *ius Quiritium* was later also referred to as *ius civile* because Roman citizens came to be called *cives Romani*. However, the term *ius civile* is used with yet another meaning. In this early period law was formed in various ways: by custom, legislation, administration of justice and interpretation of the law that had developed in this way. Because Roman citizens were always involved in this development all these rules were referred to collectively as *ius civile*. The development of law by custom will not be considered here; legislation, administration of justice and interpretation will be discussed below.

3.2. LEGISLATION

According to Pomponius and other authors, already under the monarchy the senate and the people's assembly had been allowed to vote on laws that had been proposed by the king. These authors maintain that these so-called *leges regiae* were collected and written down at the end of the monarchy by a *pontifex maximus*, Sextus Papirius. However, it is very likely that the authors in question took it for granted that laws were made under the monarchy in more or less the same way as in their own time, and therefore their information is not very reliable. From the few fragments that remain of the *leges regiae* it is evident that they were not real laws but were pronouncements made by the king, in which he established certain norms in the religious/juridical field. It is possible that these pronouncements were made known to the people during an assembly and that the relevant texts were stored in the pontifical archives. The fragments that have come down to us – if they are authentic, that is – show that the religious and juridical elements were still very closely linked. According to Plutarch, for instance, Romulus declared that anyone who sold his wife should be sacrificed to the gods of the underworld (*Romulus*, 22.3–4).

The first important piece of legislation in the early republic is the Law of the XII Tables mentioned above (section 1.3.2), which dates from the middle of the fifth century BC. With regard to this law too there is a remarkable difference between what the historians say and what, in all probability, actually happened. Tradition has it that in 462 BC the plebeian tribune C. Terentilius Arsa proposed that the law should be written down in order to prevent it from being applied discriminately by the patrician magistrates. The plebeians struggled for eight years before the patricians gave in and sent a delegation to Athens to copy out the laws of Solon, and to other Greek cities to find out about their legislation. In 451 BC ten citizens were chosen to record the laws (*decemviri legibus scribundis*). They were given supreme political power (*imperium*) for the period in which they performed this task and simultaneously the powers of the magistrates were curtailed. In the following year, 450 BC, the *decemviri* produced a copy of the laws on ten *tabulae* (tables/tablets) but it was regarded as unsatisfactory, particularly by the plebeians. A second decemvirate is said to have added two further tablets in 449 BC. Then the twelve tables were finally approved by the people's assembly, so we are told.

The account of this part of Roman history, however, contains a number of anachronisms and inaccuracies. As a result legal historians in the early part of this century reached very different conclusions about the origin and character of the XII Tables. Nowadays it is generally assumed that (a) in 451 BC, after a number of years of conflict between the patricians and the plebeians, ten patricians were chosen to produce a written code of customary law – and particularly of the most controversial points – and that (b) this decemvirate temporarily took upon itself the leading functions in Rome. It is considered unlikely that there was a second decemvirate. Furthermore, the question of Greek influence on the XII Tables is still much discussed; no one believes any more that a delegation was sent to Greece, but some think that it may have visited Greek towns in the south of Italy. The XII Tables do have some points in common with the laws of Solon, but these are almost exclusively matters of detail.[2] It is generally considered unlikely that the XII Tables were approved by the *comitia curiata*; this assembly did not acquire legislative power until 449 BC. The decemvirate probably formulated this law without it being voted upon by the people. The XII Tables seem to be correctly dated. This can be concluded, for example, from the fact that the law mentions that the Tiber is the boundary of Rome – which was the case until the end of the fifth century BC. The purpose of codification was not, as one might think, to achieve complete equality in law for patricians and plebeians; the first step in that direction was the lifting of the ban on marriage between the two orders in 445 BC. It was not until 367 BC that plebeians could be elected as consuls.

The original text of the XII Tables has not been preserved. The tables, which according to Livy were made of bronze, according to Pomponius were made of ivory and according to modern authors were made of wood, stood in the forum.[3] They were probably destroyed when Rome was set on fire by the Celts in 387 BC. Our knowledge of the contents is based on various juridical and literary sources, the oldest of which date from the late republic. However, the authors concerned, like Cicero, Gaius and

Aulus Gellius, did not reproduce the contents in their entirety. They simply reproduced fragments that were relevant to their arguments, using a modernised form of Latin. Therefore we do not know how much of the text is missing and we do not know in what order the original clauses were arranged. The nineteenth-century reconstruction which was made on the basis of the fragments that have survived and which still underlies the modern editions of the sources of archaic Roman law can be little more than a hypothesis.[4]

The fragments of the Law of the XII Tables which have survived show that its provisions related to the whole area of legal order at the time. According to Livy (*Ab urbe condita*, 3.34.6), the XII Tables were 'the source of all public and civil law', but that was probably an exaggeration: nearly all surviving fragments relate to civil law and particularly to civil procedure (tables 1–8); only two provisions relate to constitutional law (e.g. table 9.1.2 on the prohibition of privileges) and some provisions concern sacral law (e.g. table 10 which prescribes rules for burial). Furthermore, the actual legal principles underlying the clauses relating to civil law were simply assumed and only certain points were covered in the legislation. To what extent do the clauses of the XII Tables restate existing customary law and to what extent do they represent innovations? A large number of clauses probably incorporated norms that already existed; but the law must have been adapted in those areas where social life had changed. A *pater familias*, for example, could acquire greater independence after the *gentes* had lost most of their social function; in table 5.3 the *pater familias* was given the power to dispose of his property by means of a will. In criminal law the *talio* was abolished for some crimes and replaced by a system of fixed penalties (e.g. table 8.3 relating to penalties for causing hurt or injury to another person).

The XII Tables remained relevant for a long period. Even in the second century AD Gaius wrote a commentary on them and in the sixth century some fragments of this commentary have been included in the Digest of Justinian.

3.3. CIVIL PROCEDURE

In the course of its history Roman law has known three forms of civil procedure: the *legis actiones*, the formulary system and the *cognitio extraordinaria*. The periods in which these types of procedures were in use overlap to a certain extent; the *legis actiones* were generally used during the republic, the formulary system was in use from the second century BC to the third century AD and the *cognitio extraordinaria* was used in the empire.

The *legis actiones* (literally, actions based on the law) is the oldest known form of lawsuit. It was conducted orally and was divided into two phases. The first phase (*in iure*) originally took place before a pontiff; he decided whether the parties could take legal action, and, if so, in what manner; after the *leges Liciniae Sextiae* were passed in 367 BC his task was entrusted to a magistrate, namely the praetor.[5] In the second phase (*apud iudicem*) the evidence was presented to the *iudex* who pronounced his verdict. The *iudex* was a citizen appointed as judge by both the pontiff (or praetor) and the parties concerned. No one knows for certain why the proceedings were split into two sections. A possible explanation is that in early Rome the evidence was often obtained with the help of irrational, supernatural methods such as ordeal or the taking of *auspicia* by observing the flight of birds. During the monarchy the king would probably have been responsible for deciding which method would be used to obtain evidence and arrive at the verdict; during the republic this task was probably performed by a *iudex*; the two-phase proceedings possibly developed as a result of this background. For a long time the 'state' exerted only a very minor influence. During the republic a new type of procedure, the formulary system, came into being; at first it existed side by side with the *legis actio* procedure, but in time it gradually replaced the *legis actiones*. In about 17 BC the *legis actiones* were abolished, but the procedure was still used in a few exceptional cases.

Various formal rules applied to the first phase of the *legis actio* procedure. First of all, the case could not be heard unless the two parties were present. Consequently, the position of the plaintiff had to be strengthened *vis-à-vis* the defendant; thus, according to the XII Tables (table 1.1) the plaintiff could apparently compel the defendant, by force if necessary, to take part in a lawsuit. As soon as plaintiff and defendant stood facing the pontiff or the praetor, the plaintiff had to open the proceedings by pronouncing his claim in a set form of words prescribed for the case in question. In other words he had to utter a pithy sentence that summarised his claim. The defendant had to reply, also in prescribed phrases, and finally the pontiff or magistrate intervened, again by means of specific formulas, so the case might be sent for trial before the *iudex*. Gaius tells us in his Institutes (4.12–29) that at the time of the XII Tables there were four different models for *legis actiones* and that later a fifth one was added; three *legis actiones* could be used to open a lawsuit and two could be used to enforce the execution of a verdict. Within these models various claims could be formulated, but only using prescribed phraseology. From the example that Gaius gives in his Institutes we see how strict this formalism was. According to Gaius a man had once instituted a *legis actio* against another man who had chopped down his vines. He lost his case because, in the formula he was required to pronounce, he had used the word 'vites' (= vines) instead of the word 'arbores' (= trees) which was prescribed by the XII Tables (*Inst.* 4.11).

Although there were formal rules for the *in iure* phase there were none for the second phase before the *iudex*. Both parties were heard and they could produce evidence to support their respective standpoints. It sometimes happened that a prominent citizen delivered a plea in support of one of the parties, but this did not become normal practice until the later republic.[6] With regard to evidence there were only general rules such as 'the burden of proof rests on the plaintiff'. It was up to the *iudex* to decide how much weight he would attach to the evidence produced. He could seek support for his verdict from a *consilium*, an advisory council which he appointed for that purpose when necessary. He gave the verdict orally in the presence of the two parties. It was not possible to appeal against the verdict by referring the case to a higher authority because both parties had agreed to the choice of the *iudex* and had thereby agreed in advance to accept his verdict.

If the verdict turned out in favour of the plaintiff and the defendant was not prepared to comply, the plaintiff could not turn to the state and ask for the fulfilment of the judgment: the plaintiff himself had to ensure that the sentence was carried out. Therefore he had fairly powerful measures at his disposal; with the help of the pontiff or magistrate he could restrict the personal freedom of the defendant. By using one of the two *legis actiones* formulated for enforcing a judgment he could have the defendant handcuffed until he, or someone else acting on his behalf, had fulfilled the judgment. If that had not happened within sixty days he could kill him or sell him as a slave 'over the Tiber', i.e.

abroad. In the course of the fourth century BC, however, this was forbidden and thereafter the situation of the person condemned via a *legis actio* procedure improved slowly but surely.

3.4. THE INTERPRETATION

For a century after the Law of the XII Tables had been formulated new law was developed mainly by interpreting this law, later laws and the *legis actiones* based upon them. Because there was still a close link in those days between religious and juridical rules, it is not surprising that the pontiffs were made responsible for the interpretation. As was stated earlier, the pontiffs had control over the first phase of the *legis actio* procedure and could exert considerable influence on the development of the law. They could widen the scope of a *legis actio* by interpreting it broadly or they could restrict its scope by interpreting it narrowly. The pontiffs used their knowledge and power both in procedures and in other ways. They were often consulted by citizens who wanted to know whether there were specific rules of law which applied to their particular case. In their advice, however, the pontiffs not only interpreted existing legal concepts, they also introduced entirely new institutions while pretending to give interpretations. For instance, they used a recognised form of procedure for purposes other than the one for which it was intended. In this way the *in iure cessio*, the words of which originally marked the beginning of a lawsuit concerning ownership, also came to serve as a way of transferring ownership.[7] Another well-known example of law-making through interpretation by the pontiffs is the way in which the *emancipatio* of sons was made possible. The XII Tables did not contain any provision relating to the way in which a father could set his son free from *patria potestas*, but it did contain a clause which was apparently intended to protect a son against abuse of power by his father. A father could mancipate his son to another citizen for money on the understanding that the son would be manumitted after having worked for this other person. As a result of the manumission the son returned automatically into the *potestas* of his father, whereupon the father could sell him again. Table 4.2 limited this right of the father by stating that if the father had sold his son three times, the son would be free from his power. The pontiffs used this provision to free a son from *patria potestas*. The father mancipated the son three times

24

to a friend and the friend manumitted the son after each mancipation. After the first and second mancipation the son returned
to the power of his father; after the third mancipation the *patria
potestas* ceased to exist and whenever the son was then manumitted
by the buyer he became *sui iuris* (independent). Usually, however,
the son was mancipated back to the father who thereupon manumitted the son himself. This was done so that the father acquired
patron's rights over his son and thus retained rights of succession
with regard to him. A possible reason for this kind of emancipation was that a father might have several sons among whom his
estate would have to be divided when he died; he could prevent
his estate from being split into small plots by dividing it out
among his sons during his lifetime. This example illustrates how
a provision in the XII Tables was used for a purpose that was
quite different from the original purpose, and how by means of
the interpretation of this provision a new institution, namely that
of emancipation, was created. Roman legal science eventually
developed from the interpretations given by the pontiffs.

Part II

THE LATE REPUBLIC
(367–27 BC)

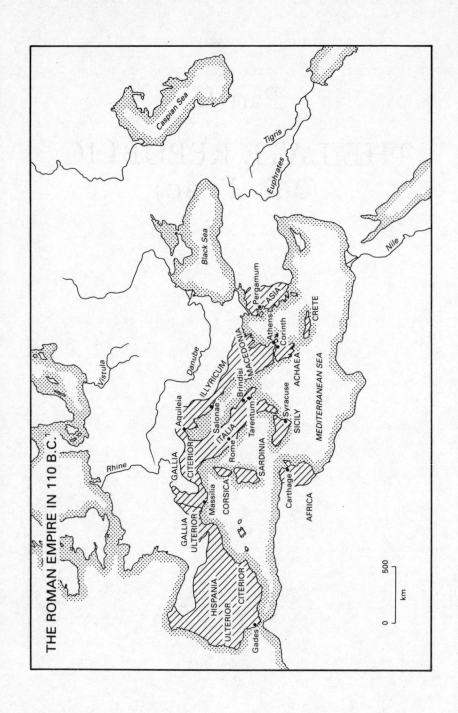

THE ROMAN EMPIRE IN 110 B.C.

4

THE LATE REPUBLIC: GENERAL OUTLINE

4.1. THE SOURCES

Considerably more is known about the late republic than about the earliest history of Rome because the sources are more numerous and more reliable. Our knowledge about this period is based mainly on literary sources; for instance, the Greek historian Polybius and the Roman historian Livy, mentioned in Part I, supply us with very valuable information. Works by writers such as Caesar and Sallust contain important information about political developments, particularly during the last few decades of the republic; because these authors write about events that occurred within their own lifetime the information they give is fairly reliable. Of course, the comprehensive works of Cicero have to be mentioned in this connection: his philosophical and rhetorical works and his speeches are important for our knowledge of the political situation in the first century BC and for our knowledge of the law in those days.

In addition to these literary sources all kinds of inscriptions have come down to us; they provide supplementary information. The most important of these are on bronze, stone or copper and reproduce laws, decisions of the senate and other documents; these inscriptions concern for instance rules relating to provincial government. Specifically juridical literature from this period is very scarce and has only come down to us indirectly, via the *Corpus Iuris Civilis* of Justinian.

4.2. THE TERRITORY

In the period between 367 and 27 BC Rome gained control of the entire Mediterranean area. At the end of this period a large part of the world as far as it was known at the time was under Roman rule. This expansion was not the work of one man and cannot be compared to the rapid conquests made by Alexander the Great, but it was the result of several centuries of conflict and persistent effort.[1]

4.2.1. The conquest of Italy

When in 367 BC the Romans changed the organisation of the state by means of the *leges Liciniae Sextiae* and thereby practically put an end to the conflicts between patricians and plebeians, they were able to concentrate once more on expansion. First of all, with the help of the Samnites the Romans defeated the Latin league which had been enviously watching the growing power of Rome and had demanded greater political power in the alliance; the alliance was dissolved and in 338 BC Latium came completely under Roman domination. Then, after a number of battles, the Samnites were defeated; their land as well as that of the Etruscans and the Celts who had allied themselves with the Samnites was conquered by Rome. By the beginning of the third century the Romans were the undisputed masters of central Italy.

During this period Rome had acquired more and more influence in the south of Italy; ultimately this was what prompted the largest Greek city, Tarentum, to declare war on Rome. Tarentum received assistance from King Pyrrhus of Epirus (in present-day Greece). King Pyrrhus defeated the Romans several times, but ultimately, after an indecisive battle, left the Tarentines to their fate. Thus the Romans were able to quickly subjugate the south of Italy as well (275 BC). In this way they established their authority over the whole of Italy, i.e. from the Po valley, where the Celtic tribes still lived, down as far as Sicily.

Some of the towns in the south were annexed, and with others Rome made various kinds of treaties and alliances. In addition a large number of new *municipia* and *coloniae* were founded. The administration of these towns was left mainly to local authorities, but the latter were not completely autonomous; for instance, they were forbidden to make alliances with anyone except the Romans.

The Romans treated the inhabitants of *coloniae* and some annexed towns in different ways. Some were granted complete Roman citizenship, some were granted citizenship without voting rights and others were not granted citizenship at all. It was not until 89 BC – and then only after several years of bitter fighting (the so-called Social War or War of the Allies) – that Roman citizenship was granted to all people living in Italy south of the river Po.

4.2.2. The conquest of the Mediterranean area

Of the great powers in the Mediterranean area Carthage (a town on the coast of present-day Tunisia) was the one that ruled the western part. Carthage was founded by the Phoenicians and Rome had had contact with Carthage since the second half of the fourth century BC and was linked to it via various treaties (made between 348–306 BC). Hitherto Rome had had very little contact with the other powerful empires such as Macedonia, Egypt and Syria, which had developed following the collapse of the empire of Alexander the Great (in about 323 BC). It was only in the third century that the Romans began the struggle which eventually – some three centuries later – was to lead to the Roman domination of the entire Mediterranean area. This expansion took place in the following way:

- The first Punic (Phoenician) war (264–241 BC); this gave Rome its first province, Sicily.
- In the second Punic war (215–201 BC) Rome succeeded in breaking the power of Carthage, conquered part of the Iberian peninsula and established control over the western part of the Mediterranean.
- Between 200 and 190 BC Rome subjugated the Celts in Northern Italy.
- After the second Macedonian war (200–197 BC) – the first one was part of the second Punic war – the Romans put an end to the Macedonian control of the Greek city-states and took control themselves.
- War against Antioch III, king of Syria and Asia Minor (192–188 BC). Rome was able to break the power of this king and obtain control of the eastern part of the Mediterranean by means of a system of alliances.

31

- After the third Macedonian war (171–168 BC) Macedonia became a Roman province in 148 BC and Achaia in 146 BC.
- At the end of the third Punic war (149–146 BC) Carthage was completely destroyed and Carthaginian supremacy in the field of commerce was crushed.
- Annexation of Pergamum (in the north-west of present-day Turkey) when King Attalus III left it to Rome in his will (133 BC).
- War with Iugurtha (111–105 BC): Numidia in the north of Africa was annexed by Rome.
- Between 88 and 63 BC Rome waged three wars against Mithridates of Pontus (in the north-east of present-day Turkey); he wanted to drive the Romans out of Asia Minor and Greece. Mithridates was defeated, Rome regained control of Greece and gained control of Asia Minor, Armenia, Syria and Judaea.
- Conquest of Gaul by Julius Caesar (58–53 BC).
- Annexation of Egypt by Octavian in 30 BC.

These developments are reflected in the new name given to the Mediterranean: it began to be referred to as *mare nostrum* (our sea), an expression which had originally been reserved for the Tyrrhenian Sea following the Roman conquest of Sicily, Sardinia and Corsica.

Because it turned out to be impossible to govern these newly conquered territories from Rome, the task was entrusted to magistrates appointed for that specific purpose, and from the second century BC to ex-magistrates chosen from and by the senate. These governors, who represented the authority of the Roman state in the province assigned to them, had duties in the military and administrative sectors and were responsible for the administration of justice. Where possible the existing territorial organisation was maintained. During the republic the inhabitants of the conquered territories were not granted Roman citizenship; nevertheless, they had to pay tax to Rome. Although the Romans dominated the conquered peoples militarily and economically they did not always do so culturally. From the second century BC Rome became strongly influenced by Greek culture and particularly by Greek literature, philosophy and the fine arts.

4.3. THE POPULATION

When it was stipulated by the *leges Liciniae Sextiae* in 367 that one of the two consuls had to be a plebeian, the dividing line between patricians and plebeians hardly existed any more: from then on the main distinction was simply between rich citizens and poor citizens. The economic changes which occurred from the third century BC onwards gradually altered the social relationships. New orders developed, but these are not easy to classify because the citizens within the various orders (except for the highest stratum) did not form a homogeneous group. Three orders can be distinguished: the senatorial aristocracy, the *equites* and the middle and lower classes.[2]

4.3.1. The senatorial aristocracy

Those families which had one or two of their members in the senate enjoyed the highest standing in Roman society. To be a member of the senate one probably had to be very wealthy; in any case it was the task of the two censors – who estimated a person's wealth and on that basis assessed that person's military and financial obligations – to determine who could become a senator; by the end of the fourth century BC the censors could not, without good reason, disregard anybody who had held a high position in the magistrature (e.g. had served as consul, praetor or curule aedile). At the end of the second century BC someone who had been a plebeian aedile or a tribune was also entitled to become a senator. Of course it was also possible to gain admittance to the senatorial aristocracy by letting oneself be adopted by an old senatorial family; for instance, adoption could be in the interests of such a family when it was about to die out.

The wealth of senators consisted mainly of estates in Italy and the provinces; traditionally this was the only known form of wealth in Rome. Since a *lex Claudia* which was passed in 213 BC senators were even forbidden to own ships that could carry more than 300 amphores, i.e. ships of sea-going capacity; they were probably also forbidden to participate in contracts with the state to collect taxes. On the other hand, those senators who held high ranks in the army often received a considerable share of the spoils of war and were able to acquire land in the conquered territories for little or no money.[3]

4.3.2. The equites

In the later republic the *equites* formed the second class in Roman society. The class originated among the horsemen who had formed the cavalry since the army had been reorganised under King Servius Tullius. During the republic they were chosen by the censor from among the citizens on the basis of their financial, physical and moral strength. For a long time there was no distinction between *equites* and senators: senators often served as cavalrymen. This situation did not change even in the third century BC when the horsemen were found to be less effective in battle.

The *equites* began to form a separate class when the above-mentioned *lex Claudia* forbade senators to engage in commerce. From then on much of the commerce fell into the hands of the *equites*, whereas the senators concentrated on politics. The *equites* did not become a completely separate class until the senators were excluded from the eighteen cavalry centuries in about 120 BC. At that time the position of the *equites* became stronger than that of the senators in many respects.

The *equites* formed a very diverse group from all layers of society: they were made up of officers, large land-owners, *publicani*, members of leading families in the *municipia*, etc. Because the *equites* were allowed to serve as magistrates it was relatively simple for them to become members of the senatorial class; therefore most of the *homines novi* in the senate had first belonged to the class of the *equites*.

4.3.3. The middle and lower classes

The middle and lower classes of the population were formed by all citizens who belonged neither to the senatorial class nor to the *equites*. The small top group, consisting of the aristocracy of the *municipia* and of the towns in the provinces, dominated the political, cultural and economic life of these places; these people were faithful supporters of Rome and gradually strengthened their links with the capital. These were the groups that would provide the senators under the principate.

People slightly lower down in the hierarchy belonged to the lower middle class: in the towns they were mainly artisans and in the country they were the small landowners; people from this group who succeeded in amassing wealth could easily move up to the local aristocracy or even to the *equites*. This class also included the agricultural workers and – in the cities – the masses who were unable to support themselves. This urban proletariat was completely dependent on the state or on certain very wealthy citizens and because its members readily accepted bribes they constituted a serious threat to political stability; this became particularly obvious in the latter days of the republic.

Finally, as a result of Roman conquests large numbers of slaves streamed into Rome and Italy. In antiquity it was standard practice for prisoners-of-war to become slaves. However, it was not only defeated opponents who became slaves; so did the civilian population of the conquered territories. Moreover, until the first century it often happened that pirates raiding ships and unprotected harbours kidnapped people and sold them as slaves, for instance at the large slave-market on the island of Delos. It is not possible to state precisely what percentage of the population were slaves, but by the end of the republic it must have been quite high. Estimates vary from 25 per cent to 50 per cent of the population of Italy; in the provinces the percentage was generally much lower.[4] The living conditions and the social standing of these people could differ tremendously; sometimes they were worse than those of free Roman citizens, sometimes they were better. In particular, slaves from the eastern Mediterranean area, who had often been well educated before being sold as slaves, could have a good life: a slave could become a manager of a business, a teacher or a doctor. Others, however, were put to work in agriculture, in the mines or in theatres, and they often had a miserable life. Of course it was possible for all slaves to be manumitted by their masters and then to live on as Roman citizens; this frequently happened, particularly in the second and first centuries.[5]

4.4. ECONOMY

It is impossible to tell whether Rome's imperialistic expansion was the cause or the result of changes in economic conditions. But there was clearly a very strong interaction between economic and political developments.[6]

As Rome extended its power over Italy it was greatly helped by the fighting spirit and discipline of the farmers. Initially Roman control strengthened their economic position. The extensive agricultural areas which were added to Roman territory and became the property of the Roman state were used to found fortified agrarian settlements. Citizens, if they so wished, could easily obtain land there and by reason of their permanent presence in the conquered territories Roman authority was upheld. In the third century Rome expanded so rapidly that there were not enough people to populate the new territories. The result was that some land remained unallocated. Part of this land could be rented from the state; the rest was divided into large plots and offered for sale at a low price. Because these plots were too large to be worked by one family (in the north of Italy, for instance, plots were fifty hectares), it was only wealthy Romans who were able and willing to exploit this land with the help of tenants and/or slaves. Both in Italy and in the provinces large estates (*latifundia*) developed; the owners, however, often lived in Rome and were interested primarily in high profits. Some small farms survived along with the new *latifundia*. This was mainly because when military campaigns came to an end (small) plots of land were often allocated to veterans who had been honourably discharged from the army after twenty years of service.

In the towns the economic development led to the setting up of all kinds of private businesses which specialised in making things or providing a service. Most of these businesses were run by free Roman citizens working for themselves or working as paid employees of the owner; some were run by slaves. The Romans found it advantageous to use slaves because slaves, unlike Roman citizens, could not be recruited for the army. A plentiful supply of slaves was available and if they were well-trained the results were positive. However, the use of slave labour also had a negative effect: there was less incentive for technical development and the slaves themselves were generally not interested in the results of their work. Most of these businesses were small; in antiquity there were hardly any large-scale industries, mainly due to the high costs of transport by land.

Overseas trade increased, particularly in transport from the provinces to Italy. Seaports developed along the Italian coast, the most important one being Puteoli near Naples. However, the Romans themselves did not engage in this activity, leaving it to the Phoenicians and the Greeks. For a long time the expansion of shipping was hindered by pirates. At the beginning of the first century several actions were undertaken, but it was only Pompey who succeeded in sweeping the Mediterranean clear of them (67 BC); then the countries around the Mediterranean were able to form a huge common market where trade knew no frontiers.[7]

Another important economic activity was the implementation of government tasks by private individuals. Many kinds of government tasks such as the construction of roads, aqueducts and buildings, the organising of transport, collecting of taxes, supplying the army with food and the exploitation of mines (so-called *publica*) were in fact not performed by the Roman state because it lacked the necessary manpower and resources. Instead these tasks were allocated to private individuals, the so-called *publicani*. Most of them formed a company for the purpose of spreading the risks and raising the huge funds that were often required for these works. The company which received the contract was generally the one which at a public meeting submitted the lowest tender for the works or services concerned. The *publicani*, however, wanted their company to make a good profit and they were often notorious for their greed and cruelty.

Finally it should be mentioned in this connection that the late republic saw the development of money and banks in Rome. Such things were known much earlier in the eastern countries, in Greece and in the Hellenistic world. When the Romans conquered these countries they took possession of the large stocks of gold and silver belonging to their victims, and entered the banking business themselves. Romans became established in the large commercial centres where they provided facilities for people to deposit their money; they also arranged for payments to be made and they granted credit. At the beginning the coins that were used had been minted overseas, e.g. by Greek cities. The oldest known Roman coins date from the beginning of the third century BC. From the second century BC onwards, however, Roman coinage was in general use and it soon even superseded all other types of coinage in the Hellenistic world.

5

THE LATE REPUBLIC: THE STATE

The political structure of Rome in the second half of the republic did not differ essentially from its political structure in the early republic. Supreme power was in the hands of the senate; the magistrates had to ensure that the various governmental tasks were carried out. In the assembly the magistrates were chosen and votes were taken on bills proposed by the magistrates.[1]

5.1. THE SENATE

During the late republic the Roman senate was a paragon of shrewdness, tenacity and perseverance; these qualities made it possible for Rome to conquer and rule the world as it was known at the time. Even though a number of senators could not resist the temptations offered by the newly arrived riches and turned to a life of luxury and ease, the senate as a whole managed to keep control up to about 100 BC.

Very little is known about how the senate was formed. According to a *lex Ovinia* of 312 BC two censors had the task of forming the senate and it is possible that this was also the method used before that time. This law decreed that in forming the senate the censors had to choose the 'best men from each class'; this is generally taken to mean that both patricians and plebeians had to be chosen and that anyone who had served as a magistrate (a consul, a praetor or an aedile) was a possible candidate. As a result persons who did not belong to the senatorial class but had been chosen as magistrates because of their knowledge and influence could also become senators. Because these *homines novi* had to spend a large amount of money in order to be elected and were therefore generally very wealthy, they had no reason to press for fundamental social and political changes. Consequently the political character of the senate remained unaltered: conservative and chauvinistic.

The senate met under the leadership of one of the senior magistrates, generally a consul. At the beginning of the meeting the subject for discussion was announced by the consul; he then asked the most important senators for their opinion, in accordance with the seniority of their ranks, and finally a vote was taken. The decisions of the senate were referred to as *senatus consulta*.

During the republic the senate extended its powers. It had long been the rule that decisions made by the assembly with regard to matters such as legislation and the election of magistrates were not valid until they had been approved by the senate. After a *lex Publilia Philonis* had been passed in 339 BC, however, the proposals relating to legislation had to be approved first by the senate. In other words, draft laws could not be submitted to the *comitia* until they had been approved by the senate; this ruling probably did not apply to the *plebiscita* which came into being in the *concilium plebis*. In the third century BC a *lex Maenia* stipulated that proposals regarding the election of magistrates also had to receive the prior agreement of the senate. Hitherto these changes are usually regarded as a restriction of the powers of the senate because they shifted the final decisions from the senate to the assembly. However, it seems more likely that in fact they strengthened the position of the senate: from then on the *comitia* could only take decisions that were acceptable to the senate.

As Roman power expanded, the tasks of the senate increased; in the field of foreign policy these tasks consisted of appointing Roman envoys and receiving foreign ambassadors, ratifying international treaties, declaring war and making peace. In addition, the senate supervised military operations and the administration of the conquered territories. As a result of these conquests it became increasingly difficult to control the treasury; taxes had to be levied, prices had to be fixed, and Rome's food supply had to be guaranteed. Finally the senate also had to look after the mental well-being of the citizens: if corrupting influences, particularly from non-Roman religions, threatened to undermine the strength and stability of the people the senate took severe counter-measures. A prime example is the action taken by the senate against the sect of the Bacchantes in 186 BC.[2]

5.2. THE MAGISTRATURE

As mentioned earlier, new rules with regard to the magistrature were introduced in 367 BC by means of the *leges Liciniae Sextiae*. The new rules referred mainly to the highest offices. Two consuls were to hold the highest office in the magistrature and it was stipulated that from then on one of these was to be chosen from the plebeians. At the same time the supervision of civil litigation (*iurisdictio*) was entrusted to a new magistrate, the praetor. Other magistrates were the censor, the aedile and the quaestor. There was no official hierarchy in these functions: each magistrate was responsible for his own decisions. In practice, there emerged an order in which the offices were held; one first became a quaestor, then an aedile or tribune, then a praetor and finally a consul. The office of censor was usually held by someone who had already been consul; it was the most prestigious of all magisterial functions. In addition, it became standard practice to have a gap of several years between magisterial appointments; this was to permit legal action to be taken against an ex-magistrate.

The top magistrates, now called consuls, were chosen by the *comitia centuriata* from the Roman citizens. They were given a variety of powers. First of all, they were given *imperium*; this included command of the army, the authority to recruit troops, appoint officers and distribute the spoils of war. Further, they had the *ius edicendi*, the right to issue binding regulations (*edicta*). A third important power wielded by the consuls was the *coercitio*; this was a general power which helped consuls to maintain public order and impose penalties for civil disobedience. Finally, they could summon the assembly and the senate and put forward proposals to these bodies. The consuls' powers, however, were not unlimited; for instance, like all magistrates they held office for only one year (the annuity principle) and the office was always held by at least two persons who had identical powers (the collegiality principle); furthermore, they could veto each other's actions as well as those of lower magistrates (right of intercession). In the late republic the consuls were mainly active as generals, aspiring to the glamour of victory and seeking a large share in the booty. In times of crisis each consul had the right to appoint a dictator who ranked higher than himself, his colleague and all other magistrates; a dictator however could not remain in office for longer than six months. This form of dictatorship did not occur after 200 BC. Although both Sulla and Julius Caesar proclaimed themselves dictators in the first century BC they were not appointed in the regular manner and their term of office was not restricted to six months.

The office of praetor could originally be held only by patricians but since 337 BC plebeians had also been eligible. Like the consuls the praetor was elected in the *comitia centuriata*. He also had *imperium* and the right to issue edicts. The praetor's task was *iurisdictio*: he had to do what had traditionally been done by one of the pontiffs, namely decide during the first part of a lawsuit whether the parties were to be allowed to put their case to a judge, whom he (the praetor) had authorised, and, if so, in what way that was to happen.[3] In the early days there was only one praetor, but in 242 BC a second one was appointed for the purpose of supervising the civil litigation between Roman citizens and foreigners and between foreigners. He was the *praetor qui inter peregrinos ius dicit*, a title which afterwards was shortened to *praetor peregrinus*. From then on the other praetor was responsible solely for the *iurisdictio* between Roman citizens; because according to certain laws he could not be absent from Rome for more than ten days during his term of office, he was called *praetor urbanus* (from *urbs* = city).[4] At the beginning of the first century BC Sulla increased the number of praetors to eight. Six of them were given the task of supervising the newly instituted criminal courts, while the other two praetors, *urbanus* and *peregrinus*, retained the *iurisdictio* in Rome and in Italy; outside the capital they were represented by the *praefecti iure dicundo*.

The two censors occupied a special position in the magistrature: they had no *imperium* and therefore were not top magistrates, but they were not subordinate to the other magistrates. In addition to their original tasks (making up the census list and appointing senators) they were put in charge of the public sales at which *publica* were leased (collection of taxes, exploitation of mines, etc.) or let (in the case of land belonging to the state).

The *leges Liciniae Sextiae* also introduced some changes into the aedileship. Two new aediles were appointed; these were additional to the original two aediles who were assistants to the tribunes. To distinguish them from the original plebeian aediles the new magistrates were referred to as curule aediles. They were chosen by the *comitia tributa*. Although the four aediles did not have exactly the same rank they had the same tasks, e.g. the maintenance of public roads and buildings in Rome, the supervision of the water supply, the provision of grain and the organisation of certain public games. The curule aediles also had to supervise the functioning of the public markets; this task is particularly interesting since it included *iurisdictio* over the sale of slaves and cattle; by issuing edicts on the law of sale the aediles contributed considerably to the development of Roman private law.

Like the aediles, the quaestors, who were traditionally assistants to the consuls, were chosen by the *comitia tributa*. About 267 BC their numbers were doubled, so then there were eight quaestors and at the beginning of the first century BC Sulla even increased their number to twenty. The quaestors could be required to perform a variety of tasks; these included supervising the aerarium, directing criminal proceedings before the *comitia* and assisting senior magistrates outside Rome.

When the differences between the patricians and the plebeians died down in the course of the fourth century BC the tribunes became magistrates for all the Roman people. They acquired the right to be present at meetings of the senate and later they even acquired the right to summon the senate and make proposals to it; we do not know precisely when this happened. From the end of the second century BC the tribunes, just like the other magistrates, became members of the senate on completing their term of office. From then on even patricians could become tribunes. They were no longer chosen by the *concilium plebis*; their election then took place in the *comitia tributa*. One of the traditional powers of the tribunes was the right to invalidate the actions taken by magistrates and other tribunes. The right of intercession turned out to be a powerful weapon in the political turmoil of the last 100 years of the republic, particularly because among the ten tribunes there was always bound to be at least one who was closely linked to the senate. Apart from a short period under Sulla, the tribunate continued well into the principate. It even formed one of the pillars on which the first emperors based their power.

5.3. THE ASSEMBLIES

Although the assemblies played an important role as from the fourth century BC – they chose the magistrates and voted on draft legislation – no real democracy developed in Rome as it had done in some Greek cities, e.g. Athens in the fifth and fourth centuries BC. Of the four types of assemblies that existed at the beginning of the republic three were still functioning about 367 BC. The *comitia centuriata*, the *comitia tributa* and the *concilium plebis*. The *comitia curiata* was still in existence but the meetings were no longer attended by all citizens; the earlier tasks of the *comitia curiata* were now performed by the thirty representatives of the *curiae*.

The difference between the two *comitia* on the one hand and the *concilium plebis* on the other hand diminished, slowly but surely. The number of patricians remained more or less constant, whereas the number of plebeians had increased dramatically after the territorial expansion: as a result the patricians in the *comitia* formed a decreasing percentage of the Roman people. When it was decreed by the *lex Hortensia* in 287 BC that from then on the plebiscites would be binding for all Roman citizens and they would thus be equated with the *leges*, this did not cause a large-scale political shift.

By the late republic a remarkable situation had developed. There were three organs with equal powers to make decisions that were binding for the citizens; two of these, the *comitia centuriata* and the *comitia tributa*, consisted of the same people, although they were organised in different ways. The *concilium plebis* was made up of more or less the same people as the two *comitia* and was organised in the same way as one of the *comitia*, namely the *comitia tributa*. Which of the three assemblies was summoned depended on which magistrate it was who wished to put a proposal to the people: it was the consul who summoned the *comitia centuriata*, the consul or the praetors who summoned the *comitia tributa* and a plebeian magistrate who summoned the *concilium plebis*. In practice, it was usual for laws to be formulated in the *concilium plebis*, because the tribunes generally had more time for and more interest in legislation than the consuls who often had military commitments. The various magistrates were still chosen by the assemblies which had traditionally had the right to do this.

5.4. THE FALL OF THE REPUBLIC

At the end of the second century BC there was a crisis in the political and social system of the republic.[5] The drastic changes in the socio-economic and political life in Rome in the third and second centuries led to such tension and political instability that the traditional republican regime collapsed. The factors that led to this instability, however, were not identical for the various elements that made up the population of the Roman empire.

In the conquered territories the violence and greed of the Romans fanned the flames of nationalism among the local people and caused large-scale rebellions, particularly in Greece and Asia Minor. Rome's allies in Italy, who had suffered greatly as a result of the second Punic war but had not shared in the spoils of war after Hannibal's defeat, were not satisfied either; they did not even have Roman citizenship but were more or less second-class citizens. Among the Roman citizens themselves conflicting interests in the socio-economic field increased steadily. Members of the senatorial aristocracy wanted to maintain the established order which had allowed them to get rich by sharing in the spoils of war and by acquiring land from the state. Among the senators there was a growing trend towards luxury and individualism; this was in sharp contrast to traditional Roman austerity and readiness to serve the state. Most of the senators lacked the vision required to tackle the problems which were beginning to develop. The same applied to the *equites*; they had been able to feather their own nest in the existing situation and therefore wanted to retain their privileges. The small landowners, on the other hand, were not satisfied; the continuing wars and the long period of compulsory military service (up to thirty years) made it almost impossible for them to keep their businesses running. The owners of large estates, however, did not have this problem because they had their land worked by slaves, who were not eligible for military service. The population of Rome had increased steadily because of the influx of impoverished farming families, veterans from the army, non-Roman merchants and artisans and because of the growing numbers of freed men and women, most of whom were not of Roman origin. Some of these people succeeded in making a reasonable living, others however soon joined the ranks of the unemployed urban proletariat. The latter were very dissatisfied with the existing situation and were therefore inclined to give their support to anyone who suggested that their prospects could be improved. The slaves, who had to do the heavy work and were often very badly treated by their masters, were of course not satisfied with their lot either; slaves rebelled on several occasions and in several areas, e.g. Sicily and Asia Minor. Military force had to be used to quell these uprisings.[6]

There was considerable discussion in the senate concerning what policy should be pursued. The majority of the senators, who were known as the *optimates* (literally, 'the best'), were opposed to any radical changes. A minority then tried to force through some changes with the help of the assembly. These senators, who were called *populares* because they relied on the assembly of the people, were led by Tiberius Gracchus.[7] When Tiberius Gracchus served as a tribune in 133 BC he introduced a bill in the assembly whereby the small rural proprietors would be reinstated and – indirectly – the power of the Roman army would be restored. To achieve this goal, state-owned land would have to be given to the poor. By this time most of the state-owned land had fallen into the hands of the large landowners who for the most part regarded it as their own property. Tiberius Gracchus proposed to re-introduce the norms that had been laid down in an earlier law (which had fallen into disuse) concerning the size of the state-owned piece of land that a citizen could occupy and the number of animals he could graze on that land. If citizens had more than the permitted amount of land, the extra would have to be divided into small sections and allocated to other persons who had no land.

Gracchus' proposal encountered a great deal of resistance but in the end it was accepted. However, Gracchus manoeuvred so clumsily and overstepped his authority as a tribune to such an extent that he seriously weakened his own position. By continually violating the established constitutional procedure and by basing his actions on the will of the people he gave the impression that he was trying to acquire power for himself. When he tried to get re-elected as a tribune, although that too was against the regulations, he was murdered by a number of senators. His death, however, did not mean the end of the political unrest. Ten years later Tiberius' brother Gaius Gracchus tried to continue the reforms. He attempted to win the support of the *equites* by promising to strengthen their position *vis-à-vis* the senators. Although he acted more cautiously than his brother and achieved a number of successes Gaius Gracchus failed in the end and, like his brother, had to pay for his exploits with his life (in 121 BC). In the next few years the reforms of the Gracchi were carried out, but in a much altered form. Power in the senate was undoubtedly back in the hands of the *optimates*.

There was no change in the situation until – a decade later – the Roman army experienced a series of defeats. For instance, it was defeated by King Iugurtha in Numidia (North Africa), and by the Cimbri and Teutones in Gaul; the *optimates* were held responsible for these defeats. In 107 BC one of the leaders of the *populares*, C. Marius, succeeded in getting himself elected consul. After defeating King Iugurtha and the Cimbri and Teutones he returned to Rome as a very powerful man. However, when he claimed state-owned land where he could establish some colonies for his ex-soldiers, the senate, which was still dominated by the *optimates*, refused to co-operate.

Marius' strongest opponent was L. Cornelius Sulla. He was appointed consul in 88 BC and was charged by the senate to lead the army against Mithridates VI, king of Pontus in Asia Minor, who had persuaded large parts of Asia Minor and Greece to rise up against the Romans. The assembly, however, decided that Marius must have control of the army. A civil war broke out between Marius and his supporters on the one hand and Sulla and his soldiers on the other. After several years of conflict Marius was defeated. In the years that followed Sulla became a dictator and conducted a reign of terror (82–79 BC). When he died one year later there was a power shift in the senate in favour of the *populares*. One of their most important leaders was Cn. Pompeius (Magnus), a very successful general. Not only did he succeed in eradicating piracy in the Mediterranean area, but he also managed to defeat Mithridates and reorganise the administration of the conquered territory in Asia Minor, Syria and Palestine. When, upon his return to Italy, he tried to look after his veterans, he – like Marius before him – encountered strong opposition from the senate. Thereupon he formed a triumvirate with two senators, C. Julius Caesar and M. Licinius Crassus, his aim being to divide up the power and bypass the senate (60 BC). This triumvirate was renewed in 56 BC but when Crassus was killed in 53 BC in the war against the Parthians, the relations between Pompey and Caesar rapidly deteriorated. In 49 BC another civil war broke out: Pompey was supported by the senate and Caesar by the people. It was not until more than four years later – after the Roman legions had faced each other on several occasions – that Caesar was able to defeat his opponent (45 BC). During this period Caesar had already had himself appointed dictator several times and in 45 BC even for an unlimited period. This dictatorship aroused a great deal of opposition in the senate and in 44 BC Caesar was murdered by a number of leading senators. These senators, however, had no alternative plan for governing the Roman empire. It was another seventeen years before Augustus resolved the crisis by creating a new form of government, the so-called principate.

6

THE LATE REPUBLIC: THE LAW

6.1. INTRODUCTION

Due to the expansion of Roman power and the changes that this expansion brought about in the socio-economic field the old legal system was no longer adequate. Archaic law, as was mentioned earlier, was closely bound up with religion and consequently it was very formalistic and exclusively Roman; the latter was nothing out of the ordinary in view of the fact that Roman territory was still very limited in size. The late republic saw a number of important changes in the law which can be summarised by the terms secularisation, internationalisation and liberalisation.[1]

As early as 367 BC the supervision of civil litigation, which had hitherto been in the hands of the pontiffs, was passed to the praetor and, to a limited extent, to the curule aediles; in addition jurists who were not necessarily pontiffs began to give *responsa* to citizens. A change that was remarkable for the times was the internationalisation of Roman law within the frontiers of the Roman territory. The granting of Roman citizenship had certainly not kept pace with the enlargement of the Roman sphere of influence. As a result more and more people belonging to other nations but living in Roman territory did not have Roman citizenship and therefore could not participate in the Roman *ius civile*. Because these foreigners, who were referred to as *peregrini*, had no access to the old *legis actio* procedure the praetor began to adapt the proceedings in the second century BC. The new procedure that developed from this was called the formulary system; it could be used almost equally by Roman citizens and *peregrini*. By virtue of his *ius edicendi* the praetor began to introduce new legal remedies which were available to both Roman citizens and

48

peregrini and also satisfied the new demands of legal practice, for in those days Rome, with its port of Ostia, began to become a very important centre of trade. These changes led to the development of a new complex of Roman private law which came to be known as *ius praetorium* or *ius honorarium* (from *honor* = magistracy).[2] The *ius honorarium* functioned side by side with and was later even interwoven with the *ius civile*: the relationship between the two types of law was rather like the relationship between equity and common law in English law.

The praetor was not solely responsible for the creation of this new form of private law. At the same time a new way of dealing with Roman law, and particularly Roman private law, known as Roman legal science, developed.[3] By giving *responsa* and engaging in several other practices the jurists helped to develop private law; they also began to record the *responsa* they had given in writing, arrange them in a certain order and publish them. This literature has become the most important and most original product of Roman culture: by means of this literature the Roman jurists exerted a worldwide influence on the law, an influence that is still clearly visible today.

It was not until the last century of the republic that penal law began to develop: the number of punishable offences and the number of courts were increased. It is striking that whereas the new elements in penal law were based largely on legislation, private law developed mainly within the framework of the administration of justice and legal science. In the following section something will be said about legislation and about the development of penal law; thereafter civil procedure and legal science will be dealt with in detail.

6.2. LEGISLATION

Traditionally the *comitia centuriata* had been the body that was authorised to make laws that were binding for all citizens. Furthermore, the *concilium plebis* could make general decisions, but originally they were binding only for plebeians. It was not until 287 BC when, due to territorial expansion, there were more plebeians than patricians, that the plebiscites were declared binding for all the people by virtue of the *lex Hortensia*.[4] From then on legislation was formulated more and more by means of plebiscites and often a plebiscite was even referred to as '*lex*'. Tradition had it that a law could not come into force until it had been approved by the senate. In 339 BC this rule was reversed and as a result proposed legislation had to be approved by the senate before the magistrate could put it to the assembly. Until 287 BC this may not have applied to plebiscites but then it probably did. In this way legislation passed definitively into the sphere of influence of the senate.

In the first century BC, when the Roman republic was caught up in an administrative crisis and the assembly had lost a good deal of its influence, it sometimes happened that a proposed law which had been approved by the senate was no longer put to the assembly but came into force immediately; on the other hand in those days plebiscites were sometimes formulated which had not been previously approved by the senate and were later declared invalid by the senate. In *Topica* V, 28 Cicero mentions both the senatorial decrees and the *leges* as sources of the law; in an inscription which probably contains fragments of the *lex Iulia municipalis* of 45 BC *leges*, plebiscites and senatorial decrees were put on a par as sources of the law. From the middle of the first century AD hardly any new laws came into being by means of *leges* or plebiscites; senatorial decrees, however, have long been used to create law.

In general the laws rarely had anything to do with private law. A well-known example of a law that did is the *lex Aquilia*, a plebiscite which probably dates from 286 BC; this law dealt with various types of unlawful damage to property obliging the perpetrator to pay a fine to the owner. Most of the laws related to politically disputed issues; a good example is the so-called *Tabula Bembina*, an inscription on a bronze plaque, nine fragments of which have been preserved. On one side of the plaque there is the text of a *lex repetundarum* and on the other side there is the text of a *lex agraria*. Nowadays it is assumed that this bronze plaque was first used about 120 BC for one of the laws to curb extortion by provincial governors and that when this law was superseded by another law, the back of the plaque was used in 111 BC for a law on land reform which was to replace the earlier legislation of the Gracchi with regard to this subject.

6.3. CRIMINAL LAW

So little is known about the criminal law in the early republic that the topic was not discussed in the previous chapter. However, in order to gain a proper understanding of how criminal justice was administered in the late republic, one needs to have some knowledge of the earlier history. It should be realised that public criminal law in Rome traditionally covered a more restricted area than modern criminal law. A large group of offences was regarded as being harmful to the individual citizen but not to the state; the perpetrators were therefore not prosecuted by the state. These so-called *delicta privata* included theft, defamation of character and since the *lex Aquilia* of 286 BC unlawful damage to someone's property. In such cases the injured party had to institute a civil procedure. If the defendant was found guilty he could be forced to pay a penalty to the injured party. *Delicta privata* were regarded as part of private law.

Offences such as treason or murder had long been part of criminal law. They were referred to by the term *crimina publica*. There are various interpretations and reconstructions of the way in which murder was dealt with. According to Mommsen and Jones the proceedings took place in the presence of a magistrate and anyone who was condemned to death by him could appeal to the *comitia centuriata*.[5] This view has been challenged in various ways.[6] The most recent view on this subject is the one put forward by Santalucia; he maintains that since the XII Tables, only the *comitia centuriata* had the authority to condemn a person to death after he had been found guilty by a *quaestor parricidii*.[7] According to Santalucia this was the procedure followed not only in cases of murder but also in cases of treason (against the state), in cases where a judge had conspired with one of the contending parties, in cases where false evidence had been given, if there had been arson or a spell had been cast on someone's harvest. Minor offences, however, like the burial of a corpse within the walls of a city and the holding of nocturnal meetings were punished by the magistrates.

About 100 BC, when Rome had grown into a large town with all the associated problems, this system was no longer adequate. Two measures were taken in order to improve the situation. First of all, low-ranking magistrates were appointed, the *tresviri capitales*, who judged cases, reported by citizens, involving violent crimes, arson, the making and possession of poison, etc. They judged slaves and foreigners and possibly also Roman citizens from the lower strata of society.

Secondly, special permanent courts were set up in connection with offences which because of their nature or because they involved so many people were regarded as a threat to the security of the state. Initially this happened only occasionally, but in 149 BC the *lex Calpurnia* established the first court for a particular type of offence, namely the *quaestio de repetundis*; its task was to deal with cases of extortion by Roman governors in Italy or the provinces. Thereafter a few more *quaestiones perpetuae* were established. They came under the authority of specially appointed praetors. A court consisted of several scores of jurors who all came from the senatorial élite. One of the reforms instituted by the Gracchi was to recruit jurors for the courts exclusively from the *equites*; Sulla then revoked this revolutionary decision and after much ado Julius Caesar finally stipulated that both senators and *equites* could serve as juror. Furthermore, within the framework of his political reforms Sulla reorganized the permanent courts and increased their number. Thereafter there were six courts: for murder and poisoning, for forgery of wills and other documents, for high treason, for bribery during elections, for extortion in the provinces and finally for embezzlement of public funds.

We know something about the procedure in the criminal courts because some of the speeches made by Cicero when he acted as advocate or prosecutor in such lawsuits have survived. Every respectable citizen, not only the injured party, could lodge a complaint against someone. If the praetor accepted the complaint, a jury was set up by drawing lots. The course of the lawsuit was not determined by the judge, as in English law, but by the parties and their advocates. The plaintiff had to prove that the defendant had committed the crime; if he was unsuccessful he ran the risk of being accused himself because he had knowingly lodged a false complaint. If he was successful he would receive a considerable reward: if, for instance, the defendant was sentenced to death and his property confiscated, then the accusor was entitled to a share of this property. It is not surprising that in time the system was abused and some people even made a profession of accusing rich fellow-citizens. Finally it was the jury who decided whether the accused was guilty or not and what the penalty would be, if it was not evident from the law.

6.4. CIVIL PROCEDURE

6.4.1. The introduction of the formulary procedure

As was mentioned earlier, in the late republic the praetor set about creating a new way of civil litigation, the formulary procedure, and began drawing up new legal norms. We have very little factual information about how or when this happened. We do know however that the introduction of the formulary procedure did not automatically lead to the abolition of the old *legis actio* procedure. The latter was even modernised to a certain extent in the third and second centuries BC and continued to exist until the beginning of the principate.[8]

With regard to the abolition of the *legis actio* procedure, all we know is that according to Gaius (*Inst.* IV, 30) this occurred by virtue of a *lex Aebutia* and two Julian laws. The Julian laws concerned were the *leges Iuliae iudiciorum publicorum et privatorum* of emperor Augustus, dating from 17–16 BC, which are also known from other sources. By one of these laws Augustus abolished the *legis actio* procedure except for jurisdiction by the *centumviri* (see under section 6.4.3) and for some other special procedures. We do not know the date or the purpose of the *lex Aebutia*. It is generally accepted, however, that the law dates from the second century BC. There are various opinions about its purpose. Nowadays it is taken for granted that the *lex Aebutia* was the first law to allow the procedure by *formula* to be used for claims which until then could only be made by means of the *legis actiones*. In these cases – it is not yet possible to ascertain which claims exactly were involved – it was possible for the plaintiff to choose whether he would use the old or the new procedure; however, because the procedure by *formula* was more advantageous and therefore was generally the one chosen, the *lex Aebutia* in fact put an end to those *legis actiones*. A problem, however, was that because these *formulae* were not based on a law, something already settled in a formulary action could be judged again in a *legis actio* procedure. The *leges Iuliae* must have removed this possibility by abolishing nearly all *legis actiones*. Thereafter, all claims protected by the *ius civile* and all claims protected by the praetor could be judged definitively in a procedure by *formula*.

6.4.2. The first phase of the lawsuit: *in iure*

Just like the *legis actio* procedure, the procedure by *formula* consisted of two phases. The first phase took place in the presence of the praetor (*in iure*); the purpose of this phase was to open the case. The second phase took place in the presence of the judge (*apud iudicem*) and its purpose was to obtain a verdict. The most important innovation introduced by the formulary system when compared to the *legis actio* procedure was that the praetor was no longer bound by the words of the (five) *legis actiones*, but could interpret them and make changes, and even introduce new legal remedies for relationships that were not recognised by the *ius civile*. Another important change was that the praetor fixed the legal remedy in a written *formula* and parties no longer had to state their dispute in certain prescribed words, with all the risks that such a procedure involved.

The procedure by *formula* began when parties that had a dispute put their problem to the praetor (or in certain cases to the aedile) requesting him to appoint a judge who could settle their dispute. The praetor first had to check whether the parties were qualified to be a plaintiff or a defendant in a legal action on the basis of the facts they had submitted; if they did not qualify, then the praetor refused the action (*denegatio actionis*); if they qualified, then he consulted the edict. In this edict, which he had issued on the basis of his *ius edicendi* at the beginning of his term of office and which in principle was applicable for the whole year (*edictum perpetuum*), he had collected all the legal remedies that he was prepared to grant together with the text of the associated *formulae*. If the edict contained no action for the dispute in question and the praetor thought that that was as it should be, then he rejected the parties' request. If the edict did contain an action which was already known from the *ius civile* or had been created by a previous praetor or by himself, then he gave permission to initiate the proceedings. The praetor and the opposing parties chose a judge and they prepared a *formula*.

A *formula* generally consisted of three parts: the appointment of the judge, a description of the conflict formulated by the plaintiff (*intentio*) and the authorising of the judge to pass a verdict (*condemnatio*). The *intentio*, other sections and the *condemnatio* were always contained in one sentence which was drawn up according to a fixed scheme. The *formula* for an action where the cause was a loan of money, for instance, ran as follows:

> *XX iudex esto. Si paret Numerium Negidium Aulo Agerio sestertium milia dare oportere, condemnato, si non paret absolvito.*
>
> XX must be the judge. If it appears that the defendant ought to pay to the plaintiff 1000 sesterces he (the judge) must condemn him; if this does not appear, then he must absolve him.

In this case the judge was charged merely to examine whether the claim of the plaintiff was true; if the praetor considered that this might lead to an unfair result he could, at the request of the defendant, incorporate a defence (*exceptio*) in the *formula*. If, for instance, the defendant did not deny the existence of the debt but asserted that the money was sued for in contravention of an informal agreement, then the *formula* would be worded thus:

> *XX iudex esto. Si paret Numerium Negidium Aulo Agerio sestertium milia dare oportere, et si inter Aulum Agerium et Numerium Negidium non convenit ne ea pecunia peteretur condemnato, si non paret absolvito.*
>
> XX must be the judge. If it appears that the defendant ought to pay to the plaintiff 1000 sesterces and if it has not been agreed between the plaintiff and the defendant that the money should not be sued for, he must condemn him; if this does not appear, then he must absolve him.

The defence 'and if ... not be sued for' was worded in a conditional clause. This meant that if the judge concluded that the claim was perfectly good according to the *ius civile* but that the defence was justified, he would reject the claim. As soon as the opposing parties agreed that the *formula* reflected their dispute accurately, the *litis contestatio* took place. Parties agreed to accept in advance the verdict passed by the judge named in the *formula* and the praetor pronounced an (oral) decree in which he charged this judge to pass a verdict.

If the edict did not contain an action for the dispute in question but the praetor thought that the parties should nevertheless put their dispute to a judge, then either he could adapt an action set out for a similar case, for instance by means of a fiction (*actio utilis*) or he could formulate 'ad hoc' a new action, for instance by incorporating the actual facts of the dispute in the *formula* (*actio in factum decretalis*). Another important category of new actions was that of the so-called *iudicia bonae fidei*: the praetor assumed that in certain legal relations such as *emptio venditio* (sale), *locatio conductio* (hire), *societas* (partnership) and *mandatum* (mandate) the obligation was not created by the use of ritual words or by the performance of prescribed acts but by *fides*, namely the duty of people to keep their word. The *formula* where the cause of the action was a sale, for instance, ran as follows:

> *Quod Aulus Agerius de Numerio Negidio hominem quo de agitur emit, qua de re agitur, quidquid ob eam rem Numerium Negidium Aulo Agerio dare facere oportet ex fide bona, eius iudex Numerium Negidium Aulo Agerio condemnato si non paret absolvito.*

Because the plaintiff bought the slave in question from the defendant which matter is the subject of this action, the judge must condemn the defendant to convey to or do for the plaintiff whatever is in accordance with good faith; if it does not appear he must absolve him.

Clearly, by substituting a word like 'hired' for 'bought' the praetor could make the same *formula* apply to other contracts.

In this way a new category of contracts was devised which could be concluded purely by agreement, no matter how they were expressed (consensual contracts) and in which the obligations of the parties were determined by *bona fides* (good faith). It is obvious that the legal remedies granted by the praetor for that purpose (*iudicia bonae fidei*) were very important for economic life and that they gave a completely new look to the law of obligations. Literary works such as the plays of Plautus show that this development must have been completed by 200 BC.

The praetor could issue other legal remedies besides actions and exceptions. On the basis of his *imperium* he could issue an order or an injunction; he could, for example, forbid someone to disturb the possession which the plaintiff had acquired in a lawful manner (*interdictum*). Furthermore, if someone had, for instance, been induced by threats to mancipate a slave the praetor could, at that person's request, grant restitution and thus declare the conveyance null and void (*in integrum restitutio*). The *formulae* for all the legal clauses were eventually included in the edict and standardized. The strength of the system was that because the *formulae* were worded so pithily they were not only accurate but they could also be adapted to new cases. Standard *formulae* that had proved their value in practice were taken over by successive praetors; in time they formed the firm core of the edict, the so-called *edictum tralaticium*. In about 50 BC the last new action was added to the edict and this brought to an end the creation of new law by means of the praetorian edict.

For a long time the praetor was almost completely free to decide whether he wished to apply, in a specific case, a legal remedy that he had incorporated in his edict. It was only the other senior magistrates and the tribunes who could exercise their veto in such cases, by virtue of their right of intercession. The praetor's freedom of decision was officially curtailed in 67 BC when, at the suggestion of a certain Cornelius, a tribune, a law was passed stipulating that the praetor had to keep to the edict that he had issued at the beginning of his term of office. In spite of this *lex Cornelia de iurisdictione*, however, the praetor was still free to introduce new legal devices in specific cases and to refuse devices which he had promised in the edict.

6.4.3. The second phase of the lawsuit: *apud iudicem*

The purpose of the *apud iudicem* phase was to obtain a verdict. This phase is either not dealt with at all in the literature or it is treated very superficially. However, it deserves fuller treatment because not only was it important for the various parties involved in a trial but it could also serve a general purpose. By accepting or rejecting a claim concluded in a *formula* the judge could make the praetor alter the *formula* concerned and thus contribute to the development of private law.

Generally the second phase of both the *legis actio* procedure and the procedure by *formula* took place in the presence of only one judge; in certain cases, however, there could be a panel of judges. At the end of the third century BC the *legis actio* type of procedure was extended in that two new courts were established; the *centumviri* (literally a hundred men) and the *decemviri stlitibus iudicandis* (ten men for the trial of cases). Emperor Augustus allowed these two courts to continue even after 17 BC when he abolished the *legis actiones* as the regular kind of procedure. On the basis of scanty evidence from the period of the principate it is assumed that the *centumviri* dealt with claims concerning inheritances with a minimum value of 100,000 sesterces and possibly also with disputes about the ownership of land and about guardianship, whereas the *decemviri* tried cases where someone's liberty was at stake. Hardly anything is known about the way in which these courts functioned. What is certain is that the inheritance trials in the presence of the *centumviri* attracted a great deal of attention. This was not only because of the splendid speeches that were sometimes delivered at these trials but it was also because scandalous revelations were made there about the private lives of wealthy citizens.[9]

The administration of justice was not organised by the state; there was only an official list of Roman citizens who could in specific cases be appointed by the praetor as judges (*album iudicum*). Initially the list contained only senators, but following the reforms instituted by the Gracchi it also included members of the *equites*. In the formulary system the parties were free to choose a judge whose name was not on the official list, provided that person satisfied certain general criteria. Because the judges were private persons they could only give a binding verdict if they had been formally authorised to do so by the praetor; the praetor gave his authorisation at the end of the first phase of the lawsuit via the aforementioned decree.

During the second phase of the formulary procedure the parties could produce evidence and try to convince the judge that they were in the right. Various types of evidence could be used, e.g. statements made by the parties (sometimes under oath), statements by witnesses and written evidence. The general rule still was that: 'the burden of proof rests on the plaintiff', but the judge was free to allow exceptions to the rule. The parties could have their points of view defended by someone else, i.e. an advocate. In principle, all citizens could serve as advocates, but in practice the citizens who performed this task – at least in important cases – belonged to the senatorial class or to the *equites*. Normally the advocates were not paid for their services – although they occasionally received a small token payment – but by serving as advocates they hoped they would win support in the elections to the magistrature or would enhance their reputation in some other way. The advocates usually pleaded in accordance with the rules of Greek rhetoric which had been taught in Rome since the second century BC. These rules consisted mainly of the status system which had been developed at that time by Hermagoras of Temnos and which included a catalogue of disputes and the speeches relating to them. An important part of the training in rhetoric was to learn what arguments one could use to support a case.[10]

The strongest arguments were considered to be based on the facts; for instance, one could deny the stated fact, or one could accept the fact but assert that the law or legal device that had been invoked was inapplicable or one could argue that it was applicable but that there were good reasons that justified the stated fact. If these arguments did not apply in a specific case, then one had to try to find arguments that were based on the law; for instance, perhaps it could be claimed that the words of the law, the will or the contract in question were not clear and should be interpreted more broadly than hitherto. Alternatively, it could be claimed that the words were clear but that they had been written by the legislator, testator or parties for another purpose than stated by the plaintiff; the latter argument could become more convincing if the advocate could refer to precedents, in other words to the fact that in similar cases the law, the will or the contract had also been interpreted in accordance with that purpose. Because in their speeches the advocates gave different interpretations of the remedy that had been included in the *formula*, they demonstrated how wide-ranging this remedy actually was. If the way in which a specific action, exception, etc., was formulated or promised in the edict led in practice to unfair and therefore undesirable verdicts, then the praetor in a subsequent case could word the action differently.[11] As soon as a workable formulation was found it could form a definitive part of the praetorian edict. In this way the advocates through their speeches and the judges through their verdicts made an important contribution to the development of Roman law.

At the end of the lawsuit the judge pronounced his verdict, either on his own or with the help of a *consilium*. He was bound by what he was charged to do in the *formula*. For instance, if he had had to find out whether the defendant owed something to the plaintiff, then his verdict had to include a condemnation or an acquittal; in the former case the verdict always led to the payment of a certain sum of money (*condemnatio pecuniaria*). When it was a question of the dividing up of common property, then the verdict included an adjudgment (*adiudicatio*). Because the parties had agreed to accept the judge's verdict, it was binding and they could not appeal to another judge.

6.5. LEGAL SCIENCE

It is generally accepted that Roman legal science began in the second century BC, under the influence of the Greek philosophers. Until that time there had been interpretation of laws and legal remedies in connection with the administration of justice. The new development was that young Romans from the senatorial class were taught methodically how to compose and deliver various types of speeches; these included political speeches, eulogies and the most difficult type: pleading in court. Initially much of the tuition was given by Greek teachers of rhetoric who gave considerable attention to grammar, style, logic and presentation. It was in that context that the Romans became acquainted with Plato's dialectic method; by means of this method they learnt to divide juridically relevant facts into *genera* and *species* and to define these facts and thus to distinguish and categorise juridical concepts. In addition, they became acquainted with the syllogism (or reasoned conclusions) and in this way learnt to form juridical concepts in a deductive manner. There was soon a small group of leading Roman citizens, the jurists, who belonged to the senate and had a very specialised knowledge of Roman law. These were the people who, following in the wake of the pontiffs, were largely responsible for the development of Roman legal science.[12]

The activities of the Roman jurists are described by Cicero as *respondere*, *agere* and *cavere* (*De oratore* 1.48.212). They show that the jurists did not form a separate class in society that kept aloof from legal practice and from politics, as is often maintained, but that their opinion was regarded as valuable just because they were part of Rome's most powerful constitutional body, the senate. *Cavere* (literally, to take precautions) meant the drafting of texts to be used in legal practice; these could be *formulae* drawn up in connection with a lawsuit by a jurist either serving as magistrate or as a member of the senate advising the magistrate. *Cavere* could also mean the drafting of deeds, for instance deeds of sale and wills. Here the jurists developed standard clauses, for instance the so-called *cautio Muciana*, which seems to have been drafted by Q. Mucius Scaevola (beginning of the first century BC); the *cautio Muciana* was the promise that the legatee had to make to the heir, namely that he would return the legacy if he were to fulfil the condition which was attached to the legacy.[13]

Agere (literally, to act) meant serving as advocates in a lawsuit.

As mentioned earlier (see section 6.4.3), the speeches of the advocates often dealt with the interpretation of laws and legal devices. Unfortunately only very few of the speeches dealing with private law have survived; these include the speeches *pro Tullio* and *pro Caecina* by Cicero. From the oratorical works of Cicero we can follow the main lines of a famous inheritance lawsuit, the so-called *causa Curiana* in which Q. Mucius Scaevola and C. Licinius Crassus served as advocates.[14]

Respondere (literally, to answer) meant giving an opinion on a legal problem to citizens, to jurisdiction magistrates and to judges. Sometimes those opinions were ratified by a verdict, sometimes they were not. Very few of the *responsa* given by the republican jurists have survived either. We know that from the second century BC some leading jurists began making collections of *responsa* that they had given and that had been applied in practice. A need had arisen for such collections because in Rome the administration of justice was not organised by the state (the praetor always appointed an *ad hoc* judge) and consequently the verdicts given by a judge were not collected on behalf of the state. In their collections the jurists sometimes summarised cases that were important in their eyes and reported the verdict or opinion given in those cases; sometimes they also formulated an abstract rule of law on the basis of an actual case. In so doing they often omitted to mention the motives for the verdict because these were not relevant for the purpose for which the collection was made.[15] Hitherto the jurists had collected *formulae* for lawsuits, but now they collected *responsa* and verdicts based on a *responsum* in which new law had been created. Well-known books (or rather scrolls) about the *ius civile* are those by M.P. Cato Licinianus (chosen as praetor for the year 149 – he died before taking office), Manius Manilius (consul in 149 BC) and the aforementioned Q. Mucius Scaevola (consul in 95 BC). Other jurists from the last few decades of the republic include C. Aquilius Gallus (praetor in 66 BC), S. Sulpicius Rufus (consul in 51 BC) and P. Alfenus Varus (consul *suffectus* in 39 BC, i.e. chosen as an interim consul upon the death or resignation of one of the consuls); Rufus was the first of these jurists to use the praetorian edict instead of the *ius civile* as his frame of reference. Unfortunately the works of these jurists have not survived intact, but we do have access to fragments since they are cited by later jurists.[16]

As can be seen from the foregoing, Roman legal science

developed largely from legal practice. The Roman jurists formulated abstract juridical concepts under the influence of Greek philosophy. However, they were not inspired by a specific theoretical concept and they did not seek to construct systems of abstract theories; they started with an actual case and tried to find a just solution that was acceptable in practice. The reason why Roman jurisprudence developed under the influence of Greek philosophy and yet is clearly Roman in character is that the Greek influence was not effective until the second century BC; by that time Roman law had developed sufficiently to withstand confrontation with Greek law. Finally one may well wonder why it was the Romans rather than the Greeks who developed legal science. A possible reason is that the Greek cities preserved their autonomy and their own legal systems and, as a result, Greek law was greatly influenced by local conditions. The Romans on the other hand founded what for those days was a vast empire in which law played a leading role and helped them achieve their imperial ambitions. The Romans became the founders of legal science because they were able to combine their organising talent and their legal talent with the tenets of Greek philosophy.

Part III

THE PRINCIPATE
(27 bc–284)

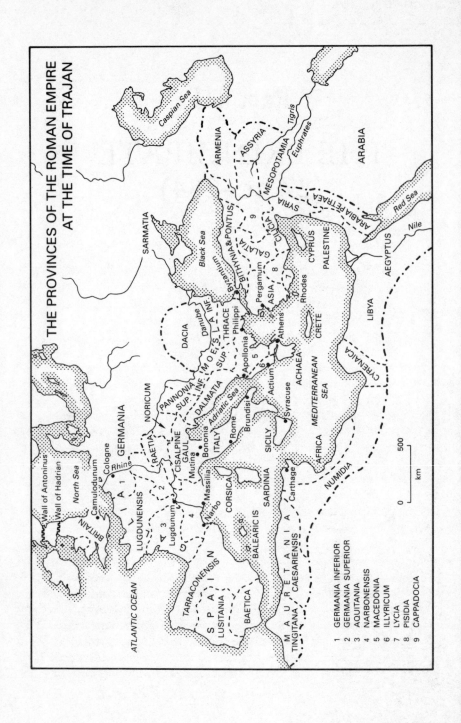

THE PROVINCES OF THE ROMAN EMPIRE
AT THE TIME OF TRAJAN

1 GERMANIA INFERIOR
2 GERMANIA SUPERIOR
3 AQUITANIA
4 NARBONENSIS
5 MACEDONIA
6 ILLYRICUM
7 LYCIA
8 PISIDIA
9 CAPPADOCIA

7

THE PRINCIPATE: GENERAL OUTLINE

7.1. THE SOURCES

Much more is known about the first three centuries of the empire, usually called principate, than about the republic. The many literary sources of the time provide a great deal of information on this period as do the innumerable inscriptions that have survived. Because the sources are both extensive and varied we can obtain a reasonably reliable picture of the principate.

The political events of the period have been dealt with by historians like Tacitus and Suetonius (end of the first century) and Cassius Dio (beginning of the third century). Their works are important primarily in as much as they relate to the period in which the historians themselves lived. Other literary works such as the poems of Martial and Juvenal and the letters of Pliny the Younger, who were all contemporaries of Tacitus, and the short stories of Aulus Gellius (middle of second century) mainly give information about daily life in Rome.

The inscriptions from the principate relate to a wide variety of subjects. For instance, the political testament of Emperor Augustus, in which he gave an official account of his reign, can still be seen today on the walls of the former temple of 'Roma et Augustus' in Ankara. A large inscription dating from the second half of the first century, which was recently found in Seville in the south of Spain, contains a law relating to the administration and civil procedure in a number of *municipia*. In addition, inscriptions (or parts of inscriptions) are found from time to time in the catacombs underneath the Via Appia in Rome. These inscriptions originally adorned the sepulchral monuments of rich citizens who were buried beside this road, just outside the city boundary. Some of them contain testamentary dispositions of the deceased person and in one case even a whole testament, providing us with valuable information on the law of succession.

Literature of a specifically juridical nature from this period has come down to us via the *Corpus Iuris Civilis* of Justinian, which dates from the sixth century; the best known juridical literature that has come down to us separately is the Institutes of Gaius, a textbook dating from about 160 AD. Our knowledge about the law in the first three centuries is also based on documents which have been preserved on wax tablets and on papyri which contain, among other things, contracts and wills.

7.2. THE TERRITORY

The Roman empire attained its maximum size in the principate: it included not only the area around the Mediterranean but also large parts of central and western Europe where the Danube and the Rhine formed the principal frontiers.[1] Augustus (27 BC–14 AD) and his successor Tiberius (14–37) conquered Raetia, Noricum, Pannonia and Moesia, which are parts of modern Switzerland, Austria, Hungary and Bulgaria respectively. For a short time, Germany, as far as the Elbe, was also in the hands of the Romans, but when, in 9 AD in the Teutoburgian Forest, a Roman legion was routed by the German tribe of the Cherusci and completely destroyed, the Romans withdrew to the left bank of the Rhine. Thereafter they made the Rhine the northern boundary of their empire. It was not until almost a century later that the Flavian emperors, and particularly Domitian (81–96), again tried to conquer the southern part of Germany, this time successfully. During the reign of Domitian the Romans conquered England and Wales as well. The 'pacification' of these regions had already begun in the days of Emperor Claudius (41–54). At that time the local tribes, however, had been able to successfully resist subjugation by the Romans. Finally Agricola managed to subdue them so that they transferred their allegiance to Rome. Scotland was conquered as well, but the northern part was abandoned because keeping it would have required too much man-power. Emperor Trajan (98–117) succeeded in conquering Dacia, present-day Romania, and thereby added a large region north of the Danube to the Roman empire; in addition, in the east of the empire he crossed the Euphrates and subjugated Armenia, Assyria and Mesopotamia, but his successor Hadrian (117–138) made the river Euphrates the frontier again. This emperor also gained fame by having a stone wall built between England and Scotland to ward off invasions by Scottish tribes.

The emperors themselves organised the administration of the newly conquered territories; the administration of the existing provinces remained with the senate – they were now called senatorial provinces – but the emperors increasingly took over the administration of these provinces as well.

Towards the end of the republic Roman citizenship extended over the whole of Italy.[2] Thereafter, this right was granted slowly but surely to people in the provinces too, either collectively (e.g. to the population of a town) or individually (e.g. to soldiers given honourable discharge from the army). Partly as a result of this, the differences between Italy and the provinces gradually disappeared. Roman citizenship, which had formerly been a symbol of nationalism, now became a status symbol. At the same time Italy came to be administered more and more like the provinces; Emperor Trajan, for instance, put the towns of Italy under his control. At the end of the second century the only remaining difference between the inhabitants of Italy and the inhabitants of the provinces was that the former were exempt from land tax. Finally, in 212 Emperor Antonine, nicknamed Caracalla, granted Roman citizenship to practically all free inhabitants of the empire. According to Cassius Dio, Caracalla took this step for fiscal reasons: certain taxes which had formerly applied only to Roman citizens would now bring in more revenue. In a political sense this so-called *constitutio Antoniniani* was not so important; in a juridical sense, however, it was important. Not only did it lead to the application of Roman law in the whole empire but it also led to the adaptation of Roman law to local law, which was mainly Greek law, and thus to the merging of Roman and Greek law.

As long as the frontiers of the empire were not seriously threatened from the outside, little effort was required to guard them and the empire could become wealthy and prosperous. At the beginning of the third century, however, the political situation along the Rhine, the Danube and the Euphrates began to change quite suddenly and it then became clear that the frontiers of this extensive empire were too long to be defended adequately. As a result there was a long period of confusion and uncertainty which did not end until Emperor Diocletian (284–305) fundamentally reorganised the empire and made it defensible and governable again.

7.3. THE POPULATION

The transition from republic to principate, which constituted a political revolution, also brought about changes in the social structure of the Roman empire.[3]

An upper class was formed by the senatorial aristocracy and the *equites*, whereas the urban aristocracy from outside Rome constituted a middle class; the rest of the population still formed the lower class. These classes were interwoven in the sense that a web of patron-client relationships existed which had developed during the republic and continued on much the same basis into the third century. The centre of the web was now of course formed by the emperor and his court.[4]

7.3.1. The senatorial aristocracy and the *equites*

The senatorial aristocracy and the *equites* together formed the upper class.[5] During the late republic the senatorial aristocracy consisted of those who had been chosen to serve as quaestors or as higher magistrates, and their agnate descendants up to and including the third generation. From now on, however, the magistrates were no longer chosen by the *comitia* but by the emperor. When Augustus came to power he replaced a number of senators by men from his own ranks; he chose mainly prominent persons from the *municipia* and the *coloniae* in Italy. This policy was continued by his successors, but they also admitted prominent persons from the provinces. In the third century, therefore, the senatorial élite no longer had any connection with the old aristocratic families of the republic or the time of Augustus.[6]

The financial situation of the senators also changed in the principate. In the past most of the senators had been large landowners. At the time of Tiberius (14–37) and Claudius (41–54) and particularly during the reign of Nero (54–68) many of them fell victim to the emperor's greed: their capital was confiscated or had to be left to the emperor in their wills. In this way the emperor became the largest landowner in the empire.

The *equites* now belonged to the upper class too. During the late republic they had been a kind of lower aristocracy of businessmen. They had primarily been engaged in trade, in levying taxes for the state and the like and had preferred to invest their profits in agriculture. During the empire the *equites* began to play a central role in the imperial administrative machinery. Within this class a hierarchy now developed which was determined by the rank persons had reached in the bureaucracy. Those who had held the highest positions in the army or in the administration formed an élite within the *equites* which was comparable to the highest ranks among the senatorial aristocracy. Unlike the regular *equites* in the *municipia* and in Rome itself who formed the lower ranks of the *equites*, the bureaucratic élite were highly esteemed in society and exerted great influence on the government.

From the first century members of the *equites* were also often admitted to the senate. In the long run the difference between the *equites* and the senatorial élite gradually disappeared: members of both classes now took part in the administration. Both classes consisted of well-to-do persons and the *equites* were sometimes even better off than the senators.

7.3.2. The urban aristocracy

The governors of the towns in the Roman empire, together with their families, formed a middle class in Roman society. A town was governed by a senate, called *ordo decurionum*. Members of the *ordo* were not paid by the central administration; they were selected on the basis of their social and financial position. A dishonourable profession or a 'criminal record' was an obstacle to membership and since the time of Tiberius it had been only freeborns who could become *decuriones*. To become a member of the *ordo decurionum* one probably had to have capital over a certain amount. We know that in the town of Comum in northern Italy, for instance, the minimum capital required was 100,000 sesterces. However, whether such a criterion was observed or not, the *decuriones* had to be rather wealthy: they had to share responsibility for public works and magisterial functions and they were personally responsible for the tax that the town was required to pay. Since the *decuriones* were recruited from the wealthy families, their office gradually became a matter of hereditary right and duty. When in the third century the economic and political situation deteriorated and the central administration grew weaker, the *decuriones* were responsible for cohesion and stability at provincial level. Then the position of *decurio* was no longer so attractive; because of the increasing pressure of taxation the function which had once been an honourable one, became a heavy burden that few people wished to shoulder.

7.3.3. The rest of the population

As in the days of the republic, the rest of the population consisted of all those who did not belong to the upper classes. They included the artisans, the farmers and farm labourers, the masses who could not earn a living and the slaves. But this group too underwent some changes during the principate. First of all, this group no longer consisted solely of citizens who were originally Roman; many of the innumerable slaves who had been brought to Italy during the late republic had in the meantime been manumitted by their owners and had thereby acquired Roman citizenship. Some of them succeeded in holding down reasonably well-paid jobs, and they and their descendants became respectable Roman citizens. Secondly, the number of people who could not earn their own living rose considerably; they moved to the large towns and became part of the urban proletariat. Because these people constituted a potential threat to political stability, food was distributed regularly and games and impressive spectacles were organised. This 'bread and games' treatment was meted out to the urban proletariat in Rome as well as in the other large towns of the empire.[7]

7.4. ECONOMY

In the first two centuries of the principate the Romans experienced a period of great prosperity. Agriculture and industry flourished and as a result a great deal of trading went on. Now that the entire Mediterranean area and a large part of western and central Europe were under Roman rule there was nothing to prevent a free exchange of products.[8]

In about 50 BC much of the large-scale landownership which had been a feature of Italy under the late republic came to an end: large numbers of the *latifundia* were confiscated and split up into medium-sized farms. A certain amount of large-scale land-ownership continued, but mainly in the provinces. At that time Egypt was the granary of the Roman empire, the main products of Italy being wine and olive oil. Initially, these were exported in large quantities to Spain, Gaul and Africa. However, in the second half of the first century the Roman colonists in these provinces began to produce and export wine and oil themselves. As a result these countries were no longer a market for Italy. Because the countries in the eastern Mediterranean had long been self-supporting in wine and oil there was no demand for Italian products there either. During the first two centuries of the principate agriculture brought prosperity to the provinces but not to Italy itself.

Because fewer countries were conquered, the supply of slaves dwindled. As a result the price of slaves increased and slave labour became expensive. Consequently large landowners preferred to lease parts of their estates to tenants. A tenant was given a farm and land and sometimes also tools and equipment. The tenancy was usually granted for a period of five years, the rent being paid annually. From the second century onwards the tenant was not required to pay rent that year if there was a poor harvest or the harvest failed due to circumstances beyond his control; in such cases the tenant could be exempted from rent by or on behalf of the emperor. Because a tenant therefore no longer had to run great risks those small farmers who were still independent found it attractive to rent a farm. As a result the number of independent farmers, both in Italy and in the provinces, declined still further.

Artefacts had been manufactured in Italy since the beginning of the second century BC. At the beginning of the principate, there was an enormous increase in the production of artefacts; terracotta pottery (the famous *terra sigillata*), metal pots and pans, glass, woollen materials and toilet requisites were produced in large quantities and exported to all parts of the empire. Nevertheless, Italy was unable to compete with similar products originating in countries in the eastern Mediterranean; the glass from Syria was better, Alexandria supplied the whole known world with papyrus, linen, perfume and similar goods, and finer woollen goods were made in Asia Minor than in Italy. In the second century Italy lost its lead in the west as well: there Gaul, followed by Germany, took over the production of pottery, glass and bronze utensils. In Italy only small workshops survived which supplied goods exclusively for the local market.

As under the republic, most of these goods were transported by sea, and only a few went overland. The land route received a boost when the Roman emperors extended the network of roads.

By the end of the second century it covered the whole empire; the tracks and sometimes even the roads themselves are still visible today. Trade relations extended even beyond the frontiers of the empire; in the second century there must have been well-used trading routes via the North Sea, the Danube and the Vistula. Furthermore, in those days Greek and Syrian merchants even had regular trading contacts with China; of the two routes involved, one being a land route, the other a sea route, it was the one over the Indian Ocean that remained important because ships could use the trade-winds. This sea route led to close contacts with the west coast of India where Roman products were traded for spices, precious stones, etc.

During the republic a number of governmental tasks such as the collection of taxes in the provinces, the construction of roads and the organisation of transport were 'farmed out' to private persons, the hated *publicani* and their companies. But by the beginning of the principate the situation had begun to change. In the provinces like Egypt and Gaul, which were under the direct authority of Augustus, the land tax (the most important form of tax) was levied directly by the local administrators supervised by an imperial official; the other tasks were put in the hands of the urban administrators. This system, which had operated long before the Romans arrived in Egypt, was gradually introduced into other provinces and finally into the whole empire. Indirect taxes, however, continued to be collected by tax-farmers well into the third century.[9]

8

THE PRINCIPATE:
THE STATE

The political structure of the Roman empire had changed fundamentally as a result of the civil wars that had swept the country
in the last 100 years of the republic. Real power was now in the
hands of the emperor. The elements that had formed the political
structure during the republic – the senate, the magistrates and the
assembly – acquired a different function or they disappeared. The
senate, whose experience in administration was almost indispens-
able, retained its administrative function – though it was far less
prominent than before – and acquired an additional task in the
field of legislation and the administration of justice. The functions
of the magistrates were gradually eroded. The assembly, which
had lost its original function since the extension of the empire,
hardly convened at all. The administrative tasks that these organs
had traditionally performed were gradually taken over by imperial
officials. Under the principate the army began to constitute an
important element in the political structure of the Roman empire.

8.1. THE EMPEROR

8.1.1. The first princeps

It is impossible and old-fashioned to try and describe the essence
of the principate in simple terms. The phenomenon can best be
explained by the events which followed the murder of Julius
Caesar in 44 BC and which led Augustus to seize power for an
indefinite period.[1] In 44 BC the prevailing problem was that the
empire could no longer be governed according to the republican
constitution. The three most important leaders at the time were
Mark Antony, Gaius Lepidus and Caesar's adopted son Gaius

Julius Caesar Octavianus, the later emperor Augustus, who then was still under 20 years of age. In 43 BC Antony, Lepidus and Octavian decided to share power by forming a triumvirate. Since each of them had at his disposal, and was financially responsible for, a fair-sized army it was comparatively easy for them to persuade the assembly to give them power for a period of five years in order 'to restore the republic'. Five years later this power was extended (probably again by the assembly) for another five years. By the end of this second period the relationships between the *triumvires* had changed dramatically. Lepidus was forced by Octavian to accept the less important post of *pontifex maximus* and was thus side-tracked, whereas Antony and Octavian did not relinquish their special powers. At the time Antony was in the eastern Mediterranean with a Roman army and Octavian was in Italy.

The tension came to a head when Antony, although still married to Octavian's sister Octavia, married Cleopatra, Queen of Egypt, and thereby gave people the impression that he wanted to found in the eastern Mediterranean a Hellenistic kingdom that was independent of Rome. At the suggestion of Octavian the senate decided to declare war only on Cleopatra so that formally a civil war between Octavian and Antony could be avoided: Octavian was put in charge of the troops. Before leading his army into battle Octavian made many Italians and inhabitants of the western provinces swear an oath of allegiance to him.[2] Octavian fought and defeated Antony and Cleopatra at the battle of Actium (Actium being an island off the west coast of Greece) in 31 BC; in the following year Octavian conquered Egypt. For a long time afterwards Egypt was considered so important, and therefore risky, that senators were not allowed to visit it without special permission from the emperor.

Octavian remained for a while in the eastern Mediterranean for organisational reasons. Upon returning to Rome in 27 BC he relinquished his special powers and, as he said later, he gave the republic back to the senate and the Roman people. However, the result of this gesture was that the senate and the assembly began bestowing on Octavian a range of powers and titles which placed him in a unique position. Most of these were already known from the time of the republic but they now acquired a new dimension through their form and number. Some of these powers and titles were completely new. In any case, the result was that Octavian, who now received the honorary title Augustus, in fact became an absolute monarch, *Caesar Augustus*.

8.1.2. The principles of imperial power

Straightaway, i.e. in 27 BC, Augustus was given responsibility for Spain, Gaul and Syria for a period of ten years; this so-called *imperium proconsulare* not only gave him control over these provinces but it also gave him command of the armies in these countries.[3] Of the powers that Augustus acquired later two were vitally important: the *imperium proconsulare maius* and the *tribunicia potestas*. Augustus was granted these two powers in 23 BC when he relinquished the consulship which he had held until then. The *imperium proconsulare maius* gave him supreme power in all the provinces and therefore placed him above even the governors of provinces which were still under the authority of the senate; this power was granted to him for life. The *tribunicia potestas* gave Augustus the powers of a tribune, but with two striking differences: this power was not granted for a year but for life and in addition he was immune to intercession on the part of other magistrates. In his capacity as tribune he could summon the assembly and propose laws, he could summon the senate and he could veto decisions taken by the magistrates.

Other duties and powers assigned to Augustus were the *imperium consulare* (19 BC), whereby he acquired just as much power as the consuls in Rome and Italy, and the *cura annonae* (22 BC) whereby he became responsible for the food supply, which was of great political importance, particularly for the city of Rome. On various occasions he was made a censor, which enabled him to have a say in the composition of the senate. Finally, after the death of Lepidus in 12 BC, Augustus also received the title of *pontifex maximus*, a title which gave him honour and dignity rather than power.

Perhaps even more important than all these powers and titles bestowed on Augustus was the personal authority, *auctoritas*, he enjoyed. Augustus had acquired this prestige on the basis of his military and political successes. In his political testament, the *res gestae divi Augusti*, in which Augustus described what he had done for Rome during his life and what honours and powers he had received in return, he stated that he had had just as much power as the other magistrates but had had more *auctoritas*. Probably it was this combination of legal and extra-legal authority which constituted the strength of his emperorship.

8.1.3. The succession

Because the power of Augustus was formally based on a number of special magisterial functions, a successor could not automatically take office. On the other hand, if the problem of the succession were not settled immediately the stability of the empire could be in jeopardy. This was why Augustus, during his forty years in office, had let the assembly grant special powers such as the *tribunicia potestas* and the *imperium proconsulare* to persons whom he regarded as suitable to succeed him. When Augustus died in 14 AD the only survivor of this group of persons was his adopted stepson Tiberius, and the senate and the people had no hesitation in proclaiming Tiberius as emperor.

During the principate emperorship is always linked with the magistrature. As a result the succession remained problematical for a long time, even when emperorship as such was no longer disputed. In the course of time the succession was dealt with in various ways: by inheritance and by selection of a new emperor by the former emperor, the senate or the army. The dynasty of the Julian-Claudian house, founded by Augustus, came to an end in 68 AD with the suicide of Nero. In the following year the emperorship passed to three persons in succession before the general Vespasian made a successful bid for power. In 79 AD he was succeeded by his son Titus (79–81), who was in time succeeded by his brother Domitian (81–96). When Domitian was murdered he left no son to succeed him; the senate therefore chose, from among its own ranks, a new emperor, Nerva (96–98). Because Nerva was already quite elderly and wanted to have personal control of the army, which was becoming restless, he adopted Trajan, a successful general from Spain; Trajan then succeeded him as emperor. This system of so-called adopted emperors turned out to work exceptionally well. The system was applied well into the second century; there was even one case where an emperor, Antoninus Pius (138–161), excluded his own son from the succession. When Marcus Aurelius (161–180) was succeeded by his son Commodus, who turned out to be insane, political stability came to an end. In the next 100 years one emperor followed another in quick succession; only Septimius Severus (193–211) and Alexander Severus (222–235) were able to survive for longish periods. Under their rule it was the army who decided who would be emperor. After the death of Alexander Severus it sometimes happened that various legions simultaneously proclaimed their own general as emperor and the final decision had to be made on the battlefield. This state of anarchy did not cease until Diocletian became emperor in 284 AD. His predecessors, Carus, Carinus and Numerianus (282–284), had not even bothered to acquire the *tribunicia potestas*, so formally the principate had then already ended.[4]

8.2. THE SENATE

The position of the senate in the principate was totally different from its position under the republic: whereas the senate had been the most powerful organ in the Roman empire until the first century BC, power was now concentrated in the hands of one person, the emperor. This shift in power, which occurred quite gradually, naturally had a marked influence on the position of the senate: it affected not only its composition and its way of functioning but also its tasks.[5]

In the last 100 years of the republic the composition of the senate was subjected to many changes. On the one hand the patrician families had suffered badly in the civil wars and the number of senators from their ranks was still low; on the other hand the revolution had brought a large number of people from plebeian families into the senate. At the very beginning of his reign Augustus purged the senate at least twice; in 29/28 BC and in 18 BC, by virtue of his powers as censor, he removed fifty and 140 senators respectively, reducing their number to 600. At the same time he filled the ranks of the senate with persons whom he regarded as suitable. He did this not only indirectly by exerting influence on the election of magistrates – performing a magisterial function had long been the only way of becoming a member of the senate – but also directly by admitting to the senate citizens who had not fulfilled any of the prescribed magisterial functions. He chose mainly prominent persons from towns in Italy. The later emperors continued with this policy. Under Vespasian (69–79) it was mainly persons from the *equites*, the urban aristocracy and the western provinces who became senators. In the second half of the second century new politics based on Hellenistic culture began and prominent persons from the eastern provinces were also admitted to the senate. In the third century, therefore, all parts of the empire, with the exception of Egypt, were represented in the senate.

The form in which the senate met remained basically unchanged during the principate; this was determined by the rules of customary law. We know that Augustus passed a law, *lex Iulia de senatu habendo*, introducing some new rules concerning the way the senate should function. Unfortunately, the content of this law has not come down to us directly; our information stems from several authors who mention that among other things the law stated how often the senate should meet, the number of senators required for a quorum and the penalties imposed on senators for failing to attend a meeting.

The emperors had a dramatic influence on the powers of the senate. As stated earlier, in about 25 BC the senate had transferred its most important powers to Augustus; these powers related to home and foreign policy, waging war, the administration, the supervision of legislation and to the magisterial elections. Nevertheless, Augustus and his successors did not discount the senate completely. Tiberius in particular saw to it that the senate was given new tasks to perform in the administrative sphere and acquired new responsibilities with regard to legislation and the administration of justice. Not surprisingly, the part of the administration relating to the senatorial provinces remained in the hands of the senate, as did the control of the aerarium, the former treasury. Furthermore, during the reign of Tiberius the task of electing magistrates was transferred from the *comitia* to the senate, and even in the legislative sphere the senate began to play the role formerly played by the *comitia*: the senatorial decree now took the place of the *lex*. The emperors also involved the senate in the administration of justice. Although the senate had been involved in a number of special cases dealt with before the beginning of the principate, in about 20 AD it started to serve regularly as *forum privilegiatum* in criminal cases.

The senate was able to retain its tasks and duties up to the end of the second century. After the death of Marcus Aurelius in 180 AD, however, there were emperors who had little contact with the senate. The administrative functions were entrusted increasingly to the *equites*, i.e. to persons from the class of knights. Although from that time onwards the senate no longer had any real power, membership of that esteemed institution was still sought after and was regarded by many as the climax of a political career.

8.3. MAGISTRATES AND OFFICIALS

8.3.1. The magistrates

The weak spot in the magistrature was the system of collegiality and annuity and the resultant lack of continuity and decisiveness. Although this system had worked fairly well in the days of the republic when the Roman territory was not so large and the senate formed the binding element, it was no longer effective in the later days of the republic. Changes were called for; these could be accomplished most easily and therefore could be carried out first in the imperial provinces. There the tasks that used to be performed by magistrates were assigned to imperial officials. The other magisterial functions continued to exist, although they were dismantled slowly but surely. Some of them, in particular the consulate and the tribunate, were used by the emperors as a basis for their power and thereby lost their original character.[6]

The only task that the consuls retained was the chairmanship of the senate. As a compensation the consuls were given several tasks connected with imperial jurisdiction.[7] The emperors hardly interfered at all with the praetorship: of the eight praetors two retained the (civil) *iurisdictio* and the other six remained chairmen of the special criminal courts. During the principate another ten praetors were appointed; their task was to apply the new imperial laws. The duties of the censor were now performed by the emperors themselves, either formally if the office had been assigned to the emperors specially, or informally. Just like the consulate, the function of tribune also lost its meaning when the emperors based their power on that office too and as with the consuls the tribunes were given several tasks in the imperial administration of justice. Among the lower magistrates the aediles lost their most important tasks, the *cura urbis* and the *cura annonae*, which passed to the imperial officials; the only duties they retained were the supervision of the market and the *iurisdictio* in that area. From the time of Nero the supervision of the aerarium, the state treasury, which had long been the chief task of the quaestors, was entrusted to two officials appointed by the emperor.

8.3.2. The officials

The position of the imperial officials was quite different from that of the magistrates. They were appointed by the emperor but were not granted *imperium* or *potestas*. The only powers they received were those delegated to them by the emperor. As a result the emperor could remove these powers from them at any time; the powers also lapsed upon the death of the emperor. The officials were selected on the basis of their abilities, and came not only from the senatorial élite but also from the *equites*. The principles of collegiality and annuity did not apply to these imperial officials. In addition, the officials were paid for their work according to their rank.

The most important officials were the *praefectus praetorio* and the *praefectus urbi*. From the time of Augustus the praetorian prefect was the head of the imperial bodyguard. He enjoyed the emperor's confidence and was therefore often very influential. During the principate the praetorian prefect also acquired jurisdictional powers in the whole empire except for the area that included Rome and 100 miles beyond its boundary. At first these powers were delegated to him by the emperor; later he exercised these powers in his own right. In the third century leading jurists like Papinian and Ulpian held office as praetorian prefects. The city prefect was originally the representative of the emperor in Rome when the emperor was away. He was quickly made responsible for maintaining public order in Rome and several cohorts were put at his disposal for that purpose. In addition, like the praetorian prefect, he was granted jurisdictional powers, but these powers were for matters in Rome itself and within a 100-mile radius of Rome.

During the reign of Claudius (41–54) the emperor's personal secretariat became so large that he established four departments or chanceries: the *a rationibus* for economic affairs, the *a memoria* for the records, the *ab epistulis* for the emperor's official correspondence and the *a libellis* for dealing with petitions from citizens. Much to the annoyance of the senate, Claudius appointed freedmen as heads of these chanceries. Most of them, however, were very well educated men from the eastern provinces of the empire. Upon their manumission they had acquired the emperor as their patron and as a result owed him respect and allegiance. Emperor Domitian also appointed members of the *equites* to these functions, but it was not until the reign of Hadrian, when the chanceries were reorganised, that the heads were selected exclusively from the *equites*. The *equites* also played a greater part in the control of the imperial treasury (the *fiscus*), into which flowed the taxes levied in the imperial provinces and from which the emperor paid his officials.

Finally Augustus and his successors also used a traditional Roman device, namely the *consilium* or the advisory council. Before any important decisions were taken with regard to public and private functions Romans were accustomed to consult with family and friends. The emperors did this too; in connection with political and military problems and with problems relating to the administration of justice they always formed an ad hoc *consilium* of trusted friends and experts. Particularly senators whom we know as jurists often participated in the *consilium*; Salvius Julianus, for instance, was a member of Hadrian's *consilium*. By this time the *consilium principis* had become a permanent and salaried body whose members were appointed for life.

8.4. THE ARMY

Whereas in the first two centuries of the principate the political structure was formed mainly by the emperor and his officials and by the senate, the most influential element in the third century was the army. Since about 100 BC the army had no longer consisted exclusively of Roman citizens doing compulsory military service but also included some professionals. The officers, however, as in the past, came from the senatorial aristocracy and the *equites*: they served in the army as part of their political career. The army soon developed into an exceptionally effective but expensive instrument.[8]

Compared to the size of the empire the army was really quite small but its power was so great that in wartime Roman generals considered that a *ratio* of one Roman soldier to two to four enemy soldiers was adequate. The army was usually stationed along the frontiers, the largest concentrations being on the Danube, the Euphrates and the Rhine. For centuries the chief 'weapon' had been the heavy infantry which was organised in legions. The legions were supported by local troops consisting mainly of cavalry. In the third century the main emphasis shifted to heavily armed cavalry. The effectiveness of the army was increased by strict discipline and thorough training; any legion that gave up a fight or mutinied was 'decimated': every tenth soldier was clubbed to death by his fellow-soldiers. In addition, every ordinary Roman soldier was also an engineer and in conquered territories the Romans not only built fortified camps but they also linked them together by a network of military roads which permitted rapid troop movements. The frontiers were strengthened where necessary, e.g. in England, Germany and North Africa. Since the army was so effective it also constituted a dangerous political factor; it could only be properly controlled if the soldiers were paid adequately and on time. When one emperor succeeded another, the army had to be 'bought over', which did not always make economic sense.

During the civil wars at the end of the republic and during the first two centuries of the principate the army was occasionally of overriding importance. In a struggle for power the only person who emerged victorious was the one with a loyal army. This became apparent in various ways: directly from the victories of, for example, Augustus and Vespasian, indirectly from the adoption by Emperor Nerva of the successful general Trajan whom he thereby designated as his successor. In the third century and particularly after the death of Alexander Severus in 235 it occurred regularly that generals of various armies were pronounced emperors by their troops and that the decision about who could in fact be emperor was made on the battlefield. Because it often took years for an emperor to defeat his opponents it sometimes came about that tiny realms were formed and managed by a former Roman general; this happened mainly in frontier areas, for example in the north-west of Gaul and in England. In the period between 235 and 285 there were about sixteen official emperors and many more unofficial emperors or usurpers. This period is also referred to as the period of the soldier emperors. Diocletian was the first general who managed to bring the whole Roman empire under his power and keep things that way for at least twenty years. The changes that he introduced into the organisation of the empire and that in many respects had been prepared by his predecessors determined the political structure of the Roman empire in the last few centuries of its existence.

9

THE PRINCIPATE:
THE LAW

9.1. INTRODUCTION

The beginning of the principate was marked by sweeping changes in the law. Whereas under the republic the senate basically had been responsible for lawmaking, power now shifted to the emperor and law too came into his sphere of influence. The process, however, was a gradual one, as can be seen in legislation, the administration of justice and in legal science.[1]

Laws were still made by the *comitia* and the senate, but the emperors, by virtue of their special powers, could influence the content of the laws. In the long run the emperors themselves began enacting laws. Ultimately, the republican methods of legislation fell into disuse: the *leges*-plebiscites by the end of the first century and the senatorial decrees by the beginning of the third century.

In the principate justice continued to be administered via the *formula* procedure in the case of disputes coming under private law (and in certain cases by means of *legis actiones*) and by means of the *quaestiones* in the case of criminal offences. At the same time, however, a new form of procedure, called the *cognitio extraordinaria*, developed. This was used by or on behalf of the emperor in connection with both types of case.

Legal science was still in the hands of the jurists. Their activities now concentrated on the giving of opinions. Here too the emperors interfered by granting certain leading senators the right to give, on their behalf, opinions on legal problems (*ius respondendi*); in the case of a lawsuit these opinions were binding for the judge. This *ius respondendi* probably limited the number of jurists giving opinions. In the second century the emperors let opinions be given in their own name as well. As under the republic, the jurists themselves collected the opinions they gave; a relatively large part of these collections has been preserved via the Digest. In addition, some jurists also published introductory textbooks, the most important one being the Institutes of Gaius.

Nowadays the law of this period is normally referred to as classical law. There are two main reasons for this: firstly, the jurists of the principate did much to develop and elaborate Roman law and, secondly, since the rediscovery of the Digest in the eleventh century the law of this period has been normative for later generations of jurists.

9.2. LEGISLATION

9.2.1. Leges and plebiscites

In the late republic there were no longer any clear-cut distinctions between the various types of assemblies and even the *concilium plebis* hardly differed from the *comitia*. In this period plebiscites were often formulated at the suggestion of the tribunes; these plebiscites were then referred to as *leges*.

As mentioned earlier, the *tribunicia potestas* was one of the main pillars on which Augustus – at least formally – based his power; he, and after him in particular also Emperor Claudius (41–54) used their authority as tribunes to make a number of important innovations. Their laws, just like those of the republic, had a political character. In 18 BC, for instance, laws were formulated relating to marriage and divorce (*lex Iulia de maritandis ordinibus*) and to bribery during elections (*lex Iulia de ambitu*); in the *leges Iuliae iudiciorum publicorum et privatorum* of 17 BC the administration of justice was reorganised. In 9 BC the above-mentioned *lex Iulia de senatu habendo* came into being; it regulated the way in which the senate was to meet. Because the law relating to marriage encountered a great deal of resistance Augustus suggested to the consuls M. Papius and Q. Poppaeus that they should propose a new law, so they did. The content of this *lex Papia Poppaea*, which dates from 9 AD, is difficult to distinguish from that of the *lex Iulia de maritandis ordinibus* and often they are referred to in one breath as the *leges Iulia et Papia Poppaea*.[2] Both laws show, however, that Augustus wanted to encourage the marriage and procreation of Roman citizens and that he wanted to protect the senatorial élite.

Emperor Claudius, who is known to have been rather fond of old republican forms, abolished the agnatic *tutela* of women by means of a *lex*, i.e. the *lex Claudia*.[3] The last *lex*, referred to as such in the sources, is a *lex agraria* of Emperor Nerva (96–98), which assigned land to poor Romans.

9.2.2. The senatorial decrees

In the first century BC, as mentioned earlier, it did occasionally happen that a proposal put forward by one of the magistrates, which had been ratified by the senate, was no longer put to the *comitia* but came into effect immediately. One reason for this was that the *comitia* functioned so badly. At the beginning of the principate more and more laws originated in this way, the senate replacing the *comitia* in this respect. Just as under the republic, a senatorial decree could result from a question put by a magistrate. From now on, however, the senatorial decrees were in most cases drawn up on the initiative of the emperor. It is known, for instance, that Augustus on occasion charged the consuls to ask the senate's opinion on a specific point. From the time of Emperor Claudius the senatorial decrees on juridical matters were usually prepared by the emperor's officials and the proposal concerned was read out in the senate by or in the name of the emperor (*oratio principis*); various senators then expressed their opinions and a vote was taken. Because the emperor exerted so much influence in the senate, the senate never failed to agree to the main lines of the proposal. In the second century the senatorial decrees became a formality whose sole purpose was to ratify the emperor's proposal. The juridical literature of the time often referred only to the proposal. A well-known example is the *oratio Severi* from the year 206, which includes a relaxation of the ban on the exchange of gifts between husband and wife.[4]

At first the senatorial decrees mainly concerned problems pertaining to criminal law. A famous or rather infamous example is the *SC Silanianum* of 10 AD; this decree aimed to repress the frequent killing of masters by their slaves. It stated that when the identity of the murderer(s) was unknown, all the slaves who had lived in the same house as their master had to be tortured and condemned to death; if the victim's heir omitted to have the murder investigated, he would no longer be entitled to the inheritance.[5]

In the middle of the first century the senate started to introduce innovations into private law: the first known decree of this kind is the *SC Velleianum* which forbade women to stand surety for debts of others, including their husbands.[6] The number of innovations brought about in this way increased in the middle of the second century and reached a maximum by the end of the century. The senate introduced for instance a legal right of succession between mothers and children.[7]

In the third century emperors no longer submitted their proposals for approval by the senate and in this way the senatorial decrees disappeared formally as a source of law.

9.2.3. Imperial legislation

Not only did the emperors contribute indirectly to legislation by way of *leges* and senatorial decrees, but they themselves also created new law. Because in a formal sense they had no legislative power, at first the emperors had to base this power on the magisterial functions they performed. One of them, the *imperium proconsulare maius*, was particularly suited for this purpose, because it authorised the emperor to issue *edicta* (general pronouncements) and *mandata* (instructions given by the emperor to his officials). The emperors also created new law in another way: whenever citizens put legal problems to the emperor relating to private or criminal matters, the (written) answers, the *rescripta*, were binding because they were given by the emperor. This was also the case when the emperor or his representative acted as judge: the sentences, *decreta*, had the force of law because they were given by the emperor. The edicts, rescripts and decrees are referred to in the sources by the collective name *constitutio*. Nowadays it is normal to add the mandates as a fourth category, because they too sometimes contained new rules of law. Because the decrees and rescripts did not originate within the framework of legislation and at first were not of general validity, they need not be discussed here. They will be treated in sections 9.3.3 and 9.4.1. We will now look more closely at the edicts and mandates.

The edicts of the emperors resembled those of the magistrates with regard to form but differed from them considerably with regard to content. The difference was due to the fact that the emperor held various magisterial functions simultaneously for life whereas the magistrates usually fulfilled only one function for a year and therefore their power was much more limited. Consequently edicts of magistrates were only valid during the period they were in office, whereas the imperial edicts did not lapse at the end of the emperor's reign, which generally coincided with his death: the latter were of unlimited validity and did not have to be constantly renewed. Another difference between the edicts of the magistrates and those of the emperors was that the magistrates could only issue edicts within their own sphere of power; the imperial edicts referred to everything that had to do with the state. In practice the emperors primarily issued edicts in the field of public law. The most well-known edict is the above-mentioned *constitutio Antoniniana* in which Emperor Caracalla granted Roman citizenship to all free inhabitants of the empire.

The mandates were instructions issued by the emperor to his officials and especially to provincial governors. Because originally the instruction was strictly personal it resembled the contract of mandate in private law. Like the contract it lapsed upon the disappearance of either the principal or the delegate; therefore when the emperor died or the official was replaced, the instruction had to be renewed. In this way gradually a whole body of instructions developed (*corpus mandatorum*) which were more or less of general validity. These mandates mainly concerned the provincial administration and particularly its financial side, and in addition some dealt with matters pertaining to private and criminal law. New rules were introduced particularly in connection with soldiers and administrators; because mandates could be relied upon by other citizens as well, they began to be regarded as a form of legislation. A good example of a mandate is the so-called soldiers' will. Julius Caesar had already allowed soldiers to make a will without being bound by the regulations that applied to the wills of ordinary citizens. In the first century various emperors (e.g. Titus and Nerva) renewed this privilege. Finally Emperor Trajan allowed this informal type of will to retain its validity for a year after the soldier had been honourably discharged from the army. Thereafter the privilege was not renewed, but the soldiers' wills continued to exist.[8] This indicates that in the second century the mandate was regarded as forming part of imperial legislation.

9.3. THE ADMINISTRATION OF JUSTICE

9.3.1. The criminal trial

At the end of the republic there were two juridical procedures for criminal law: serious crimes were tried by special standing tribunals (*quaestiones perpetuae*), other crimes were dealt with by lower-grade magistrates, the so-called *tresviri capitales*. In the first few decades of the principate the tasks of the *tresviri capitales* were taken over by officials in the service of the emperor; the tribunals continued to exist for quite a long time after they had been reorganised and even expanded by Augustus.[9]

As early as 17 BC Augustus had regulated by law how the tribunals were to be composed and how they were to function. The list of potential jury-members, the *album iudicum*, was composed in a new way, the *equites'* participation being increased. Furthermore the minimum age for jury service was lowered from 30 to 25, so that there would always be enough jury members available. By the end of his reign, probably in 18 AD, Augustus added two new tribunals to the six existing ones: the *quaestio de adulteriis* and the *quaestio de annona*. The first had to pass judgment in cases of adultery involving a married woman or an otherwise honourable woman and in cases of procurement. The second had to pass judgment in cases of hoarding or speculation which led to a rise in food prices.

The tribunals had a number of disadvantages which were not adequately dealt with by the innovations of Augustus. First of all, a citizen could only lodge a complaint about a crime if there existed a tribunal for that crime. Secondly, it sometimes happened that in one case several persons were involved who had committed various crimes. In such a case it would have been more efficient to have all the persons involved tried by one jury. In addition, the penalties that could be imposed were often regarded as being too mild for the type of crime committed. Therefore, the work of the tribunals was first supplemented but soon taken over by the new criminal court of the emperor and his delegates. In about the year 200 all *quaestiones perpetuae* had disappeared.

9.3.2. The formulary procedure

In the first few centuries of the principate the formulary procedure was still the usual way of taking legal action in disputes relating to private law. The proceedings were also essentially the same as they had been under the republic. In the first phase the praetor decided whether parties could submit their dispute to the judge and if so in what manner. The trial itself took place in the second phase, which consisted of the production of evidence, the pleas by the advocates and finally the judge's verdict. In practice, however, the dividing line between the formulary system and the *cognitio*-procedure was not always observed and now and again elements of the *cognitio*-procedure were applied in a procedure that was conducted by means of formulas. The only thing that altered in the formulary procedure was the function of the praetorian edict.

For a long time the praetorian edict continued to be an important source of law, but no more new legal remedies were incorporated; very occasionally the formulation for a legal remedy was changed and sometimes the edict was altered in accordance with what had been decided by a *lex* or senatorial decree. About the year 130 it became almost impossible to alter the edict, for then Emperor Hadrian gave Salvius Julianus, the most famous jurist of his time, the task of drawing up a definitive version of the praetorian edict; from then on only the emperor would be able to change it. In practice, this measure was probably not very important, for contemporary sources do not mention it. Our oldest sources on the subject date from the end of the fourth century, and their credibility has been questioned. What Emperor Justinian tells us in the sixth century about the measure is unclear and contradictory.[10] Therefore we really know very little about the task assigned to Julian and the way in which he carried it out.[11]

Although the edict was no longer a source of new law, its importance did not decline. It was used as a source of law for legal practice for a long time, even after the formulary system had fallen into disuse. From the third century the edict was referred to as the *edictum perpetuum*, although the term was no longer used in the former sense of the edict which was issued by the praetor at the beginning of his period of office and which in principle was valid for a whole year; the term was now used in the sense of the definitive version of the edict produced by Julian. The formulary procedure itself was abolished by law in 342.

The edict has not been preserved in its original state and the content can only be reconstructed on the basis of the information given in the juridical literature of the classical period. The leading German Romanist, Lenel, made a plausible reconstruction in 1883; this went through two revisions and from 1927 the second revision has been regarded as the standard edition.[12] Lenel's reconstruction indicates that the clauses of the edict were probably in a certain order which was dictated by the course of the trial, but only in the part involving the praetor. Modern jurists who are not familiar with the rules of the formulary procedure find this order difficult to understand. Lenel's reconstruction also shows that the terminology is not always consistent; the explanation for this is simple, if one realises that the clauses of the edict were formulated by different persons over a period of 150 years and were not adapted by Julian. The reason that the edict was not preserved may be connected with the fact that in their collections of *responsa* the jurists always quoted the relevant words from the edict, with the result that the edict itself became superfluous.

9.3.3. The cognitio extraordinaria

The *cognitio extra ordinem* or *cognitio extraordinaria* is a collective name for all those legal procedures in which the trial consists of one stage only and in which judgment is given by the emperor or by an imperial official acting on behalf of the emperor. The disputes that were settled by means of the cognition procedure could be of very different kinds: not only could they be about matters concerning private law and criminal law, but they could also be disputes between citizens and government officials.

The *cognitio* had originated during the republic and was first used in the provinces. One of the tasks of the provincial governor was the administration of justice. Criminal offences were generally dealt with by the governor or his representative, but he could not sentence Roman citizens to capital punishment. In disputes pertaining to private law the governor performed the tasks which in Rome were entrusted to the praetor. Sometimes the governor also passed judgment or he delegated the task to one of his subordinates (*iudex pedaneus*). This happened for instance in the case of disputes between persons who did not have Roman citizenship or in the case of disputes between Roman citizens when there were not enough citizens who could serve as judges. When the governor was investigating a case – criminal or private – himself, he did not use the ordinary procedure but applied the *cognitio extraordinaria*.

When in 27 BC the *imperium proconsulare maius* was granted to Augustus a number of provinces came directly under his control. Augustus delegated the day-to-day management, including the administration of justice, to officials in his service (*legati Augusti pro praetore*) and they then exclusively used the *cognitio extraordinaria*. In the senatorial provinces, where the *cognitio* had also sometimes been used, this example was followed increasingly and by the second century the *cognitio* became the normal form of trial there as well. The *cognitio* was used in Italy and in Rome from the beginning of the principate, but as yet not on a regular basis. This happened only in the third century, and by then the *cognitio extraordinaria* had become the ordinary form of procedure in the whole empire.

The decisions of the emperor as judge in the first instance or in the case of an appeal (*decreta*) did not have force of law in a formal sense but – because they emanated from the emperor – they did carry authority and they could be referred to in later trials. Initially a precedent of this kind was not binding for a judge, but since the time of the Severi (end of the second century) the power relationships had changed so radically that an imperial decree had the same status as a law and a judge who had to pass judgment on a similar case could no longer deviate from that decree.

The introduction of the *cognitio extraordinaria* not only meant that judgment was now given by the emperor or one of his officials but it also marked the beginning of many other kinds of changes. With regard to disputes pertaining to private law the judge now played a more active role particularly with regard to the summons. Whenever a defendant refused to appear before the judge, the judge himself could summon him, and if the defendant still refused to comply the judge could condemn him by default; in a formulary procedure, on the other hand, it was the plaintiff who had to see to it that the defendant appeared in front of the praetor and a sentence by default was absolutely out of the question because there could be no trial without the agreement of the defendant. Secondly, in the cognition procedure it was possible for both parties to appeal against the verdict; now that the parties were no longer allowed to choose their own judge, they could not be expected always to accept his verdict without question. The judge was now an official who worked in a hierarchical structure headed by the emperor, so parties could appeal to a senior judge or to the emperor himself. As mentioned earlier, there was not always a strict distinction between the cognition procedure and the formulary system, and from the beginning of the principate it sometimes happened that parties that had fought each other within the framework of a *formula* procedure appealed to the emperor or his subordinate against the sentence that had been pronounced.

The *cognitio* procedure also brought about a number of changes in criminal law. Tribunals other than the *quaestiones* began to judge criminal cases. The senate, for instance, developed into a tribunal dealing with more or less political cases. At first it was mainly trials connected with *laesio maiestatis* (insulting the Roman people and/or the Roman emperor) or with extortion perpetrated by governors in their provinces which were brought before the senate. Tiberius allowed all kinds of other crimes to be tried by the senate, but the accused were generally senators or members of the senatorial élite. In this way the senate developed into a *forum privilegiatum* for crimes committed by persons from their own class. During such trials the senators fought each other fiercely, but to the world at large they kept an appearance of unity. Fascinating reports of trials before the senate are to be found in Tacitus' work and in the letters of Pliny the Younger who repeatedly took part in such trials, serving as advocate or judge. As from the reign of Commodus the activities of the senate were drastically curtailed and a few decades later the senators were no longer involved in criminal trials at all.

Another tribunal was the court of the emperor and his delegates, particularly the prefects. In Rome and in the zone within a 100-mile radius of Rome the city prefect, by virtue of delegation on the part of the emperor, had his own authority in minor criminal cases. In the course of time his power was extended so much that towards the end of the second century he was entitled to judge all criminal cases. The praetorian prefect became responsible for the punishment of crimes elsewhere in Italy. In the senatorial provinces this task was performed by the governors. They had long been authorised to act as judges in lawsuits against *peregrini*, but in cases against Roman citizens their authority was fairly limited: they were not entitled to condemn citizens to death unless the latter had first been given the opportunity to have their case judged in Rome. In the imperial provinces the administration of criminal justice was in the hands of special representatives of the emperor (*legati Augusti*). Already in the first century the emperors began to allow those *legati* who were in charge of an army in their province, to condemn to death a soldier, a Roman citizen, without the soldier having the right to bring his case before a tribunal in Rome. When the number of people with Roman citizenship increased and it became practically impossible to deal in Rome with all cases involving capital punishment, this so-called *ius gladii* (literally, the right of the sword) was granted more and more often to other provincial governors and was made applicable to civilians as well. By the beginning of the third century the governors were fully authorised to act as judges in all kinds of penal cases in their provinces, not only in the first instance but also in cases of appeal.[13]

Another difference between the *quaestiones* and the *cognitio extraordinaria* was that the latter had a predominantly inquisitory character. The trial was started by the 'state'; no formal accusation by a citizen was necessary except for the old *crimina publica*. Traditionally any citizen could bring such an accusation. However, the old rules relating to this public accusation were now changed so profoundly that by the end of the principate all that was left was a sort of complaint which could be put forward by the injured party. Furthermore, in the *cognitio* procedure the judge could conduct investigations on his own initiative and by any means at his disposal. Only the senatorial court adhered to the accusatory form of procedure used by the *quaestiones*.

Thirdly the *cognitio* knew no fixed penalties. The judge or court was free to determine the form and measure of the punishment. He could, for instance, take into account the circumstances in which the crime was committed, the personal or social condition of the accused, etc.; but he could not set a convict free, for that was a prerogative of the emperor and the senate.

9.4. LEGAL SCIENCE

9.4.1. The activities of the jurists

There is a certain degree of continuity between the legal science of the late republic and the legal science of the principate. As in the republic the jurists of the principate were leading senators with an exceptionally good knowledge of and great interest in the law. They often held high political office; the new element was that they could function not only as magistrates (e.g. as consul, praetor, governor of a senatorial province) but from the second century they could also be imperial officials (e.g. they could serve as city prefect or as praetorian prefect). Another new feature was that they could now participate in the emperor's *consilium*. As far as legal science was concerned, the jurists were still engaged in *cavere*, *agere* and *respondere*. The fact that the highest power in the Roman empire was now in the hands of the emperor naturally had an influence on these activities.

Cavere, the drafting of texts, underwent some changes at this time. Developing formulas for the formulary procedure was no longer one of the regular tasks of the jurists because the edicts of the praetors and the curule aediles now contained adequate legal remedies. Drawing up formulations for the practice of law was still part of their activities, but only a relatively small part. The classical Roman jurists show their ability to draft texts very clearly in the field of the law of succession, especially in the endless variety of legacies which they invented and which occupy five books of the Digest (D. 30–34.4).

Agere (serving as advocate) remained more or less the same. Whenever jurists interpreted laws and formulas in their pleas it made little difference to them whether they were participating in a formulary procedure or in a lawsuit before an imperial official or the senate. Unfortunately the speeches of the jurists made when serving as advocates have not survived. We do still have access to the *Controversiae* of Seneca the Elder, which are practice speeches from the beginning of the first century, and we can consult *De Institutione Oratoria* of Quintilian, which is the standard work on the training of orators, dating from the year 95; it too deals mainly with forensic speeches. Furthermore, in a number of letters Pliny the Younger describes the speeches he made as advocate during extortion trials in the senate; on some occasions he spoke on behalf of a province which accused an ex-governor of extortion and on other occasions he spoke in defence of an ex-governor.[14]

Respondere (giving opinions) was now the major legal activity of the jurists. As under the republic they themselves collected their opinions; these collections will be dealt with in the next section. We shall now discuss the way in which the jurists gave their opinions. The principal source of information is the afore-mentioned Enchiridium, the overview of the history of Roman law which the jurist Pomponius compiled in the middle of the second century and which is included in the Digest of Justinian (D. 1.2.47–53). The first change mentioned by Pomponius has to do with the so-called law-school. Under the republic the jurists had formed a *secta* or *schola* in the senate in which they discussed the problems that had been put to them, under the leadership of the person with the greatest authority in law. At the time there were still no rules about the persons who could give *responsa* and no rules about the topics on which or the manner in which *responsa* were given. Pomponius relates that at the time of Augustus a second *schola* emerged in the senate around M. Antistius Labeo in addition to the existing school around Ateius Capito. These two senators had very different characters and consequently they had completely opposing views in the political and juridical field. Capito was a great supporter of Augustus, whereas Labeo did not want anything to do with the politics of Augustus; Capito was a traditional jurist who put into practice what he was taught, whereas Labeo was an innovator and was reputed to be an excep-tionally gifted jurist. A vast quantity of literature has appeared over several centuries about the differences between the schools.[15] The resulting theories have one thing in common: they are all based on the hypothesis that the law-schools were 'schools of thought'; they had to do with legal science, i.e. the theory of law.

The second change mentioned by Pomponius is the introduction by Augustus of the *ius publice respondendi ex auctoritate principis*. This part of Pomponius' text is generally regarded as corrupt and has been interpreted in many different ways. The discussion concentrates on two questions: how did this privilege work and to whom was it granted? Most authors believe that the *ius respond-endi* meant simply that the jurists in question could give opinions in the name of the emperor, i.e. with more authority than other jurists; they were in a sense 'jurists for the crown'.[16] According to some other authors, however, this privilege consisted of an exclusive right; only the jurists who were granted this right had the emperor's permission to give opinions which were then binding for the judge. Opinions differ even more regarding the second question: to whom was the privilege granted? Some authors maintain that the *ius respondendi* was granted to only a few jurists and only by the first emperors, Augustus and Tiberius. However, others believe the privilege was granted to various jurists up to the reign of Hadrian; others again think that after Hadrian the number of jurists who received the right increased.

Recently Tellegen has pointed to the fact that Pomponius mentions the *ius respondendi* in the context of the law-schools and suggests that the two are linked: Augustus would have introduced the *ius respondendi* in the *lex Iulia de senatu habendo* of 9 BC for the benefit of the head of the law-school.[17] This jurist would then have the exclusive right to give opinions on his, Augustus', authority on behalf of the senate. Because the opinions would be based on imperial authority, they would be binding for the judge. By coupling his personal authority to the authority of the leader of the law-school Augustus hoped he could restrict the giving of opinions by the jurists and thereby promote unity and security in law. However, there was a problem about who was actually to be granted this right. As leaders of their respective schools both Labeo and Capito were possible candidates for the *ius respondendi*. However, they were such rivals that there was a danger that if they both received the *ius respondendi* they would be constantly at loggerheads and thereby create legal instability. Since the situation was so problematical and since Pomponius remarked that Sabinus was the first to be informally granted by Emperor Tiberius the right to exercise the *ius respondendi*, Tellegen concludes that Augustus himself never granted this privilege to anyone. Tellegen's reconstruction is based on the hypothesis that the law-schools did not have to do with the theory of law but with legal practice. This reconstruction seems plausible because it fully explains Pomponius' text as included in the Digest, and because it solves problems regarding the *ius respondendi* and the law-schools which have hitherto appeared to be insoluble.

After mentioning the introduction of the *ius respondendi*, Pomponius goes on telling about the jurists and their law-schools. Sabinus had succeeded Capito as leader of the traditional school, although he was not a member of the senate; this was an exceptional situation that is even reported twice by Pomponius.

Emperor Tiberius granted him the right to use the *ius respondendi*, possibly by way of experiment. The *ius respondendi* was first granted in a normal way to Sabinus' successor, Cassius, who was a member of the senate; this would explain why in the Roman literature it is Cassius, not Capito or Sabinus, who is called the founder of the traditional school. It is not known which emperor granted him the right; it could have been Nero (54–68). Since about forty controversies developed between Sabinus/Cassius and Nerva/Proculus, the leaders of the other school, it can be concluded that Nerva and Proculus had the *ius respondendi* as well. The other jurists could still give opinions, but since the Digest contains many more opinions given by leaders of the law-schools than by other jurists it would appear that the latter hardly gave opinions any more or, if they did, then less importance was attached to such opinions. It is possible that the later heads of the law-schools also had this privilege, although we only know for certain that Iavolenus Priscus had it (end of the first/beginning of the second century). A probable reason why there were far fewer controversies between the later leaders of the law-schools is that the emperors included these leaders in their *consilium* and involved them in central government. Finally Emperor Hadrian stopped granting the *ius respondendi*; in those days one of the two schools was headed by two jurists, the other by three, so there was a real danger that new schools would be formed, again threatening legal security. It is not clear whether the law-schools in the senate continued to exist after this time; nothing further is heard of them.

Hadrian now began to give opinions (or let opinions be given) in his own name, in the form of rescripts. Even before that time emperors had occasionally issued rescripts, but as far as is known, they were mainly letters addressed to towns or other communities in the province, in which a specific, administrative problem in the province was solved.[18] Hadrian was the first to use the rescript to give juridical advice. He let two chanceries prepare these rescripts: the *scrinium ab epistulis* was to deal with correspondence with officials and important persons, and the *scrinium a libellis* with letters from other citizens. In the first case the reply was sent in a separate letter (*epistula*), in the second case the reply was given at the bottom of the letter from the citizen (*subscriptio*). Probably both chanceries had registries where copies of the rescripts were kept.[19] The *scrinia* were supervised by jurists who, at least since the last few decades of the second century, were simultaneously members of the emperor's *consilium*. Hadrian and his successors therefore allowed these *scrinia* to perform exactly the same task as the leading senators had performed for a very long time and were still performing. However, since the senators were no longer granted the *ius respondendi* their *responsa* had to compete with the rescripts of the emperor. This caused no problems as long as they were members of a senate that had authority and as long as they were members of the emperor's *consilium*: then they still had sufficient personal authority. However, when in the third century the senate lost all its power and authority to the emperor and his officials and the senators no longer had any influence in the *consilium*, their *responsa* were no longer regarded as authoritative. The reason for this was not – as some writers assert – the spread of the practice of rescripts but it was the decline of the senate: it is via the rescripts that the opinions of the jurists lived on for a long time, namely until the fourth century.

Finally something should be said about the schools in which law was taught from the first century onwards. Tuition in law had always been given individually, but when a kind of civil service developed there was a need for people with a more professional juridical training, and not only at a high level. According to a text by Ulpian (F.V. 204) there must have been a school for teaching law in Rome in the second century; according to other sources there was also a law-school in Berytus, the modern Beirut, at the beginning of the third century.[20] Nothing is known about how the tuition was organised, but several textbooks that were used in these schools have survived.

9.4.2. The juridical literature

Only a small part of the collected opinions in which the classical jurists interpreted and created Roman law has come down to us directly; however, we do know about the contents of many of them indirectly, because in the sixth century, upon the order of Emperor Justinian, a comprehensive anthology was compiled from fragments of the classical juridical literature, the Digest, and this has survived. The compilers of the Digest arranged the texts of the classical jurists in a fairly systematic way; they preceded each fragment with an *inscriptio* which gave the name of the jurist and the work from which the fragment was taken.[21]

The collections of opinions of the classical jurists had different names according to the way in which the opinions were arranged. An arrangement commonly used in the republic followed the *ius civile*, which meant that those opinions were put together which dealt successively with the law of succession, the law of persons, the law of obligations and the law of things. A famous example of a volume arranged in this manner is the *Tres libri iuris civilis* of Massurius Sabinus: in its turn this served as a model for later collections which were then referred to by the title *ad Sabinum*. The opinions could also be arranged according to the rubrics of the praetorian edict, a method that had also been used earlier; the eighty-three *libri ad edictum* by the jurist Ulpian are the best known examples of this. The reason that this work consists of so many volumes is that the older literature is included and it therefore gives a comprehensive picture of the law. Other collections of opinions were, for instance, *Digesta*, *Responsa*, *Quaestiones*, *Epistulae* and *Disputationes*. Most of them consisted of two parts; in the first part the opinions were arranged *ad edictum* and in the second part the opinions were linked with the *leges*, senatorial decrees and imperial constitutions to which they referred. A famous example is the *Digesta* of Julian from the middle of the second century; it was a source of inspiration for many other jurists. Sometimes opinions relating to one theme were collected in one volume, e.g. the *liber singularis* by Modestinus about manumission and the book by Paul about the task of the proconsul; both of these books date from the beginning of the third century. Finally, works called *Regulae*, *Definitiones* and *Sententiae* have also come down to us; they contain short pronouncements about the law, originally delivered in connection with specific cases but later reformulated in the form of an abstract rule, which creates the impression that they have general validity. These works were used mainly in legal practice, for instance by advocates who wished to support their speeches with a general pronouncement of this kind, and were possibly also used in teaching. At the end of the nineteenth century Lenel, who was mentioned earlier, attempted to put back in their original order the texts of the classical jurists, which had been preserved via the Digest and other older collections; in other words he made a reconstruction of these works. This reconstruction was possible because each fragment was preceded by an *inscriptio*.[22]

Roman legal science owes its reputation largely to these collections of opinions. The opinions are characterised by the lucidity of the language and the exceptionally clear formulations. They reveal a way of juridical thinking which has been normative for many generations of jurists, right up to the present day. The Roman jurists managed to create a legal system which did not seek to apply the laws as literally as possible to specific cases, but instead they tried to find solutions that were as just and practical as possible.[23]

The collections of opinions reveal a number of characteristics that can only be explained by the fact that they originated in legal practice and were intended for use in legal practice. First of all, the opinions usually do not include any specific grounds or motives; instead the jurist often refers to similar cases that he or another jurist has dealt with. In addition, it is striking that the opinions contain very few definitions, not even of elementary juridical concepts like *dominium* (ownership), and *culpa* (negligence). According to D. 50.17.202 the jurist Iavolenus Priscus believed that definitions could even be dangerous because most of them could easily be overthrown, in other words they could nearly always be turned round to mean the opposite. Apparently Priscus was inspired by his experience in the practice of law. Finally, the opinions only rarely include explanations based on legal history; apparently a jurist only referred to law in the past, e.g. the law of the XII Tables (and its later application), if he thought that it would provide useful support for his arguments. The opinions were predominantly practical; this meant that when Roman law was rediscovered in the Middle Ages it could be used as a starting point for the development of a common European legal science.

In addition to these opinions, introductory textbooks on law, called *Institutiones*, have come down to us. The oldest known legal textbook, the Institutes of Gaius, dates from about 160. In this book the law is treated systematically and is divided into law relating to *personae* (law of persons), *res* (law of things, law of succession and law of obligations) and *actiones* (law of actions). After Gaius, other authors including Marcian and Ulpian wrote juridical textbooks that are divided in the same way. Fragments from these books are known via the Digest of Justinian. The Institutes of Gaius have come down to us directly. In 1816 the German historian Niebuhr discovered in the chapter library of Verona that a manuscript containing letters by St Jerome, dating from the seventh/eighth centuries, also contained another text.

His fellow-countryman, Von Savigny, the famous legal historian, recognised this other text to be the Institutes of Gaius. The manuscript turned out to be a palimpsest, i.e. the letters by St Jerome were written on top of the original text. Attempts to reveal the entire text of Gaius were not completely successful (only 80 per cent), but thanks to later discoveries (in Egypt) in 1927 and 1933 of fragments of Gaius' Institutes various gaps could be filled. The Verona manuscript dates from the fifth century, whereas the original dates from the middle of the second century, but recent research has shown that the later manuscript does indeed contain classical Roman law.[24]

The Institutes of Gaius are of very great importance, for various reasons. First of all, Gaius describes in a systematic way the most important legal concepts of his time with their history. His trichotomy of the law in the law regarding persons, things and actions has become famous. A major problem with Gaius' Institutes, however, is that the text is sometimes very short and compact and was intended for contemporary readers who were familiar with all the facts and circumstances. Because the modern reader lacks this background information, he finds some passages confusing rather than informative. Secondly, Gaius' Institutes is the only juridical work from the principate which has come down to us in practically its original form. It was not adapted by later jurists and still contains descriptions of legal concepts which were no longer applied in the fifth century; for instance, it is mainly through the Institutes of Gaius that we know about the *legis actio* type of lawsuit. Thirdly, the Institutes of Gaius are of indirect importance for later European legal science. They served as a model for the Institutes which Emperor Justinian published in the sixth century and which formed part of the reception of Roman law since the Middle Ages. When private law was systematised in the seventeenth and eighteenth centuries by, for instance, Dutch, German and French lawyers, they generally followed the system of Justinian's Institutes, and therefore indirectly the Institutes of Gaius. The same holds for the French Civil Code of 1804 which was based on their work, and for its derivatives.

9.4.3. The most important jurists

Not much is known about the lives of the classical Roman jurists. The most important sources of our knowledge are Pomponius'

Enchiridium, a number of inscriptions and literary works by authors like Tacitus, Pliny the Younger, Aulus Gellius and Cassius Dio.[25]

Of the early classical jurists (those who lived between the end of the first century BC and about 80 AD), the first one who should be mentioned is M. Antistius Labeo. He lived at the beginning of the principate and was one of the political opponents of Augustus. He held the office of praetor but did not become a consul. According to Pomponius this was because he refused the position when offered it by Augustus; according to others, however, it was because he was *not* offered the position. Labeo was an exceptionally gifted and original jurist and a second *schola* formed around him in the senate; this *schola* was additional to the traditional one led by Ateius Capito. When Labeo died (between the years 5 and 22) he left 400 scrolls; some of them concerned the law of the XII Tables and pontifical law, and others consisted of collected opinions. His opinions were edited and commented upon until the third century by various jurists including Paul.

As mentioned earlier, Massurius Sabinus occupies an exceptional position among the jurists.[26] He was not a member of the senate, did not make his career in politics and was not even elevated to the *equites* until later in life. Nevertheless, because he had an exceptionally good knowledge of the law he was the leader of the earlier school of Capito. Emperor Tiberius allowed him to use the *ius respondendi*. He was the first jurist to use this privilege. Sabinus is known mainly because of his *Tres libri iuris civilis* which Pomponius, Paul and Ulpian later used as a framework for their own work.

C. Cassius Longinus belonged to a leading plebeian family. He was a direct descendant of one of the murderers of Julius Caesar, but he was also related by marriage to the imperial house. Cassius liked to boast that, via his mother, he was a great-grandson of the republican jurist S. Sulpicius Rufus. Cassius was praetor, became consul in the year 30 and was a provincial governor several times between 40 and 49. In addition to his important political career Cassius was also a successful jurist: his knowledge of the law was unequalled in those days and he was also the leader of the traditional school. It was probably because he was the first to be granted the *ius respondendi* in a regular way that his school was later called the *schola Cassiana*. Only a few of Cassius' opinions have come down to us; they have survived because they were cited by later authors.

The first of the jurists in the high classical period (from about 80 to about 180) was Iavolenus Priscus.[27] Iavolenus was a very versatile man. He had a career in the army (he was commanding officer of various legions), in politics (he was consul in 86), in administration (he was governor of three provinces) and in law; he was leader of the Cassian school and had the *ius respondendi*. He was also a member of the *consilium* of Emperor Trajan. Iavolenus published his opinions in *Epistulae* (fourteen books) and in his *Libri ex Cassio*; fragments of these are included in the Digest and have therefore survived.

Salvius Julianus was a very important, if not *the* most important, jurist of the second century. On the basis of an inscription he is believed to have been born in Hadrumetum in the province of Africa. Like most of the other jurists, he too had an impressive political career under the emperors Hadrian, Antoninus Pius and Marcus Aurelius. He held many offices including those of praetor, consul, pontifex and governor of various provinces and he was a member of the now permanent *consilium* of the emperor. At the request of Hadrian, Julian produced a definitive edition of the praetorian edict in about 130. He was the last known leader of the Cassian school. Julian gave many *responsa*; they are collected in his *Digesta* which contains ninety scrolls. Apparently this work was considered to be very important, for later jurists like his pupil S. Caecilius Africanus quote liberally from it and those who compiled the Digest of Justinian also used it constantly.

P. Iuventius Celsus (*filius*) also had a brilliant career in politics; in 129 he even became consul for the second time. He took part in the *consilium* of Emperor Hadrian and was governor of Thrace. Like his father, P. Iuventius Celsus (*pater*), he was leader of the Proculian school. He collected his opinions in *Digesta* (thirty-nine books), *Epistulae* and *Quaestiones*. Celsus is famous particularly for his pithy statements. It was he who produced the classical definition of law: *ius est ars boni et aequi* (D. 1.1.1.pr).

Sextus Pomponius is known particularly as the author of the *Enchiridium*. In this work, which dates from the reign of Emperor Hadrian, Pomponius deals with, among other things, the origin and history of Roman law, from the monarchy up to his own day. The fragment in question is incorporated in its entirety in the Digest of Justinian and is important because it is the only one of its kind. It is not known whether Pomponius had a political career or whether he himself gave opinions. He certainly made some comprehensive compilations of opinions such as those *ad Sabinum* and those *ad edictum*, and he wrote various monographs. Numerous fragments have been preserved in the Digest.

All we know about Gaius as a person is that he lived in the second half of the second century. Interest in Gaius and his life has increased considerably since a manuscript of his Institutes was discovered at the beginning of the nineteenth century (see end of section 9.4.2). There have been all kinds of hypotheses about his origins and the place where he lived and about the question of whether he had any political career, but so far no convincing evidence has been found to support any of the hypotheses. In addition Gaius published various collections of opinions, fragments of which have been preserved in the Digest. Perhaps one can conclude from that that he was a member of the senate.

The most highly esteemed of the late classical jurists (about 180 to about 230) is Aemilius Papinianus. All that we know about his political career is that he was head of the chancery *a libellis*, that he was praetorian prefect from 203 until his death in 212 and that by virtue of this function he was a member of the imperial *consilium*. He was murdered upon the order of Emperor Caracalla because, it was rumoured, he refused to condone the fact that Caracalla had had his brother and fellow emperor Geta murdered. Papinian gave opinions on many occasions and these are collected in *Quaestiones* (thirty-seven books) and *Responsa* (nineteen books). In these books he also reported opinions of other jurists and even decisions taken by the emperor and the prefects. In the post-classical period these collections were regarded as the most important source of Roman law. This explains why fragments have survived, over and above those contained in the Digest of Justinian.

Just like Papinian, Julius Paulus held high office; his positions included being head of the chancery *a memoria* and during the reign of Alexander Severus he was praetorian prefect. He too was a member of the emperor's *consilium*. Of his numerous works the most comprehensive are his eighty(!) books *ad edictum*. In addition he published sixteen books *ad Sabinum*, *Responsa*, *Quaestiones* and innumerable monographs concerning, for example, codicils, certain *leges* and the tasks of senior officials and also a textbook. In the later Roman empire fragments from Paul's work were collected in a book which became known as *Pauli Sententiae* and which must have been very popular. The fact that a large part of the Digest of Justinian, namely one-sixth, consists of texts by Paul indicates the great importance that was attached to his work in the post-classical period.

The last important jurist in the late classical period is Domitius Ulpianus.[28] We know that he came from Tyre in Phoenicia. He was a pupil of Papinian and like Papinian made his career according to the official hierarchy; he held several posts including head of the chancery *a libellis*, city prefect and praetorian prefect. When serving as praetorian prefect in 223 he was murdered by members of his own praetorian guard. Like Paul, Ulpian published much juridical literature: eighty-three books *ad edictum*, fifty-one books *ad Sabinum*, numerous monographs and finally *Responsa*. Because he often cites other jurists, one gets the impression that Ulpian was trying to make the older literature superfluous; if that is the case, then he was certainly successful, for the compilers of Justinian's Digest used his work more than the work of any other jurist; almost half of the Digest (41.56 per cent, to be precise) is made up of fragments from Ulpian's work.

Part IV

THE DOMINATE
(284–565)

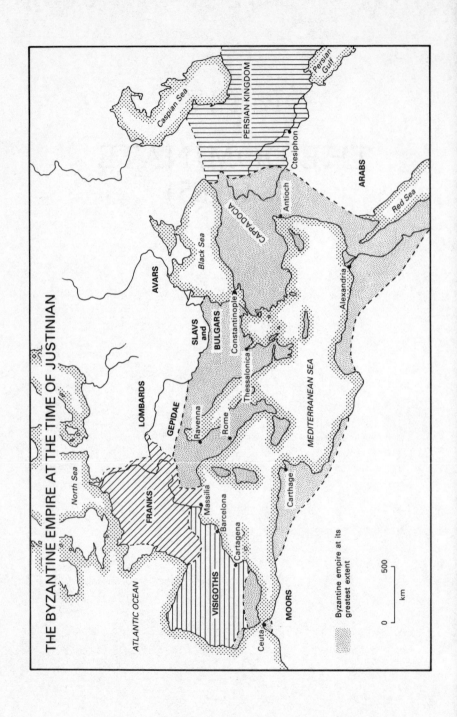

THE BYZANTINE EMPIRE AT THE TIME OF JUSTINIAN

PERSIAN KINGDOM

Persian Gulf

Caspian Sea

Ctesiphon

ARABS

CAPPADOCIA

Antioch

Red Sea

Black Sea

AVARS

Alexandria

Constantinople

SLAVS and BULGARS

LOMBARDS

GEPIDAE

Thessalonica

MEDITERRANEAN SEA

Ravenna

Rome

North Sea

FRANKS

Massilia

Barcelona

Carthage

ATLANTIC OCEAN

Cartagena

VISIGOTHS

MOORS

Ceuta

Byzantine empire at its
greatest extent

500

km

0

10

THE DOMINATE: GENERAL OUTLINE

10.1. THE SOURCES

There is an abundant supply of source material for the dominate, but the information given by these sources is not always complete or reliable.[1] Important historians who wrote about this period of Roman history were Ammianus Marcellinus (fourth century) and Procopius (sixth century). The only part of Marcellinus' work that has survived is his report on the period 359–378 in which he puts special emphasis on the reign of Emperor Julian (361–363), an emperor for whom he had great admiration. Julian is known as the 'Apostate' because he opposed Christianity and tried to restore the old Roman traditions. Procopius described the wars that Emperor Justinian waged against the Persians, the Visigoths and the Vandals between 529 and 553; in addition, in one of his works, which was probably not published officially, he denounced the private lives of several important persons, including Justinian.

The works of Christian authors like Lactantius and Eusebius (third/fourth centuries) form a special category of sources. Lactantius wrote about the persecution of the Christians in the time of Diocletian; Eusebius, who was bishop of Caesarea, wrote a history of the church. In view of the close links between church and state at this time these works also give important information about everyday life. On the other hand, the fact that these authors, because of their religious background, are somewhat prejudiced against certain persons and events means that the information given in their work is less reliable.

Another important source of information is the so-called *Notitia dignitatum*, which dates from the early fifth century; it is an official handbook in which the staffs of the various government departments and army units are listed and therefore it is our chief source of information on the organisation of the empire under the dominate. Of the various epigraphs and papyrus scrolls that have come down to us from these times the most important is the so-called price-edict of Emperor Diocletian (284–305); in order to combat currency depreciation he stipulated maximum prices for the most common goods and services and saw to it that inscriptions bearing these prices were displayed in many places in the Roman empire. From fragments found in a variety of places, it has been possible to reconstruct the whole text and as a result we can obtain greater insight into the social and economic conditions prevailing in the Roman empire at the time.[2]

We are also fairly well informed about the development of law and legal science in the dominate. Various juridical manuscripts from the fourth and fifth centuries have survived, some complete, some incomplete; an example of the latter category is the *Fragmenta Vaticana*. Another important source, dating from the sixth century, is the *Leges Romanae Barbarorum*; one of these laws is the *lex Romana Visigothorum* which includes both the legislation of Roman emperors and fragments from works of classical jurists. By far the most important source of our knowledge about the law of this period is, however, the so-called *Corpus Iuris Civilis* which was compiled between 530–534 on the orders of Emperor Justinian. It contains an enormous collection of texts by classical jurists as well as a large quantity of imperial constitutions from the second century up to and including the time of Justinian himself; these collections were arranged in the same way as those of the classical period. In addition, it contains an introductory textbook on law, which is based on the Institutes of Gaius.

10.2. THE TERRITORY

When Diocletian became emperor in 284 the Roman empire was considerably smaller than the area over which Emperor Trajan (95–117) had once ruled. In the north various Germanic tribes like the Franks, the Saxons and the Burgundians tried, with varying degrees of success, to become established within the borders of the empire. The Goths no longer accepted the Danube as the frontier and in the east the Persian kings of the house of the Sassanids conquered large parts of the Roman empire with the help of their heavily armed cavalry. One of Diocletian's greatest achievements was to reorganise the government and the defence of the empire so efficiently that the Roman empire survived in its entirety for at least another 100 years and the eastern part even for more than 1000 years. Admittedly this stability involved the loss of some territory, but the ultimate frontiers were strategically so much better in that they could be adequately defended in the long term. The Rhine and the Danube formed the northern frontier; in Africa and the Middle East Roman rule was restricted to the coastal areas.

In the course of the fourth century the empire was ravaged by a number of civil wars and by invasions of barbaric tribes. In 395 the empire was finally split into two parts; a western part with Rome as its capital and an eastern part with Constantinople as its capital. The West-Roman empire soon had to cope with invading Germanic tribes. By the beginning of the fifth century Gaul had been conquered by the Franks and the Burgundians, Britain by the Angles and Saxons and Spain and North Africa by the Vandals. In addition, large numbers of Visigoths settled in the West-Roman empire, firstly in Italy but finally in Aquitaine (south-west France) and Spain. About the middle of the fifth century the Huns led by Attila threatened to invade Gaul, but a West-Roman general called Aetius was able to prevent this with the help of the Visigoths. Several decades later, namely in 476, the leader of the Ostrogoths, Odoacer, finally brought the West-Roman empire to an end by defeating the emperor Orestes and by deposing his son Romulus Augustus, nicknamed Augustulus.

As a result of the splitting up of the Roman empire, Italy and the western provinces gradually lost their Roman character. The East-Roman empire, which was much stronger economically, was able to survive. There was still cohesion there due to the common culture, although this was basically Greek, and to the common religion, since Christianity had become the state religion. This last phase of the (East-)Roman history is also called the Byzantine period.[3] There was one Byzantine emperor who succeeded in restoring parts of the old empire to its former glory: in the sixth century Emperor Justinian, helped by his generals Belisarius and Narses, reconquered some parts of the former West-Roman empire, namely Italy, southern Spain and North Africa. However, it proved impossible to occupy these territories permanently, and after a few decades most of them were lost again. In the seventh and eighth centuries the Arabs conquered the southern part of the

Byzantine empire, namely Syria, Egypt and North Africa, and in the ninth century they conquered Spain. However, it was not until 1453 that Constantinople, the capital of the Byzantine empire, fell.

10.3. THE POPULATION

The social structure of the later Roman empire is characterised by its exceptional rigidity. This was due to the economic crisis of the third century and the measures taken by the emperors to combat it. The emperors increased the influence of the state, for instance by obliging the citizens to perform all kinds of tasks for the benefit of the state, by making these tasks hereditary and by creating a huge bureaucracy to try and keep things under control. The upper class was less affected by this policy than the lower classes of the population.[4]

The senatorial class no longer consisted mainly of a few families of ex-magistrates and large landowners and their next-of-kin, as it had done under the principate; now it was made up of persons who were or had been senior officials and of their descendants. At the same time it became usual for the emperor to appoint to the senate well-to-do persons who had been active in the provincial government, high-ranking soldiers who had finished their careers, jurists who had held high positions in the administration of justice and other persons of distinction. Senators now came from all parts of the empire and together they formed a very heterogeneous group. When in 357 Constantius II set up a second senate in Constantinople seats were given mainly to citizens from the eastern part of the empire, whereas the Roman senate consisted of persons from Italy and the western provinces. It sometimes came about that certain senators were not even of Roman origin but were Germans, Persians, etc. In the senate in Rome, where a number of members were still proud of the fact that they were descended from old Roman families, there was scarcely any integration. In Constantinople, on the other hand, integration occurred much more smoothly.

In the principate the *equites* had been involved in the imperial administration and had therefore belonged to the upper class. In the dominate their position was at first strengthened as a result of the administrative reforms of Diocletian, but things changed when Emperor Constantine opened up to the senatorial élite the functions that originally could be performed solely by *equites*. As a result the *equites* lost their political power and their social standing; they were allotted the same status as low-ranking officials and were addressed accordingly.

The urban aristocracy (*curiales*) theoretically still formed a privileged class, but their position was no longer an enviable one. As urban administrators they had the same rights and duties as before, but as a result of the economic crisis of the third century it became more and more difficult for them to fulfil their obligations. Because of this many *curiales* tried to evade their duties, but such attempts were severely punished. A number of constitutions were issued for the purpose of preserving the urban administration; for instance, the status of *decurio* was made hereditary in the male line; furthermore, a person could be obliged to become a member of the *curia* when he was 18 years old. Other constitutions were aimed at making the position of *curialis* a little more attractive; for instance, illegitimate sons could be made legitimate by becoming members of the *curia*. To prevent *curiales* from reducing their financial resources it was stipulated that they could only sell property with the consent of the provincial governor. At the beginning of the fifth century a person could even be made a member of the urban administration by way of punishment! The *curiales* now formed a kind of caste from which it was difficult to escape.

The dominate brought all kinds of changes for the rest of the population as well. For example, the farmers and the artisans suffered from the economic recession and those who lived in the frontier provinces were subjected to invasions by barbaric tribes as well. Moreover, their freedom was severely restricted by high taxation and the system of compulsory trades and services. They lived in conditions close to slavery. For the urban proletariat in Rome, Constantinople and the other large cities in the empire 'bread and games' were still organised from time to time at the state's expense. The position of the slaves improved somewhat, both in a juridical and in a social sense. For instance, the killing of a slave by his master was now punished as murder. Marriages of slaves, which were invalid in law, were recognised by the church and also accepted by society. Slaves were given more power to acquire capital and increasingly they could serve as plaintiff or defendant in a trial. Although no more lands were conquered the number of slaves did not decline; quite often poverty-stricken citizens would abandon their children or even sell them into slavery. The authorities tried to counter this practice –

as is demonstrated by various legal provisions on the subject –
but in fact this turned out to be impossible.

10.4. ECONOMY

The political calamities of the third century brought to an end
the prosperity which the Roman empire had enjoyed under the
principate. The economic crisis which ensued was aggravated by
the devaluation of the coinage and the arbitrary nature of taxation.
Diocletian took several hard measures to tackle these problems.
To curb inflation he issued an edict of maximum prices and tried
to restore a stable, silver currency. Apparently, however, these
measures did not have the desired effect. Constantine was more
successful in this respect in that he introduced a new currency
unit of gold, the *solidus*; this coin was to retain its weight and
purity for seven centuries. To stabilise taxation Diocletian introduced a new tax system which met with more success – at least
from the state's point of view. It provided the emperors with huge
sums of money and not surprisingly the new system was used
throughout the dominate.[5] In theory it created security and equality before the law because tax was now levied regularly and in
accordance with fairly well-defined criteria. In practice, however,
it required a huge administrative machinery which was not available, so in the end the new system did not work very fairly and
justly. A danger of this was that it was so easy to adapt: if the
state had spent too much, it was simpler to raise the rate of tax
than to economise. In the long term the disadvantages outweighed
the advantages and the area that suffered most was agriculture.

Because tax had now to be paid annually and no account was
taken of bad harvests or similar natural disasters, the new tax
system was troublesome particularly for the independent farmers.
If after a number of bad years a farmer was no longer able to
pay his tax he had to sell his farm and become a tenant farmer
working for a landowner. Hence the number of independent farmers declined still further in this period.

Trade and industry were affected by the economic crisis as well.
Although conditions were still favourable for trade, fewer people
now earned their living from it. The main reason was that the
biggest customer, the state, did not use the private sector but had
its own firms for producing and transporting goods. All over the
empire the state had arms factories to supply the army, marble

quarries for public works and mines from which gold and silver were extracted to make coins. These activities, however, were not financed by normal taxes, but they had to be performed by specific groups of citizens in lieu of tax. For instance, the *fiscus* made the *navicularii* responsible for transporting corn from the province of Africa to Rome and from the province of Egypt to Constantinople in connection with the distribution of free food in these cities. These *navicularii* were wealthy people who either financed the construction, repair and operation of sea-going ships or who put their own ships (of a certain minimum size) at the disposal of the *fiscus*. In return, they were exempted from other tasks that were in the public interest.[6]

In spite of the dominant role played by the state in the economic life of the later empire, private individuals still engaged in trade and industry in many fields: utensils were now made chiefly for the home market, but items like woollen cloth and clothes were produced on a large scale in Egypt and Asia Minor and then exported to all parts of the empire; Egyptian corn, and wine and oil from Africa were still very much in demand. Trade did not stop at the frontiers. The markets in large cities like Constantinople, Alexandria and Rome still sold silk from China, precious stones and spices from India and south-east Asia, and slaves from Persia, Armenia and the Caucasus. The official splitting of the empire at the end of the fourth century into a western and an eastern part did not bring about any important changes in this pattern of trade.

11

THE DOMINATE:
THE STATE

After Alexander Severus, the last of the dynasty of that name, had been assassinated in 235 the empire suffered fifty years of confusion and disaster. During that time, usually called the military anarchy, there were more than sixteen official and many more unofficial emperors. It was only Diocletian who succeeded in bringing back stability and peace. His success was due to three major changes. He became an absolute monarch, he divided the empire among four co-rulers and he reorganised the administration.[1] The changes he instigated were worked out by his successor Constantine. The latter also made another important break with the past in that he tolerated Christianity which was later even recognised as the state religion.

11.1. THE EMPEROR

Emperorship in the dominate differed markedly from emperorship in earlier centuries. From Diocletian onwards, the emperor was no longer *primus inter pares*, the first among his peers, namely the senators, but he had become an absolute monarch and was elevated far above all his subjects. Since 282 the emperors had no longer asked the senate to ratify their title. On the other hand the emperors retained their quasi-republican status: they still served as consuls for form's sake and still enjoyed the *tribunicia potestas* at least in name. In fact, however, they wielded their power with the help of the army and their election had normally been arranged by their predecessor. This new type of emperorship was particularly obvious in court ceremonies. Diocletian and particularly Constantine introduced a number of rules which were taken from the instructions for the Persian court. The purpose of these rules

116

was on the one hand to impress the subjects with imperial majesty and power and on the other hand to guarantee the greatest possible personal safety for the emperor. From then onwards the emperor hardly ever appeared in public, but if he did he wore a diadem of pearls and beautiful clothes embroidered with jewels. In his presence people had to prostrate themselves (*adoratio*) and only a few senior officials were allowed to kiss the hem of his robe. Anything that was linked with the emperor – ranging from official to domestic matters – was regarded as sacred. The emperor was no longer within reach of normal mortals.

The territorial division introduced by Diocletian was not based on any plan worked out beforehand but was the result of solutions to various problems which arose at specific moments. Right at the beginning of his reign Diocletian had to deal with a revolt in Gaul and the threat of war along the Danube and in Syria. In order to solve these problems adequately he appointed his general Maximian as *Caesar*, under-emperor, and entrusted him with the special task of suppressing the Gallic revolt. Less than a year later, in 286, he even appointed Maximian as *Augustus*, co-emperor, of Italy, Africa, Spain and the northern frontier provinces. Diocletian, however, as senior-*Augustus*, retained the supreme power in the empire. Initially this measure seemed to be effective, but in 292 there was another revolt in Egypt and there was considerable unrest in Britain and North Africa. Diocletian therefore decided to appoint more under-emperors, one for Maximian and one for himself. Constantius, the father of the later Emperor Constantine, thus became *Caesar* for the north-western part of the empire in 293 and Galerius was given the south-eastern part of the empire. Then his new form of government, nowadays referred to as a tetrarchy (literally, rule by four) was complete.

By employing this system Diocletian probably had a dual purpose: he wanted administrative and defence tasks to be effectively distributed and he wanted to safeguard the succession. The first objective was certainly achieved in view of the fact that after 297 the sources make no further mention of revolts. Although Diocletian himself apparently was not an exceptionally talented general he was very good at choosing people who would wage war and govern large areas without questioning his supremacy. The second objective was not achieved. In 305 Diocletian and Maximian, at the initiative of the former, abdicated.[2] They appointed Constantius and Galerius as *Augusti* and chose two new *Caesares* for them, but neither of the two new *Augusti* had enough personal authority to keep the other emperors under control. When Constantius died only a year later, in 306, there was a struggle for power among the remaining emperors and the sons of Maximian and Constantius. It was not until 326 that the conflict was settled definitively in favour of Constantius' son Constantine.[3]

Constantine ruled alone until he died in 337, but from 317 he appointed his sons as *Caesares*. Three surviving sons succeeded their father in 337, as *Augusti*. From that time onwards the Roman empire was ruled by one *Augustus* or by two or sometimes three *Augusti*, and no more *Caesares* were appointed; instead, the son of an emperor was often elevated to the rank of *Augustus*, even at a very early age, in order to safeguard the succession. In this way the empire was ruled for another 150 years by a number of relatively stable dynasties. Often the emperors ruled together, but in fact each was autonomous in his own part of the empire. When the emperor of the West-Roman empire was deposed by the Ostrogoths in 476 this had absolutely no influence on the position of the East-Roman emperor. Of the later East-Roman or Byzantine emperors one in particular was very important for the history of Roman law, namely Justinian I. In section 12.5 more attention will be paid to him and to his activities in the field of law.

11.2. THE SENATE AND THE CONSISTORIUM

Although the senate had lost its power since the end of the second century, for the sake of tradition this illustrious body continued to exist under the dominate. As mentioned earlier, there had even been a second senate in Constantinople since the middle of the fourth century. Both senates were presided over by a senior official, the city prefects of Rome and Constantinople respectively. The two senates functioned mainly as local councils and in addition they had ceremonial tasks, for instance, the inauguration of the new emperor. Although theoretically the senate still had powers in the field of legislation and the administration of justice, as in the principate, it now had very few opportunities to use them. If a senate had proposals concerning legislation the city prefect passed them on to the emperor. Sometimes the emperor consulted the senate, but then it was only for the purpose of obtaining support for his own plans. Furthermore, the senate no longer functioned as a *forum privilegiatum* for its own members;

if a senator had to stand trial, then the trial took place in the presence of the city prefect or a provincial governor. Apparently, however, the senate in Constantinople did function as a lawcourt from time to time.

Even though membership of the senate no longer implied political power it was still greatly sought after. Senators were highly respected in society and they were exempted from difficult financial tasks in the towns from which they came. In addition, they enjoyed certain privileges in lawsuits. In return for these privileges, however, they incurred certain obligations. For instance, senators had to see to it that certain games were held in Rome and, from the middle of the fourth century, in Constantinople.

The advisory function that had been performed by the emperor's *consilium* in the principate was taken over in the fourth century by the so-called *consistorium*. Its members, who no longer sat but stood in the emperor's presence, were high-ranking officials and army officers and a number of unofficial members. The *consistorium* functioned as a kind of council of state and supreme court. It was summoned when there was a threat of a rebellion or when religious problems had arisen. It received foreign envoys and dealt with administrative and political matters. In the middle of the fifth century, however, this advisory body also began to lose its power and by the sixth century it had more or less the same ceremonial status as the two senates.

11.3. THE OFFICIALS

The dominate was characterised not only by the introduction of the absolute monarchy and the territorial division of the empire, but also by the development of a very extensive civil service with a hierarchical structure. The foundation for this was laid by Diocletian, but it was primarily Constantine who extended the bureaucratic system.[4] The reorganisation of the public administration was linked with the territorial division of the empire introduced by Diocletian. Under the tetrarchy Diocletian had divided the empire into four regions, or prefectures. Each was under the authority of an emperor (*Augustus* or *Caesar*). Each of the four emperors had a praetorian prefect to support him in military, juridical and financial matters. In addition, Diocletian subdivided the four prefectures into dioceses, each of which was governed by a *vicarius*. The dioceses were subdivided into provinces, each of which was governed by a *praeses*.

Emperor Constantine did not take over the system of the tetrarchy, but he continued the division of the empire into four sections. He also relieved the prefects of their military duties, but gave them a different task in return. They now had to govern the prefectures themselves. This meant that each praetorian prefect in his part of the empire was, along with the emperor, the highest authority to whom appeals could be made in connection with legal procedures. The praetorian prefect was also responsible for recruiting soldiers, supplying the army (with food/equipment) and in general had to supervise the work of the provincial governors. The *vicarius*, the representative of the prefect in a diocese, also served as a judge when appeals were made against sentences passed by a provincial governor, and he also supervised the work of the governors. Just as before, the governors of the provinces were required to perform tasks in the field of jurisdiction and administration and were sometimes involved in military matters. They were primarily responsible for the collecting of taxes, they supervised the state post and public works and saw to it that the orders of the central government were carried out. Rome and Constantinople were not included in this system: each was governed by a city prefect.

This hierarchy was in itself clear and easy to understand, but it became complicated because the system was not adhered to consistently. For example, certain provinces, namely Asia and Africa, were governed as before by governors who came directly under the emperor. In addition, the *vicarii* were sometimes appointed by the emperor personally instead of by the prefects and the emperors regularly passed over the prefects and the *vicarii* and turned directly to the provincial governors. When in the fifth century various vicariates were abolished and regional prefectures were set up, the administration of the empire seemed more and more like a patchwork quilt, in which the various patches could only be accounted for by history.

This effect was strengthened still further by the fact that parallel to this hierarchy Constantine had set up a separate civil service to serve the central administration in Constantinople. Four senior functionaries with the same rank as the prefects served as ministers. They were the *quaestor sacri palatii*, the minister of justice, the *magister officiorum*, whose various tasks included supervising the imperial secretariat, the state police and the post, the *comes sacrarum largitionum*, a sort of minister of the state finances, and the *comes rerum privatarum* who was responsible for the imperial treasury. Each of the last three functionaries had an extensive staff.

Not surprisingly, the complicated administrative machinery did not work very efficiently. Another point was that top officials were no longer appointed for indefinite periods, as they had been under the principate, but they now held office for only a couple of years; the city prefects even changed after about a year. Only the low-ranking officials kept their posts for a long time and they therefore provided the experience and continuity which was so often lacking at the top. Senior officials were often appointed by the emperor, either on the basis of his personal preference or upon the recommendation of the imperial household. Because these functions were associated with all kinds of income differentials, privileges and high status, they were greatly sought after. High-ranking officials were repeatedly bribed to put forward someone's name to the emperor. As a result it was not always the most suitable persons who held high office in the empire. On the other hand it sometimes happened that the emperor appointed people from the lower classes to high functions because he knew of their abilities as a result of his own experience. This happened in the case of Justinian's appointment of Belisarius as general. Belisarius had formed part of Justinian's bodyguard before Justinian became emperor. Apparently Belisarius' appointment was justified since he and another general, Narses, succeeded in reconquering parts of the earlier West-Roman empire from the Goths and the Vandals.

11.4. CHRISTIANITY

At the beginning of the principate various new cults and religions developed alongside the traditional Roman religion. They had originated in the eastern part of the empire but soon gained support in other parts, extending even to Britain. Adherents of these new religions worshipped, for instance, Isis, Mithras, the *Magna Mater* and Jesus Christ. There were various reasons why Christianity finally triumphed over the other religions – which nevertheless survived until the sixth century.[5] The reasons include the closely knit organisation of the church, the development of in-depth theological literature and the ethical norms that the Christians observed. Until the beginning of the fourth century, however, Christianity encountered opposition, which was often fierce, because the Christians refused to have anything to do with the other religions and tended to isolate themselves. Rumours abounded about their 'scandalous' rituals, and their refusal to worship the traditional Roman gods, including the emperor, meant that they could easily be reproached for their lack of solidarity with the Roman state. When times were bad, this occasionally led to acts of aggression being directed against the Christians who were then used as scapegoats. For example, in the middle of the third century, when anarchy was threatening the very existence of the empire, emperors like Decius (249–251) and Valerian (253–260) tried to restore unity and solidarity by forcing the Christians to give up their special position. They were unsuccessful and it is said that thousands of Christians were then put to death. Later emperors refrained from persecuting the Christians. Galerius, the *Caesar* of Diocletian, was an exception. When Diocletian was seriously ill in 303 Galerius took the opportunity to announce that severe measures would be taken against Christians all over the empire. In some provinces, particularly in the eastern part of the empire where Galerius himself reigned, these measures were in fact carried out and sometimes in a very cruel manner. The other emperors, however, hardly carried out any of these measures.

In 313, the tide definitely turned in favour of the Christians. In that year the two surviving emperors, Constantine (from the west) and Licinius (from the east), decided that thereafter Christians would have complete freedom of worship and that the churches would be rehabilitated. This decision became known as the 'Edict of Milan', being named after the place where the decision was taken. In 321 Constantine declared that the church was permitted to receive inheritances and bequests. Although Constantine did not let himself be baptised until he was on his deathbed, he and his successors strongly supported the Christian church; only Julian 'the Apostate' (361–363) tried to reinstate Roman rituals but finally he had to admit that Christianity had triumphed. In 391 Emperor Theodosius I declared Christianity to be the state religion.

Since the Edict of Milan, church and state had become increasingly intertwined. One of the consequences was that the church came to be organised in more or less the same way as the state. Initially Christianity had gained supporters mainly in the towns and particularly among the lower classes. As soon as a Christian community had developed in a town, the faithful chose a bishop who was then consecrated by the bishops of nearby towns. The bishops of a province used to gather regularly in so-called councils (*consilia*). As the bishops increased in number they developed a hierarchy of their own which was parallel to the administrative hierarchy in the state. From the fourth century supreme authority in the church was in the hands of the emperor. In the west he was represented by the patriarch of Rome and the bishop of Carthage, and in the east by the patriarchs of Constantinople, Antioch, Jerusalem and Alexandria. Below them were the bishops of the provincial capitals, and below them again were the bishops of other towns in the provinces concerned; the local priests in their turn were subordinate to these bishops. The areas over which the patriarchs and bishops exercised their ecclesiastical authority were more or less the same as the prefectures, dioceses and provinces ruled by the prefects, vicars and governors appointed by the emperor. Certain aspects of the organisation still exist today in the Roman Catholic church and some of the terminology is still in use there as well.

Because he saw Christianity as a potential binding element within the Roman empire, Constantine regarded it as his task to watch over the unity of the church. He tried to prevent the various doctrinal movements such as those of the Donatists and the Arians from causing schisms in the church. In this connection Constantine was the first to summon a council to which all bishops of the empire were invited; this was the famous Council of Nicaea which met in 325. Later emperors, and in particular Justinian, also tried to settle religious disputes and make their own views prevail. Neither Constantine nor his successors really managed to do this, but they did prevent schisms.[6]

12

THE DOMINATE:
THE LAW

12.1. INTRODUCTION

In the dominate, when the emperors wielded absolute power in the empire, the emperor and his officials were also in complete control of law-making. This period in the history of Roman law has rightfully been characterized as the bureaucratic period.[1]

Legislation, which in the principate had been characterized by pluriformity, now stemmed exclusively from the emperor. The content of the laws also differed markedly from the content of the laws of the principate. For instance, the law was no longer strictly Roman, but showed Greek influences. Furthermore, it is striking that imperial legislation reveals traces of so-called vulgar law; this involves a juridical style of thinking which through its simplicity and lack of subtlety is not in keeping with the traditional classical way of thinking.

As in the principate, the administration of justice was closely linked with the government. In civil and penal cases justice was still administered in principle by the emperor and – by delegation – by his officials. This basically simple system was, however, thwarted in various ways because (a) special courts were set up for specific matters and persons, (b) bishops were granted judicial powers and (c) a variety of appeal procedures developed side by side.

In those days legal science was anonymous and lacked creativity. There were no longer any jurists who, in their dual capacity as members of the senate and experts in the field of law, gave opinions on juridical problems and recorded them in writing. Their place was now taken partly by senior officials whose names are hardly known, and by professors at the law-schools. These people did not give any new opinions but made summaries and anthologies of opinions dating from the principate. At the same time collections were made of imperial legislation.

This period of Roman law culminated with the publication of Justinian's legislation. In the sixth century this emperor ordered new collections to be made of opinions of classical jurists and of imperial constitutions, and he had a new introductory textbook for law prepared. The three resulting books, Digest, Code and Institutes, all had the force of law, and were used in practice as well as in teaching. Because manuscript copies of the Digest, Code and Institutes were preserved in Italy, they could and also did form the basis of later European legal science.

12.2. LEGISLATION

12.2.1. The forms of legislation

In the course of the principate the traditional forms of legislation were ousted to make way for the imperial constitutions. The old *leges* and senatorial decrees remained valid in the dominate, but the constitution then became the only source of new law. Of the four types of constitution that had developed since Augustus – edicts, mandates, rescripts and decrees – the edicts from the fourth century onwards were the most important. Usually the edicts, now also called *leges generales*, were prepared by the minister of justice and discussed in the *consistorium*. An edict was generally issued in the form of a letter addressed to the praetorian prefect or to another senior official who then had to ensure that it was publicised. An edict could, however, be directed to a particular people or group of people, for instance to the inhabitants of a certain town. The mandates, which were originally instructions from the emperor to his officials, were incorporated in the edicts. The rescripts and decrees, now referred to as *leges speciales*, lost their separate identity. The rescript, in which the emperor or his chancery solved a juridical problem submitted by a citizen or an official, continued to be an important source of law until the time of Diocletian.[2] In 315 Constantine decided that rescripts that deviated from the prevailing law were invalid. From the end of the fourth century rescripts were no longer considered to have any general validity, so they finally ceased to be a source of new law. The decrees, which were originally decisions of the emperor taken as judge of first instance or of appeal, gradually disappeared as the emperors more and more often left their officials to deal with such matters.

Under the dominate, however, two new types of constitution appeared, namely the *adnotatio* and the *sanctio pragmatica*. The sources do not tell us precisely what an *adnotatio* was. The term leads one to assume that it was a decision of the emperor in connection with a petition and was placed in the margin of the petition. If this assumption is correct the *adnotatio* must have served almost the same purpose as the earlier rescript. No clear definition can be given of the *sanctio pragmatica* either. It generally consisted of a reply by the emperor to a petition, but this reply sometimes had a general purport. The best-known example of such a constitution is the *sanctio pragmatica pro petitione Vigilii* in which Emperor Justinian, at the request of the bishop of Rome, Pope Vigilius, solved a number of juridical problems that had arisen following the re-conquest of Italy and in which Justinian also introduced his legislation into Italy.

The administrative division of the empire into two parts, which had occurred materially since the death of Constantine in 337 and had been formalised since the death of Theodosius I, also led to a division in the legislation. Even when Theodosius I actually ruled alone for several years in the whole empire (because the West-Roman emperor Valentinian II was so young) he enacted separate laws for the two parts of the empire. In fact, it often happened that the emperor of the western part took over a constitution from his East-Roman colleague, but the reverse did not occur. The fact that after 395 the names of the two emperors still appeared in the heading for a law is probably because in a political sense the empire was still regarded as one unit.

12.2.2. The content of the legislation

Legislation in the dominate shows the intrusion of non-Roman elements and of vulgar law into official Roman law. Since Roman citizenship had been granted via the *constitutio Antoniniana* to all free inhabitants of the empire at the beginning of the third century, all these people could now participate in Roman law. However, local laws remained in force. As a result Roman law began to influence local laws and in the long run local laws also influenced Roman law. When in the fourth century the intellectual centre of the empire shifted from Rome to Constantinople, all kinds of legal concepts particularly of Greek origin appeared in the official Roman legislation. This influence is even visible in the law of persons and in family law, although traditionally that is the part of the law that changes least. For instance, Constantine began to put restrictions on the typical Roman concept of *patria potestas* by acknowledging that in one case persons *in potestate* could have proprietary rights: when a mother had bequeathed something to her children who were still under the *potestas* of their father, the father would no longer automatically become the owner but the children would get it (C. 6.60.1). Constantine was apparently making concessions to the much more restricted concept of paternal authority under Greek-Hellenistic law. Later emperors went even further. Justinian finally decreed that a child *in potestate* became owner of everything it acquired except when it acquired something from its father (C. 6.61.1).

Another difference with regard to the content of the legislation is that from the fourth century elements of vulgar law penetrated into official law. It is self-evident that in every sophisticated legal system the over-simplified interpretation of the law by lay people differs from the official law. This was the case in the Roman empire too, not only in the provinces but also in Italy and in Rome itself, and even under the principate which was the Golden Age of Roman law. The fact that aspects of vulgar law worked their way into official law should not necessarily be regarded as reprehensible and objectionable. The changes which were introduced in the later empire as a result of the vulgarizing trend satisfied the needs of the times. Examples of such changes are: the conferring of a binding force on every agreement confirmed in writing so that people were no longer tied to the traditional way in which agreements had to be drawn up.[3] Another change was the removal of the distinction between ownership and usufruct through the recognition of a kind of joint ownership. Nevertheless it is generally agreed that partly as a result of the vulgarization of the law, the intellectual level of the law was lower than in the late republic and the principate. The most striking example of the decline is the blurring of the distinction between ownership and possession, which was and still is typical of lay-thinking about law.[4]

The decline occurred in both the eastern and western parts of the empire, but after the final division in 395 vulgarization prevailed, particularly in the West-Roman empire. There, for instance, an *interpretatio* was often added to laws which summarized the content of the law in question. Now the laws already deviated from the classical law in various respects, but the interpretation sometimes underlined the content of the law in question in such an awkward manner that the summary totally contradicted classical law. In the East-Roman empire, on the other hand, the intellectual level had not declined so much and in the course of the fifth century classical law, as it had existed in the principate, could again be the centre of attention. Admittedly, this so-called classicist tendency was to be found mainly in the law-schools of the East-Roman empire, but this did not alter the fact that legislation there was at a higher level than in the West-Roman empire.

12.3. THE ADMINISTRATION OF JUSTICE

12.3.1. The courts

Under the dominate the normal administration of justice was largely in the hands of the imperial officials.[5] These officials were certainly not always professional jurists and therefore they were often assisted by *adsessores* who had had a legal training and had usually belonged to the legal profession. The hierarchy that was observed with regard to the administrative tasks performed by these officials also applied to the jurisdictional tasks they performed; it was only in Rome and Constantinople that administration and jurisdiction were organised differently.

The lowest level of jurisdiction was that performed by the urban administrators; their powers were limited. Private law disputes could only be submitted to them if the disputes concerned small amounts of money. However, this restriction could be removed if both parties wished to submit the dispute to the urban magistrates. In the area of penal law the magistrates performed only a kind of policing function.

The provincial governors administered justice in all criminal cases and in important private-law disputes; in addition they could be required to deal with appeals against sentences passed by urban magistrates. Since the provincial governors on the whole had not been given any military tasks since the end of the third century and the areas they governed had become much smaller, the administration of justice was a very important part of their daily work.

If an appeal was made against a sentence passed by a provincial governor it was handled by the *vicarius* of the diocese in which the province in question was situated or by the praetorian prefect (if he was nearer) of the prefecture of which the province formed a part. The sentence of a *vicarius* could be re-submitted to the emperor but the sentence of a prefect could not: the latter was considered to administer justice on behalf of the emperor. In exceptional cases the *vicarii* and the prefects could serve as judges of first instance, for example if one party in a trial were so powerful that there was a chance the normal judge would be intimidated.

The emperor himself was of course authorised to serve as judge in all types of lawsuit, both of first instance and of appeal, but in fact this hardly occurred. The main reason why the emperor hardly ever served as judge was that he would then come into close contact with his subjects, which was something that the late Roman emperors sought to avoid. Imperial jurisdiction therefore often took place by virtue of delegation by the praetorian prefect and the minister of justice.

In addition to normal jurisdiction there were all kinds of special legal procedures for specific matters and persons. Examples of the former were the tax problems that had to be put to the *rationalis*, the official who represented the public treasury in a diocese; an appeal against the *rationalis* could be made to the *comes sacrarum largitionum*, the minister of the state finances. An example of the latter is the privilege enjoyed by the members of the senatorial élite who could only be prosecuted by the city prefect (if they lived in Rome or Constantinople) or by their provincial governor.

In this connection mention should be made of the special procedure available to Christians which in the long term became more important than all other forms of special jurisdiction. Even before Christianity had become a state religion it was normal for Christians to put their private law disputes to a bishop; they did this in accordance with a letter from the apostle Paul to the Corinthians (1 Cor. 6, 1–8). This type of jurisdiction, called *episcopalis audientia*, was officially recognised by Constantine at the beginning of the fourth century because he proclaimed the sentences in question to be legally binding (C.Th. 1.27). The sources suggest that a person could also be forced by the opposing party to put the dispute to the ecclesiastical judge, but since 398 the consent of both parties had been necessary. This legal procedure differed from normal jurisdiction not only with regard to the court involved but also in another respect: it was not possible to appeal against a sentence passed by the *episcopalis audientia*. Nevertheless, this special form of legal procedure became very popular because the procedures were cheaper and faster than those of the ordinary courts.

12.3.2. The criminal trial

Since the third century the *cognitio extraordinaria* had been the normal procedure for criminal trials. A criminal trial usually began because there was a public prosecution.[6] It was still possible for citizens to indict someone on a charge, but this hardly ever occurred because of the high risks involved. If the trial demonstrated that the charge was unfounded, then the accuser received the same punishment as the one to which he had exposed the accused; in the principate, on the other hand, it was only the person who had intentionally made a false accusation who was punished.

The range of offences for which prosecution could be instituted was widened considerably. Both the old and the new offences were now based exclusively on imperial constitutions (*leges generales*). The new offences clearly show the changes that occurred in Roman society in the later empire. For instance, the influence of bureaucracy is clearly visible from the fact that corruption perpetrated by provincial governors in the course of their tasks in jurisdiction or in their administrative tasks was made punishable. Furthermore, economic dirigisme can be seen from the fact that the evasion on the part of *decuriones* of fiscal tasks imposed by the state was now regarded as an offence. The recognition of Christianity also gave rise to a number of new penal clauses, particularly in the sphere of marriage and sexuality; for example, Emperor Constantine decreed that a woman could only renounce her husband if he was a murderer, poisoner or desecrator of tombstones. In all other cases she would be punished by deportation and the loss of her dowry (C.Th. 3.16.1). In this connection one should also mention offences against the Christian religion, for instance dissenting from orthodox Catholicism by Manicheans, renegades, pagans and Jews; the persecution of dissenters had intensified, particularly since the last few decades of the fourth century when Christianity became the state religion.

THE LAW

The judge in the criminal procedure was bound by all kinds of rules relating to the evidence. The confession of a suspect served as proof and the judge could only sentence a suspect to death if the latter had confessed or evidence to this effect had been produced. In addition, the suspect could be tortured during the interrogation, and so could the witnesses, unless the persons involved were senators, dignitaries of the church, *decuriones* and the like. As in the principate a suspect could only be sentenced if it was absolutely certain that he had committed the crime in question: *in dubiis pro deo*, when there was uncertainty the suspect had to be given the benefit of the doubt.

The criminal trial closed when the judge gave his verdict in which he either sentenced or acquitted the accused. The penalties that a judge could impose were laid down by law and in general were much more severe than those in the principate. The death penalty was imposed frequently. Lower-class citizens and slaves could be sentenced to forced labour in the mines. Other punishments were exile (often for life), confiscation of property, and fines. Lower-class citizens and slaves could also be subjected to corporal punishment. Prison sentences did not exist; as in earlier times prisons were used solely to guard convicts for short periods, not to punish them. Under the influence of Christianity certain punishments like crucifixion and gladiatorial combat were abolished and the treatment of prisoners improved. On the other hand, all kinds of other cruel punishments persisted; these included being burnt alive and *culleus*, whereby the convict was tied up in a leather sack containing a snake or another animal and drowned in the sea.

In general, condemned persons were free to appeal against their sentences. This was impossible when crimes had been committed such as murder, adultery or violence, and if the condemned person had confessed. Condemned persons could not appeal either if it was evident that the sole reason for the appeal was to obtain a stay of execution.

12.3.3. The civil procedure

The way in which civil procedures were conducted in the late empire was characterised by the active role played by the judge in various stages of the trial. The origin of this procedure can be traced back to the principate when the *cognitio extraordinaria*

131

became increasingly popular. However, it differed in several respects from the cognition procedure of the principate.

To begin a civil procedure it was no longer sufficient for the plaintiff to issue a summons: he now needed the consent of the judge and the co-operation of an official who then made a formal note of the fact. The result of issuing a summons was that the plaintiff and the defendant had to appear in front of the judge within four months. If the defendant failed to appear he could be prosecuted for *contumacia*, insubordination. If the plaintiff failed to appear he lost his case and could only institute proceedings one more time. Under Justinian the rules for issuing a summons were slightly different: the plaintiff had to submit a *libellus conventionis* (statement of claim) to the judge concerned; the defendant had to sign the petition and to guarantee that the case would be put to the judge within two months. If he could not give this guarantee he could be imprisoned.

During the trial itself the evidence was presented as before. There were, however, different rules governing this part of the trial. On the one hand the parties were more or less free to alter the claim and the defence in the course of the trial, and the procedure ran more smoothly than before. On the other hand the judge was no longer free to evaluate the evidence produced by the parties. As an imperial official he was bound by the instructions of his superiors. It was stipulated that more weight should be attached to written evidence than to oral pronouncements and an order was established for the various forms of written evidence. Furthermore, assertions of witnesses had to be evaluated according to the social position of the witnesses concerned. Witnesses who were held in low esteem could even be subjected to torture. In trials in which one of the parties was an orthodox Christian, no heretics or Jews could be accepted as witnesses.

It was also normal in the dominate for parties to be supported by advocates; however, they no longer delivered a speech summarizing the case on behalf of their client but their activities were restricted to supporting their client with advice. Furthermore, at the beginning of the trial they, just like the opposing parties, had to swear that they were defending an honourable case which was not based on false declarations. The advocates were no longer persons from the upper class who had trained in law and oratory and had served as advocates in order to further their political careers. They were now persons who had followed instruction in law at one of the law-schools and were serving as advocates in a professional capacity. They were tied to one particular court and formed a kind of association or order. They had to obey the rules of their order but also enjoyed all kinds of associated privileges. Their tariffs were laid down by law. The advocates of the dominate were more like modern advocates than the advocates from the late republic and principate.

The proceedings were over as soon as the judge gave his verdict. Just as in the *cognitio extraordinaria*, the judge in the post-classical cognition procedure was free to sentence someone to something other than the payment of damages. The verdict had to be put in writing and made known to both parties. In principle it was now possible to appeal against all sentences, but anyone who took this step without due consideration was severely punished.

12.4. LEGAL SCIENCE

The crisis in the third century, which caused power to fall definitively and exclusively into the hands of the emperor, completely changed the nature of legal science. From the fourth century onwards it was mainly practised at the law-schools. Emphasis was no longer on the creation of new law by means of the interpretation of legal provisions, wills, etc. What was stressed now was the study and explanation of the writings of jurists of the principate. The literature that originated in this period consisted on the one hand of selections of opinions of classical jurists and rescripts from the imperial chancery and on the other hand of simplifications of these. From the fifth century onwards collections of imperial law were compiled on behalf of the state.

12.4.1. The law-schools

The history of the law-schools dates from the principate: the first law-school was probably established in Rome in the second century and followed by another one in Beirut in the third century. The purpose of these schools was to train people for functions in the civil service. When Diocletian and Constantine reorganised the government, state officials began to perform key tasks in the government and law-schools became increasingly important. In addition to the schools in Rome and Beirut, which were very highly regarded, new schools were founded in places such as Carthage, Alexandria, Caesaraea and Athens, and in 425 in Constantinople. It was particularly at the law-schools in Beirut and Constantinople that classical legal science began to be studied again and it was also at these schools that the foundation was laid for Justinian's codification of the law.

Initially tuition at the law-schools was given in Latin, but about the year 400 Greek replaced Latin as the language of instruction. Legal studies took four to five years and were divided up as follows: in the first year the Institutes of Gaius were dealt with; thereafter a study was made of the collections of opinions *ad ius civile* of the classical jurists, followed by the opinions *ad edictum*; then special attention was given to the opinions of Papinian and Paul published in other books and in the final year the emphasis was on 'modern' law. This involved discussion of the imperial constitutions from the middle of the second century up to the 'present'. The way in which instruction was given was the same as that in which it had been given at the schools of rhetoric: a text from the classical juridical literature was discussed by the teacher or professor and, when possible, compared with parallel texts. On that basis the teacher formulated general principles, posed specific juridical problems and solved them, illustrating his points with examples from juridical practice. This so-called scholastic method is rather similar to the method used by the Glossators in the eleventh century in Bologna. At the end of their studies students who had successfully completed the course were awarded a certificate entitling them to serve as advocates in the courts of urban magistrates and of higher officials up to and including the praetorian prefect.

12.4.2. The juridical literature from the third to the fifth centuries

The juridical literature of the third to the fifth centuries is characterised by its lack of creativity and by the fact that the authors are unknown. The works in question are mainly compilations of opinions and rescripts dating from the principate. Probably these works were intended primarily for use in legal education and replaced the scarce and therefore expensive manuscripts of the classical jurists, but they were also used in practice. The most important work that can be mentioned in this connection is the so-called *Fragmenta Vaticana*; as the name indicates, this consists of part (probably only a small part) of a comprehensive collection of opinions and rescripts which was discovered in the Vatican library in 1821. The collection is important mainly because it contains texts that have not come down to us in other works or that have survived only in greatly abbreviated versions. The texts are arranged according to the subject matter (for example, there are sections on sale and on usufruct) in titles, seven of which have been preserved and are more or less complete. Each text is headed by a note stating from which work of which jurist it comes or if the text is a rescript the note gives the name of the emperor who issued it. The jurists involved here are Papinian, Paul and Ulpian who lived at the end of the second century and at the beginning of the third century. All the imperial constitutions except three date from the period 205–318. It is probable that this selection was compiled in or shortly after 318 and that the three other constitutions (from 330, 337 and 372) were added later.

Another selection, currently known as the *Collatio legum Mosaicarum et Romanarum* (abbreviated to *Collatio*), also dates from the beginning of the fourth century. The manuscript itself, however, gives the title as *Lex dei quam praecipit dominus ad Moysen*, the law of God which the Lord gave to Moses. This selection closely resembles the Vatican Fragments as regards content and composition but differs from that text in that several sentences from the first five books of the Old Testament, particularly the sayings of Moses, appear at the beginning of every title. In addition it contains texts not only by Papinian, Paul and Ulpian but also by Gaius and Modestinus. Various hypotheses have been put forward regarding the name of the author and the purpose of the work. Because the biblical texts concerned are all taken from the Old Testament and not from the New Testament it is often assumed that the author was of Jewish origin and wanted to demonstrate that Roman law corresponded to or possibly even was taken from Mosaic law.

In this connection the *Sententiae* of Paul and the *Epitome* of Ulpian can be mentioned as well. The *Pauli Sententiae* consist mainly of short pronouncements and rules of this late classical jurist. It is not certain whether Paul himself ever wrote a book called *Sententiae*. It is now generally assumed that the work that we know as *Pauli Sententiae* appeared at the end of the third century and was compiled by an unknown author on the basis of texts by Paul. The book must have become popular very rapidly, because it is quoted repeatedly in other selections of the time, including the *Lex Romana Visigothorum* and the Digest of Justinian. Furthermore, Constantine mentions it as being one of the few books to which reference can be made in trials. Unfortunately, the work has not come down to us directly; we know of it only via citations in the above-mentioned collections.

The *Ulpiani Epitome* was probably a shortened version of a work by Ulpian, the *liber singularis regularum*. Until recently it was assumed that the *Ulpiani Epitome* was based on the Institutes of Gaius and some other works of classical jurists. Not long ago, however, Nelson demonstrated that this assumption was incorrect.[7] The *Ulpiani Epitome* originated in about 300. It has come down to us via a manuscript dating from the tenth or eleventh century which is in the Vatican library; unfortunately both the beginning and the end of the text are missing.

12.4.3. The collections of constitutions from the third to the fifth centuries

In the principate the rescripts important for the development of law had been published because the jurists mentioned them in their collections of *responsa*. After the death of the last classical jurist, Modestinus, in the middle of the third century, this method of publication came to an end. When Diocletian had restored peace and order to the empire in about 300 and the imperial chancery could function again reasonably well, a new way of publishing the rescripts was required. This need was satisfied by the compilation of the *Codex Gregorianus* and the *Codex Hermogenianus*. These collections resemble the earlier collections of opinions in that they were not prepared officially on behalf of the state; they are private collections. It is possible, however, that the compilers, Gregorius and Hermogenian, were senior officials who had easy access to the archives of the imperial chancery. The fact that these works are referred to by the term *codex* and not by the previously used term *liber* is connected with the form of publication: after the year 300 literary works were no longer published as scrolls but appeared in modern book form. Neither of the two above-mentioned collections has survived; part of the contents is known because very many texts from these collections were incorporated in later collections such as the Vatican Fragments and the *Collatio* and particularly in the Code of Justinian.

The Gregorian Code must have been the more comprehensive of the two; it contained constitutions from Hadrian up to and including Diocletian. These were divided into books and titles according to the subject matter. The order of the subject matter was the same as that observed by the classical jurists in their *Digesta*. The Gregorian Code was probably published in 291. The *Codex Hermogenianus* contained mainly constitutions from the year 293/294; this much smaller collection was not subdivided into books and titles but only into titles devoted to certain topics; the constitutions in it were in chronological order. The Hermogenian Code was probably published in 295.

In spite of the existence of these two collections and of the above-mentioned Vatican Fragments and the *Collatio* there was still a great deal of uncertainty in the practice of law, about which opinions and rescripts could be recognised as being authoritative. First, the texts were sometimes contradictory, and second, it was often difficult for the judges to check whether a specific text was authentic. In an attempt to put an end to this situation of uncertainty Constantine formulated some laws: in 321 he decreed that the critical remarks (*notae*) that Paul and Ulpian had made in connection with the *responsa* collection of Papinian were no longer to be used. A year later, however, he declared that the other works of Paul, and particularly his *Sententiae*, had the force of law (C.Th. 1.4.1 and 1.4.2 respectively). In the end these measures turned out to be insufficient and in 426 the East-Roman emperor Theodosius II and the West-Roman emperor Valentinian III together formulated a new law on the subject (C.Th. 1.4.3); this so-called Law of Citations stipulated that from then onwards the works of the late classical jurists Papinian, Paul, Ulpian and Modestinus and those of Gaius had the force of law and that only these could be cited in a lawsuit. If these jurists had expressed different opinions on a particular topic then the opinion of the majority prevailed; if numbers were equal, then the view of Papinian had to be followed and only if Papinian had expressed no view on the subject was the judge free to make a choice himself. The reason why it was the works of these five jurists that could be cited was probably that a number of good manuscripts of these authors were readily available; the works of the four late classical jurists were available because they were the most recent and the work of Gaius was available because his work enjoyed great popularity in the dominate.

Very soon, however, it appeared that this Law of Citations was not a definitive solution either; as a result the same emperors, Theodosius II and Valentinian III, charged a committee specially appointed in 429 first to make a collection of all *leges generales* from the time of Constantine and thus produce a supplement to the *Codex Gregorianus* and the *Codex Hermogenianus* and thereafter, from these three collections of constitutions and from the writings of the classical jurists, to compile a Code which contained no contradictions and no repetitions. The execution of this plan, however, encountered insurmountable problems and finally in 435 another committee was set up for the purpose of collecting the constitutions, starting with those issued in the reign of Constantine. These texts had to be shortened and altered where necessary. After three years, in 438, the work was complete and the collection was published under the name *Codex Theodosianus*. On 1 January 439 the Theodosian Code became law, meaning that from then on only the constitutions in that Code could be cited in a lawsuit. In practice, however, the Gregorian Code and the Hermogenian Code continued to be used. As far as the works of the classical jurists were concerned, the Law of Citations remained in force.

The Theodosian Code is divided into sixteen books which are subdivided into titles according to the subject matter. The constitutions (numbering more than 3000) appear in these titles in chronological order. In these constitutions the emphasis is not on private law (whereas it was in the *responsa* and rescripts) but on public law; the Theodosian Code is therefore very important for our knowledge of constitutional and administrative law in the dominate. Most of the Theodosian Code has been preserved; in this case too the content is known only because constitutions from the Theodosian Code were included in later collections, particularly in the *Lex Romana Visigothorum* and in the Code of Justinian. In addition there are two manuscripts, one dating from the fifth and the other from the sixth century, which contain books six to eight and nine to sixteen respectively. Various versions of the Theodosian Code have been published since the sixteenth century; at present the version that is normally used is the one edited by Mommsen at the beginning of this century.[8]

THE LAW

12.4.4. The *Leges Romanae Barbarorum*

When the last West-Roman emperor was deposed in 476, his empire broke up into several parts; Italy came into the hands of the Ostrogoths, while Spain and the south of France came under the Burgundians. In these areas the personality principle prevailed again; in other words the original population continued to live according to Roman law, while the newly arrived Germanic population used Germanic law. For the Roman part of the population this meant the continuance of the uncertainty concerning the content and authenticity of jurists' law and imperial law. Some Germanic kings therefore had lawbooks published which contained Roman law and applied only to their Roman subjects; examples are the *Lex Romana Visigothorum* and the *Lex Romana Burgundionum*. These lawbooks are very important for our knowledge of Roman law in the dominate, because they contain a number of Roman law texts which have not come down to us anywhere else. The *Lex Romana Visigothorum* was issued in 506 by Alaric II, the king of the Visigoths. It contains, among other things, extracts from the Codes of Gregorius, Hermogenian and Theodosius, an abbreviated version of Gaius' Institutes, a *responsum* of Papinian and sections from the *Sententiae* of Paul. Some of these texts are provided with a so-called interpretation, i.e. an explanation which can be anything from a paraphrase to an explanatory remark. The purpose of this lawbook was to make all other sources of law superfluous. In 654 it was superseded by a new lawbook which was to apply both to the Goths and to the Romans. As a result the *Lex Romana Visigothorum* was gradually forgotten about in Spain; in France, on the other hand, it was still applied, although officially it was no longer valid. This is also the reason why knowledge of Roman law survived in that part of western Europe, but only to a very limited extent.

The *Lex Romana Burgundionum* was also promulgated at the beginning of the sixth century, having been drawn up by the Burgundian king Gundobad for his Roman subjects. Unlike the lawbook of the Visigoths it does not consist of extracts from various works but is made up of newly formulated rules which are systematically ordered and distributed over forty-seven titles. However, these are based on the three Codes, and on the Institutes of Gaius (a shortened version) and the *Pauli Sententiae*. In addition, the lawbook contains some elements of Burgundian law.

139

The *Edictum Theoderici* can also be mentioned in this connection. This is the work of the king of the Visigoths, Theoderic II, and not of Theoderic the Great, king of the Ostrogoths, as it was long assumed to be. The *Edictum Theoderici* probably originated in the middle of the fifth century in France. It contains 154 legal rules, which, as in the case of the two above-mentioned lawbooks, are taken mainly from the three Codes and the *Pauli Sententiae*. Unlike those lawbooks, however, the *Edictum Theoderici* was applicable to both the Visigoths and the Romans in that area.

12.5. THE LEGISLATION OF JUSTINIAN

When Justinian became emperor of the Byzantine empire in 527 he had three ambitions. He wanted to re-conquer the former West-Roman empire that had been lost fifty years before; he partly succeeded in fulfilling this ambition since Italy, southern Spain and part of North Africa were brought back under Roman rule. Secondly he wanted to restore unity in the church whose existence was threatened by various schisms; he was not very successful in this respect because he was unable to disband sects like that of the Monophysites. One of the reasons he failed may have been that his wife Theodora as a member of this sect energetically defended it. Thirdly he wanted to get things organised in the legal field.[9]

Almost 100 years had passed since the compilation of the Theodosian Code. Over that period a number of constitutions from that Code and from the two older collections had become outdated and many new constitutions had been issued. Furthermore, although the Law of Citations of 426 had reduced the uncertainty concerning the content and authenticity of jurists' law, it had not removed this uncertainty. Therefore Justinian wanted to solve this problem in a definitive way. The fact that he proved so successful in this field is due primarily to two circumstances. Firstly, he had a top official, Tribonian, who had the necessary knowledge and enthusiasm to complete the work; Tribonian was head of the imperial chanceries and since 530 had himself been minister of justice[10]. Secondly, it had become a tradition at the law-schools of Beirut and Constantinople to collect and study the works of the classical jurists and to give them an important place in the curriculum (see section 12.4.1); as a result the law-schools were a storehouse of knowledge about classical law.

12.5.1. The first Code

The legislation project started only a year after Justinian had become emperor, namely in 528.[11] He then gave a specially appointed committee the task of making a new collection of imperial constitutions. The committee consisted of ten members, seven being top officials (including Tribonian), two being advocates and one, named Theophilus, being a professor at the lawschool in Constantinople. Their task was not simply to prepare a collection of constitutions that had been issued after the Theodosian Code; the new collection was also to replace that Code and even the Codes of Gregorius and Hermogenian. The committee was granted very wide powers; it could delete outdated or unnecessary elements from the texts, remove contradictions and repetitions and could even combine, alter or extend texts. The members of the committee were therefore called 'compilers', from the verb *compilare* (literally, to plunder). The constitutions were to be divided according to the subject matter and arranged chronologically in the appropriate titles. On 7 April 529 the new collection was published under the name *Codex Justinianus* and from 16 April of that year it acquired force of law. This Code only remained valid till 534; then, for reasons to be explained more fully later, it was replaced by a revised version. The text of the first Code, also called *Codex vetus* (the old Code) has not survived; an index, however, has been found on a papyrus fragment in Egypt.

12.5.2. The Digest

The next step was to remove the remaining uncertainties about classical law. It is not certain whether Justinian intended from the outset to make a new collection of classical law or whether he only decided to do this later; we do know, however, that the order to compile the Digest was given on 15 December 530, about a year and a half after the first Code had been introduced, and that on 17 November 530 a collection of fifty constitutions was published, the so-called *quinquaginta decisiones*. In this work contradictions between the opinions of the classical jurists were resolved and outmoded legal concepts were scrapped. This collection has not come down to us as a separate volume, but the content is included in the revised Code of 534.

The task in question was entrusted to Tribonian who was then the minister of justice. He was allowed to choose the members of the committee that was to support him. Tribonian selected four professors from the law-schools (two from Beirut and two from Constantinople), the new head of the imperial chanceries who was also minister of the state's finances, and eleven leading advocates. The committee was given the task of preparing, within a period of ten years, an anthology of the writings of the classical jurists, i.e. not only of the five jurists mentioned in the Law of Citations. Just like the compilers of the Code they were given very wide powers: they themselves could determine which texts were suitable for inclusion, they could delete superfluous and outdated elements and could resolve contradictions; in other words, they could shorten the texts concerned and alter them as much as they thought necessary. However, they always had to indicate from which work of which jurist a text came; these notes are of great importance for legal history, because they permit historians to reconstruct the works in question and discover how the compilers worked. In addition, Justinian stipulated that the collection was to consist of fifty books subdivided into titles: these titles were to be placed in the same order as in the Code; in other words, they had to follow the order in the edict.

By 533 the committee had already finished its work. Thanks to the zeal and enthusiasm of Tribonian and the unceasing interest of Justinian himself, the work had taken only three years instead of the stipulated ten years. On 16 December 533 the work was published under the name *Digesta* and was given the force of law. From then on the only texts that could be used in a lawsuit were the ones included in the Digest. In the introductory constitution Justinian states that the compilers worked through almost 2000 scrolls containing 3,000,000 lines and that they reduced these to 150,000 lines and thereby made a large number of major changes; however, there is some doubt about whether these remarks should be interpreted literally. On the basis of the contents, however, one can get a better idea of how the compilers tackled their work. Firstly, the headings over the texts show that the texts are taken from the work of thirty-nine jurists who lived during the period extending from about 100 BC to 300. The number of texts per jurist is extremely variable. There is only one text by Aelius Gallus from the first century BC, but there are so many texts by Ulpian that they make up over 40 per cent of the entire Digest. This discrepancy is of course connected with the fact that the works of the late classical jurists like Ulpian were the most recent and therefore the best preserved.

From the order of the texts within the various titles the German legal historian Bluhme deduced – at the beginning of the last century – that the compilers had divided the works of the classical jurists into three categories or 'masses' (German 'Massen') and that they had divided their committee into three sub-committees, each of which was required to work through one mass.[12] The masses as indicated by Bluhme were first of all the works *ad Sabinum*, i.e. those works of the classical jurists in which the order of the opinions was the same as that followed by Sabinus in his *Libri tres iuris civilis*; this category was referred to by Bluhme as the 'Sabinian mass'. Second, there were the works *ad edictum*, referred to by Bluhme as the 'edictal mass'. The third mass was the collection of opinions that had been published under various titles such as *Digesta*, *Responsa* and *Epistulae*; because this mass always begins with a *responsum* of Papinian, Bluhme called it the 'Papinian mass'. Finally, Bluhme distinguished a fourth, smaller category which he referred to as the 'appendix mass'; it contains texts from works of various kinds. Although several attempts have been made to correct Bluhme's 'mass theory', the theory is still generally accepted.[13]

Since the sixteenth century many opinions have been expressed about the extent to which the compilers altered the content of the texts. The problem became the focus of attention particularly at the end of the nineteenth century. Many German and Italian legal historians believed they could identify alterations, known as interpolations, on the basis of linguistic arguments. Because this method of textual criticism became almost a campaign it was referred to as the 'interpolation hunt'. Nowadays the critics are more restrained.[14] Passages are mainly regarded as interpolations in two cases. First, if one and the same text has come down to us not only via the legislation of Justinian but also via another reliable source like the Vatican Fragments and if the former deviates from the latter, then the Justinian text is considered to have been interpolated. Second, texts referring to legal concepts which are known to have been obsolete at the time of Justinian have often been interpolated because the compilers had to bring the text up to date.[15]

Many manuscript copies of the text of the Digest have survived but nearly all of them date from the eleventh century or later when the Glossators began to study Roman law again. However, there is one manuscript that dates from the sixth century. It was probably produced in Constantinople before 550 and is perhaps one of the seventy-five or so copies which were sent in 553 to all important government bodies.[16] According to a note on the manuscript it was in Italy in the ninth or tenth century and it is known to have been in Pisa in the twelfth century. When the people of Florence captured Pisa in 1406 they carried off the manuscript; since then it has been kept in Florence and is generally known as the 'codex Florentinus'.[17] In the last century Mommsen and Krüger used this manuscript to produce an edition of the Digest which is now regarded as the standard edition.[18]

12.5.3. The Institutes

The compilation of the Digest was not only desirable from the point of view of legal practice, but it was also extremely valuable for teaching purposes. The Digest, however, was too difficult for students just beginning their studies. So, in 533, even before the work on the Digest was complete, Justinian decided that a new introductory textbook for law would have to be written. The task was entrusted to Tribonian and to two of the four professors who were helping to produce the Digest, namely Theophilus and Dorotheus. They were asked to produce a new book on the basis of the Institutes of Gaius and using some other introductory works from the principate. This new book was to reflect the law of their own time. Where they considered it advisable, they were permitted to include a historical introduction. In November of the same year (533) their work was published under the name *Institutiones* and came into force along with the Digest on 30 December 533.

The speed with which the Institutes of Justinian were compiled is largely due to the fact that the compilers took over two-thirds of the text more or less word for word from the Institutes of Gaius. Like Gaius they divided the material into three parts: law relating to persons, law relating to things and law relating to actions. Also like Gaius, the compilers divided the material into four books, but unlike Gaius they subdivided the books into titles. Because a number of the legal concepts described by Gaius had become obsolete by then, the compilers had to adapt the text in a number of places. One of the most radical changes concerned procedural law. In the sixth century legal action was taken only by means of the *cognitio extraordinaria*, so the compilers replaced Gaius' discussion of the *legis actio* procedure and the formulary system in the fourth book of the Institutes by a much shorter description of the currently used procedure and supplemented this with a title about penal law. The Institutes of Justinian became very popular, particularly in the former West-Roman empire; the text has therefore been preserved in many manuscripts. Practically all of these manuscripts, however, date from the eleventh century or later and only one fragment, which is difficult to read, dates from the sixth century. In 1872 Krüger produced a standard edition of Justinian's Institutes.[19]

In those days copies of the Digest and the Institutes were made by hand. There was always a danger that spelling mistakes and even textual alterations would occur. To forestall this possibility Justinian took two steps. First of all he forbade the use of abbreviations and the use of figures instead of letters, for this habit had caused great confusion in the past. In addition, no explanatory remarks were to be placed on the manuscripts, because the following copyist might easily think that the remark formed part of the text and thus incorporate it in the text.

12.5.4. The second Code

At the beginning of 534 Justinian decided that a new edition of the Code was needed. The reasons for this were as follows. As the Digest and the Institutes were being compiled all kinds of new constitutions had been issued and various old ones had been abolished, so the first Code was no longer up-to-date. Another reason may have been that during the copying of the first Code abbreviations and figures had been used and because of that the text was not quite reliable. Tribonian was entrusted with the task of producing a new Code. He was assisted by Dorotheus and by some of the advocates who had helped compile the Digest. Again they were given wide powers. They could remove constitutions that were superfluous or supplement those texts that revealed gaps.[20] At the end of the same year a revised version of the Code was published under the name *Codex repetitae praelectionis* and became law. As far as we know, the second Code closely resembled the first with regard to arrangement and systematics. Both are divided into twelve books; the first book is devoted to jurisdiction and ecclesiastical matters, books two to eight to private law, book nine to penal law and the last three books to administrative law. Each of the books is subdivided into titles. In these titles the constitutions are in chronological order. The oldest of the 4000 or so constitutions dates from the time of Hadrian, the majority stem from Diocletian (i.e. about 1200) and about 400 of Justinian's constitutions are included.

The revised Code has suffered a strange fate. Not long after this Code had been introduced, manuscripts began to circulate which, in spite of Justinian's ban, contained numerous abbreviations and remarks of jurists of his day; an example of such a manuscript – at least a part of it – has been preserved on a palimpsest from the sixth or seventh century. Furthermore, between the sixth and ninth centuries the last three books of the Code were published separately, the constitutions in Greek were removed and in general the text was drastically shortened. From the ninth century these abbreviated versions were extended again by the incorporation of elements from complete manuscripts that were apparently still in existence. From the sixteenth century, at the instigation of the humanists, the Greek constitutions were reincorporated in the text. It was not until the end of the nineteenth century that a new complete edition of the Code was produced by Krüger; this is the edition that is in general use today.[21]

12.5.5. The Novels

With the publication of the revised Code Justinian had achieved his aim of putting matters in order in the juridical field. But this was not the end of Justinian's legislative activities. In the period 535–555 he issued many new constitutions; these are generally referred to as 'Novels' (from *Novellae leges*; literally, new laws). Primarily, the Novels contain innovations in the field of administrative and ecclesiastical law, but there were also many changes in private law, particularly in family law and the law of succession upon intestacy. Although Justinian wanted to collect the Novels and publish them as soon as he had issued enough of them, he was never to achieve his aim. A few private collections were prepared but no manuscript copies of these have survived. We know of these collections only via the following three works that are based on them:

1. The oldest is the so-called *Epitome Juliani*, an abbreviated version of a collection of 122 constitutions, which was produced during the reign of Justinian. The edition was probably intended for use in Italy. This is indicated by two factors: the language of the texts is Latin and the last constitution dates from the year 555, i.e. one year after Justinian had introduced his legislation into Italy.

2. Another work based on a private collection is the *Authenticum*. This is a collection of 134 constitutions from the period 535–556; these have also been translated from Greek into Latin. It is very difficult to ascertain when this collection was published. It may have originated in the sixth century, like the *Epitome Juliani*, but the oldest references date from the eleventh/twelfth centuries. According to reports, one of the Glossators, Irnerius, regarded this as the official collection of Novels which was prepared at Justinian's request for use in Italy, and it is Irnerius who gave it its name *Authenticum*. Nowadays, however, it is assumed that Irnerius' view is incorrect and that the collection is nothing more than a poor-quality translation of a so-called *kata podas*, i.e. a teaching aid used in the Justinian law-schools.

3. The most comprehensive collection of Novels is the so-called *Collectio Graeca*. It consists of 168 constitutions and includes not only constitutions of Justinian but also constitutions of his successors Justin II (565–578) and Tiberius II (578–582). It was probably compiled during the rule of the latter. Our information about this collection is based on two manuscripts from the thirteenth and fourteenth centuries, but the collection itself was not known in western Europe until the fifteenth century. After the fall of Constantinople in 1453 various Byzantine jurists fled to Italy and introduced the collection there. However, it was mainly due to the humanists in the fifteenth and sixteenth centuries that the collection became known. The standard edition of the Novels, which was produced in 1895 by Schöll and Kroll, is based on the *Collectio Graeca*.[22]

EPILOGUE

The legislation of Justinian marks the end of the first period of the history of Roman law and the beginning of the second period. Together the Digest, the Code and the Institutes give a comprehensive picture of the way in which Roman law developed from the first century BC up to and including the sixth century. Although the compilers undoubtedly altered the texts in places, adapting them to their own time, they did not make any major changes. Consequently these three works are still the most important source of our knowledge about classical Roman law.

The legislation of Justinian also marks the beginning of the second period of Roman law. It is surprising, however, that this second phase was restricted to the former West-Roman empire and initially only to certain parts of Italy where Justinian law was applied. In the Byzantine empire the legislation of Justinian remained in force until the fall of Constantinople in 1453, although much of it was in the form of Greek translations, summaries and adaptations. The most important of the translations are the so-called *Basilica* (from the Greek 'ta basilika nomima' – the imperial laws) that date from about 900. In this collection, most of which has survived, texts with related contents from the Digest, the Code and the Novels are grouped in titles. No further Latin texts were incorporated but where necessary Greek summaries dating from the early Byzantine period were added. The Byzantine form of Roman law lasted longest in Greece; not until 1946 was it replaced by a modern civil code based on the German civil code which in turn has its roots in Roman law.

In the former West-Roman empire Roman law continued to exist via the *Leges Romanae Barbarorum*. There was no change in the situation until the end of the eleventh century. During the economic revival and the cultural renaissance that occurred in northern Italy at the time, law-schools were founded in which instruction was given on the basis of the legislation of Justinian. When a manuscript copy of the Digest, dating from the time of Justinian, was discovered in Pisa in 1077 the study of Roman law received a new impetus. Because the content of the Digest is casuistic and therefore sometimes inconsistent, many explanatory remarks (glosses) were made in the margin of the texts. These remarks referred to analogous cases or resolved contradictions. The jurists of the law-school in Bologna, like Irnerius in the twelfth century and Azo and Accursius in the thirteenth century, became particularly famous for their textual comments on the Digest and attracted students from all over Europe. Later European legal science developed out of the school of the so-called Glossators and has left its mark particularly on private law in continental Europe, South and Central America and Africa.

The second period of the history of Roman law is very different from the first. In the second period law-making was influenced not only by Roman law but also by Canon law and Germanic law. From the sixteenth century onwards Justinian law was referred to as the *Corpus Iuris Civilis* to distinguish it from the *Corpus Iuris Canonici*. Another difference is that the Glossators and their successors did not regard the Digest, the Code and the Institutes as the embodiment of seven centuries of development in law with all the associated problems, but instead they regarded it as an authoritative lawbook which they, via their rational methods of interpretation, could prove to be complete in itself. What was missing in this approach was the historical dimension. However, one cannot have a proper understanding of modern law and of the way in which this has developed since the Middle Ages, partly under the influence of Roman law, unless one has some knowledge of the history of Roman law in antiquity.

CHRONOLOGICAL TABLE

	General	Political	Legal
	I The monarchy and the early republic		
1000 BC	Latins and Sabines in Latium		
850	Etruscans in Tuscany		
753	Foundation of Rome (according to tradition)	Romulus, first king	*Leges regiae*
600	Etruscans found Rome		
509	Etruscans driven out of Rome	Beginning of the republic	Private law formulated by *pontifices*
500	Re-organisation of the army; beginning of the struggle between patricians/ plebeians	Besides *comitia curiata* there are now two new assemblies: *comitia centuriata* and *tributa*	
471		Establishment of *concilium plebis* and tribunate	
450		Tribunes sacrosanct	Law of the XII Tables; criminal jurisdiction by *comitia centuriata*
387	Celts conquer Rome but allow themselves to be bought out		

Chronological table *contd*

	General	Political	Legal
II The late republic			
367		*Leges Liciniae Sextiae* with re-organisation of magistrature	Praetor and curule aediles become responsible for *iurisdictio*
339		*Lex Publilia Philonis*: bills require prior approval of senate	
338	Latin League defeated: central Italy under Roman power		
337		Praetorship open to plebeians	
286	End of struggle between patricians/plebeians		*Lex Hortensia*: plebiscites = *leges*
264–241	First Punic war, beginning of expansion in area around Mediterranean		
242			Praetor peregrinus; probable introduction of formulary procedure
218	*Lex Claudia*: senatorial aristocracy separated from *equites*		
150	West Mediterranean area and Greece under Roman power		Beginning of legal science; first collection of *responsa*; M. Porcius Cato and Manius Manilius. Setting up of permanent penal courts to deal with certain types of crime

Chronological table *contd*

	General	Political	Legal
133	Asia becomes a Roman province. Land reform introduced by Tiberius and Gaius Gracchus		
107–100	Re-organisation of the army by Marius	Marius, autocrat	Q. Mucius Scaevola
91–88	Social war: all free inhabitants of Italy receive Roman citizenship		
82–79	Subjugation of east Mediterranean area	Sulla, dictator	Increase in number of penal courts
60–56		First triumvirate	M. Tullius Cicero, S. Sulpicius Rufus and C. Aquilius Gallus
50			Last new action incorporated in edict
48–44	Conquest of Gaul	Caesar, dictator	
43–32		Second triumvirate	P. Alfenus Varus
31		Battle of Actium: defeat of Antony and Cleopatra	
30	Egypt becomes Roman province		

III The early empire

	General	Political	Legal
27 BC	Conquest of central Europe; development of urban aristocracy in Italy and provinces; extension of Roman citizenship	Augustus, first emperor; *Lex Iulia* concerning the functioning of the senate; officials replace magistrates	Imperial legislation via *leges*, senatorial decrees and constitutions. *Legis actio* procedure practically abolished, beginning of imperial jurisdiction via the cognition procedure.

Chronological table *contd*

	General	Political	Legal
			Establishment of second law-school; introduction of *ius respondendi*. M. Antistius Labeo and Ateius Capito
14–37 AD		Tiberius	
37–41		Gaius (Caligula)	*Ius respondendi* granted to C. Cassius Longinus and probably to Proculus, leaders of the law-schools
41–54		Claudius	
54–68		Nero	
68–69		'Year of the three emperors'	
69–79		Vespasian	
79–81		Titus	
81–96	England and Wales become a Roman province	Domitian	
96–98		Nerva	Last *lex* (*agraria*)
98–117	Conquest of Dacia, Assyria and Mesopotamia	Trajan	Iavolenus Priscus, Celsus
117–138	Euphrates once more becomes eastern frontier	Hadrian	Definitive version of praetorian edict by Salvius Julianus. End of the *ius respondendi*; extension of the practice of rescripts
138–161		Antonius Pius	Pomponius, Gaius
161–169		Marcus Aurelius and Lucius Verus	
169–177		Marcus Aurelius	
177–180		Marcus Aurelius and Commodus	

Chronological table *contd*

	General	Political	Legal
180–192		Commodus; senate loses political power	
193		'Year of the five emperors'	
193–198		Septimius Severus	
198–211		Severus and Antoninus (Caracalla)	Last senatorial decree
211–212	*Constitutio Antoniniana*: citizenship for all free inhabitants	Caracalla and Geta	Papinian, Paul and Ulpian
212–217		Caracalla	
217–218		Macrinus	
218		Elagabalus	Law-school in Beirut
222–235		Alexander Severus	
235–284	Loss of border areas; devaluation of currency	Crisis, period of the military anarchy	*Sententiae* of Paul and *Epitome* of Ulpian probably compiled during this period

IV The dominate

	General	Political	Legal
284–305	Roman empire regains its former frontiers. Re-organisation of government and finances, price edict to prevent inflation	Diocletian and Maximian	*Codex Gregorianus*, *Codex Hermogenianus*; imperial legislation and jurisdiction exclusive sources of new law
307–337	Constantinople, new capital	Constantine the Great	
313	Tolerance-edict of Milan relating to Christianity		

Chronological table *contd*

	General	Political	Legal
337–340		Constantine II (west)	*Fragmenta Vaticana* and *Collatio legum Mosaicarum et Romanarum*
337–350		Constans (central area)	
337–361	Second senate in Constantinople	Constantius II (east)	
361–363		Julian the Apostate	
363–364	Invasion of barbaric tribes	Jovian	
364–375		Valentian I (west)	
364–378		Valens (east)	
367–383		Gratian (west)	
375–395		Theodosius I	
391	Christianity becomes state religion		
395	Division of the empire		
408–450		Theodosius II (east)	(425) Law school Constantinople; (426) Law of Citations; (438) *Codex Theodosianus*
425–455		Valentian III (west)	*Edictum Theoderici*
476	End of West-Roman empire	Romulus (west) deposed by Odoacer	
c. 500	Ostrogoths in Italy, Visigoths in Spain and south of France, and Burgundians in northern France		*Lex Romana Burgundionum*; *Lex Romana Visigothorum*
527–565		Justinian I	
528			First Justinian Code

Chronological table *contd*

	General	*Political*	*Legal*
533			Introduction of Digest and Institutes
534			Introduction of second Code
535–555			Novels
553	Parts of former West-Roman empire re-conquered		
554			Justinian's legislation introduced into Italy
564–578	Italy conquered by the Lombards	Justin II	*Collectio Graeca* (Novels)
578–582		Tiberius II	
886–911		Leo VI ('the Wise')	Basilica
11th/ 13th centuries			Glossators in Bologna: Irnerius (±1100), Accursius and Azo (±1230)
1453	Constantinople captured by Turks: end of East-Roman empire		

NOTES

PART I FROM MONARCHY TO EARLY REPUBLIC (–367 BC)

1 General outline

1 According to E. Gjerstadt, *Early Rome. The Written Sources*, Lund, Svenska Institutet i Rom, 1973, pp. 35–6, there is archaeological evidence that the Latins did not immigrate into Latium all at one time, forming an organized ethnic unit, but they arrived in at least two separate groups. See for the history of Latium and Rome also M. Cary and H. H. Scullard, *A History of Rome*, 3rd edition, London, Macmillan, 1975, pp. 31–94.

2 M. Pallottino, *The Etruscans*, translation from the Italian by J. Cremona, ed. D. Ridgway, revised and enlarged, London, Allen Lane, 1974, p. 79. See for the Etruscan language the more recent work by G. and L. Bonfante, *The Etruscan Language*, Manchester, Manchester University Press, 1983.

3 In Etruscan law, for instance, adoption took place when the adoptive mother breastfed the adoptive child; according to U. Manthe, 'Etruskisches Recht. Die Rechtsordnung einer Minderheit', in *Minderheiten im Mittelmeerraum*, ed. K. Rother, Passau, Passavia Universitätsverlag, 1989, pp. 22–4, this ritual shows that the Etruscans originally had a matrilinear society.

4 The power of a *pater familias* over his wife and, if he had sons who were married, over their wives, was called *manus*; children and grandchildren were in the *potestas* of the *pater familias*. See A. Watson, *Rome of the XII Tables*, Princeton, Princeton University Press, 1975, pp. 47–51.

5 For instance, Gaius Julius Caesar belonged to the *gens* Julia, Gaius being his *praenomen* or personal name and Caesar the name of his family within the *gens*.

6 E. Ferenczy, *From the Patrician State to the Patricio-Plebeian State*, Amsterdam, Hakkert, 1976, pp. 15–16 gives an overview of the many theories formulated on this subject. According to Ferenczy the current view is that the patricians were the descendants of the early nobility.

157

NOTES

7 This was probably not a restatement of an existing law but was an innovation whereby the patricians sought to keep well-to-do plebeians out of the senate; cf. Watson, ibid., pp. 20–3 with references.
8 It is obvious that in this way the vote could easily be manipulated, cf. E. S. Staveley, *Greek and Roman Voting and Elections*, Ithaca, Cornell University Press, 1972, pp. 193–5. This practice became particularly important during the civil war at the end of the republic. See for the relationship between patron and *clientes* also Watson, ibid., pp. 98–110.
9 G. Diósdi, *Ownership in Ancient and Preclassical Law*, Budapest, Akadémiai Kiadó, 1970, pp. 19–42.

2 The state

1 The main function of the *comitia curiata* then became to confirm the right of a newly elected magistrate to take auspices in his official capacity and on behalf of the Roman people. See Staveley, ibid., pp. 121–3.
2 Th. Mommsen, *Römisches Staatsrecht* I, Leipzig, Duncker & Humblot, 1887 (reprinted Graz, Akademische Druck- und Verlagsanstalt, 1971), pp. 6–7. Mommsen's view is supported by, for instance, H. F. Jolowicz and B. Nicholas, *Historical Introduction to the Study of Roman Law*, 3rd edition, Cambridge, Cambridge University Press, 1972, p. 30, and Cary and Scullard, ibid., p. 62, but is rejected by, for instance, W. Kunkel, 'Magistratische Gewalt und Senatsherrschaft', *ANRW* I, 2, Berlin and New York, De Gruyter, 1972, pp. 3–22, particularly p. 14. F. Wieacker, *Römische Rechtsgeschichte* I, Munich, Beck, 1988, pp. 223–4 rejects Mommsen's theory regarding the consuls, but does not make it clear to whom the power of the king was transferred.
3 For a description of the republican constitution, see Jolowicz and Nicholas, ibid., pp. 17–57.
4 Servius Tullius imported this new technique from Greece. At the beginning of the fourth century this hoplite army underwent two substantial changes which eventually made it possible for the Romans to conquer the Mediterranean world. On this subject see L. Keppie, *The Making of the Roman Army*, London, Batsford, 1984, pp. 17–19.
5 Nevertheless women, particularly those from upper-class families, sometimes did have an influence on politics; cf. H. P. Hallet, *Fathers and Daughters in Roman Society: Women and the Elite Family*, Princeton, Princeton University Press, 1984. The many recent publications about women in Roman antiquity deal mainly with their position within the family, cf. J. Gardner, *Women in Roman Law and Society*, London and Sydney, Croom Helm, 1986; S. Dixon, *The Roman Mother*, London and Sydney, Croom Helm, 1988 and S. Treggiari, *Roman Marriage*, Oxford, Clarendon Press, 1991.

3 The law

1 On early Roman law, see Jolowicz and Nicholas, ibid., pp. 86–190 and Wieacker, ibid., pp. 185–340.

2 The details relate mainly to certain restrictions on display at funerals in table 10, which according to Cicero, *De legibus*, 2.59 and 64, are taken from the laws of Solon. For further information on this subject, see Wieacker, ibid., pp. 300–4 with references. The XII Tables are studied in a wider context by R. Westbrook, 'The Nature and Origins of the Twelve Tables', *SZ* 105 (1988), pp. 74–121. He believes that the idea of recording the law was brought to Italy by the Phoenicians from the eastern Mediterranean area. He found that the method of recording and the content of the XII Tables bear a close resemblance to the Codex Hammurapi (about 1700 BC), the Ten Commandments (700 BC) and other codifications from that area and that period.

3 Livy, *Ab urbe condita*, 3.57.10; Pomponius, D. 1.2.2.4; L. Wenger, *Die Quellen des römischen Rechts*, Vienna, Holzhausen, 1953, p. 56, note 11; according to Wieacker, ibid., p. 294, note 47, however, stone was the most likely material to have been used for the XII Tables.

4 R. Schöll, *Leges XII tabularum reliquiae*, Leipzig, Duncker & Humblot, 1868; also in P. F. Girard and F. Senn, *Les lois des Romains*, septième édition par un groupe de romanistes, Naples, Jovene, 1977, pp. 25–73; Schöll's reconstruction is based on the work of H. Dirksen, *Übersicht der bisherigen Versuche zur Kritik und Herstellung des Textes der Zwölftafelfragmente*, Leipzig, Duncker & Humblot, 1824. English translation of the XII Tables in A. C. Johnson, P. R. Coleman-Norton and F. C. Bourne, *Ancient Roman Statutes*, Austin, University of Texas Press, 1961, pp. 9–13.

5 I base this statement on the words of Pomponius in D. 1.2.2.6: '. . . Omnium tamen harum et interpretandi scientia et actiones apud collegium pontificum erant, ex quibus constituebatur, quis quoquo anno praeesset privatis. Et fere populus annis prope centum hac consuetudine usus est'. Most romanists regard this text as corrupt and take the view that already in the early republic the first phase of the procedure took place in front of a magistrate; pontiffs were only involved if they gave a *responsum* (advice) to the magistrate or to one of the contending parties. See for instance F. Schulz, *History of Roman Legal Science*, Oxford, Clarendon, 1946, p. 7; M. Kaser, *Das römische Zivilprozessrecht*, Munich, Beck, 1966, p. 22; Jolowicz and Nicholas, ibid., pp. 88–9; Wieacker, ibid., pp. 313–14. The words 'quis . . . praeesset privatis' are generally translated as 'who should give advice to citizens'. Various translators of the Digest, however, e.g. *Das Corpus Iuris in's Deutsche übersetzt von einem Vereine Rechtsgelehrter*, in C. E. Otto, B. Schilling and C. F. F. Sintenis (eds), I, Leipzig, Focke, 1839, p. 226; S. P. Scott, *The Civil Law* I, Cincinnati, The Central Trust Company, 1932 (repr. New York, AMS Press, 1973), p. 214; *The Digest of Justinian*, Latin text edited by Theodor Mommsen with the aid of Paul Krüger; English translation edited by Alan Watson, I, Philadelphia, University of Pennsylvania Press, 1985, *ad locum*, rendered these words

by 'who should be in charge of private disputes'. To me this seems the correct translation. F. De Martino, *Storia della costituzione romana* I, Naples, Jovene, 1972 (2nd edition), pp. 23–52 also maintained that the pontiffs were the predecessors of the praetor, but on different grounds.

6 Unlike lawyers nowadays, these 'lawyers' did not act in a professional capacity and they did not represent their 'clients' at a trial. Generally they were leading citizens who occasionally assisted persons who could not speak for themselves or who had difficulty in doing so and persons whose words would have little effect because they belonged to a low social class (*clientes*). It was not until the time of the later republic that other people began to make use of legal assistance. On this subject see section 6.4.3.

7 The procedure was as follows. As in the case of a real lawsuit concerning ownership, the two parties brought the object to the pontiff (or praetor). The transferee, holding the object, asserted that he was owner. The pontiff (praetor) then asked the transferor whether he made a similar claim. When the transferor remained silent or said 'no', the pontiff (or praetor) adjudged the object to the transferee.

PART II THE LATE REPUBLIC (367–27 BC)

4 General outline

1 M. Cary and H. H. Scullard, *A History of Rome*, 3rd edition, London, Macmillan, 1975, pp. 84–96 and 113–68.

2 Cf. H. F. Jolowicz and B. Nicholas, *Historical Introduction to the Study of Roman Law*, 3rd edition, Cambridge, Cambridge University Press, 1972, pp. 78–85.

3 In addition, a senator who was governor of a province could increase his wealth by extorting money from the inhabitants; however, in 149 BC it became possible for the inhabitants to sue him via a special procedure in order to get their money back: see section 6.3.

4 Regarding the number of slaves in relation to the population as a whole, see K. Hopkins, *Conquerors and Slaves*, Cambridge, Cambridge University Press, 1978, pp. 99–106, part 101.

5 S. Treggiari, *Roman Freedmen during the Republic*, Oxford, Clarendon, 1969, p. 245 demonstrates how important the freedmen were for the development in the arts and in industry and even for the change from republicanism to principate.

6 See Cary and Scullard, ibid., pp. 186–90 concerning agriculture, trade and industry in the second century BC.

7 See Cary and Scullard, ibid., pp. 250–1.

5 The state

1 See Jolowicz and Nicholas, ibid., pp. 17–57; Cary and Scullard, ibid., pp. 177–81.

2 This basically respectable ancient cult, in which only women participated, had got out of control. Shortly after the second Punic war, when

the state was still very vulnerable, the cult won many supporters in Rome. During the meetings, which were attended by a mixture of male and female citizens, freed men and women and slaves, all kinds of offences were committed in an atmosphere of secrecy. The senate thereupon decided to reduce the sect to its traditional form and decreed that those who had committed serious offences should be put to death: more than 4000 people were killed, not only in Rome but also in other parts of Italy. For several centuries these measures were cited as an example of exceptionally harsh action on the part of the senate; cf. Cicero, *De legibus*, 11.37 and Livy, *Ab urbe condita*, 39.8–19.

3 According to Pomponius, D. 1.2.2.6. The prevailing view, however, is that it was the consuls who had fulfilled the tasks which were now entrusted to the praetor; cf. Jolowicz and Nicholas, ibid., p. 48 and F. Wieacker, *Römische Rechtsgeschichte*, Munich, Beck, 1988, pp. 429–34. On the other hand, A. Watson, *The Law of the Ancient Romans*, Dallas, Southern Methodist University Press, 1970, pp. 24–5 thinks that until 367 BC it was the pontiffs who were in charge of the supervision of civil litigation.

4 As from 242 BC several more praetors were appointed; their task was to govern the newly conquered territories. The first one was appointed for Sicily. In 227 BC another one was appointed for Sardinia and Corsica, and in 197 BC two were appointed for the two Spanish provinces. In the second century it became customary for the provinces to be governed by ex-magistrates; cf. Cary and Scullard, ibid., p. 172.

5 Cary and Scullard, ibid., pp. 203–312. See also P. A. Brunt, *The Fall of the Roman Republic and Related Essays*, Oxford, Clarendon, 1988.

6 The most well-known rebellion of slaves is the one led by Spartacus which began in Capua in 73 BC and ended in 71 BC in the south of Italy. See Cary and Scullard, ibid., p. 242. Z. Yavetz, *Slaves and Slavery in Ancient Rome*, New Brunswick, Transaction Books, 1988, pp. 83–112 offers in an English translation a complete collection of the Greek and Latin sources that deal with the great slave rebellions in the second and first centuries BC; for the sources dealing with the war against Spartacus, see ibid., pp. 83–112.

7 Cf. A. H. Bernstein, *Tiberius Sempronius Gracchus. Tradition and Apostacy*, Ithaca and London, Cornell University Press, 1978.

6 The law

1 For a general survey, see A. Watson, *Law Making in the Roman Republic*, Oxford, Clarendon, 1974; Jolowicz and Nicholas, ibid., pp. 191- 320; Wieacker, ibid., pp. 388–675.

2 The term *ius honorarium* dates from the second century AD; the word *honor* refers to the fact that the praetor, like the other magistrates, did not receive any salary during the year he was in office. Regarding the terms *ius honorarium* and *ius civile* see the article with that title by M. Kaser, in *SZ*, 101 (1984), pp. 1–114.

3 The term legal science is a rather vague and modern term – it dates from the nineteenth century – but it can be used in this connection

NOTES

because the writings of the Roman jurists formed the basis for later European legal science.

4 The sources do not agree about when and how the *leges* and plebiscites acquired the same status.

5 Th. Mommsen, *Römisches Staatsrecht*, 3rd edition, Leipzig, Duncker & Humblot, 1887 (reprinted Graz, Akademische Druck- und Verlagsanstalt, 1952), pp. 163–4, and *Römisches Strafrecht*, Leipzig, Duncker & Humblot, 1899 (reprinted Graz, Akademische Druck- und Verlagsanstalt, 1955, and Darmstadt, Wissenschaftliche Buchgesellschaft, 1961), pp. 56–7; A. H. M. Jones, *The Criminal Courts of the Roman Republic and Principate*, Oxford, Blackwell, 1972, pp. 1–39.

6 Particularly by J. L. Strachan-Davidson, *Problems of the Roman Criminal Law* I, Oxford, Clarendon, 1912, pp. 138–40, and by W. Kunkel, 'Prinzipien des römischen Strafverfahrens', in *Symbolae David* I. Leiden, Brill, 1968, pp. 111–33 = *Kleine Schriften zum römischen Strafverfahren und zur römischen Verfassungsgeschichte*, Weimar, Böhlau, 1974, pp. 11–31.

7 B. Santalucia, *Diritto e processo penale nell'antica Roma*, Milan, Giuffrè, 1989, pp. 31–89.

8 An important innovation was the introduction of the *legis actio per condictionem* for the recovery of definite sums of money or definite things. Now it was no longer necessary for the parties concerned to make a *sacramentum* (or bet) in front of the praetor concerning the righteousness of their claim or defence so that it also became possible for poor litigants to take part in civil litigation.

9 For instance the case of Attia Viriola described by one of the advocates, Pliny the Younger, in his letter VI 33; for a juridical commentary on this letter see J. W. Tellegen, *The Law of Succession in the Letters of Pliny the Younger* I, Zutphen, Terra, 1982, 108–18.

10 See G. Kennedy, *The Art of Rhetoric in the Roman World* (300 BC–AD 300), Princeton, Princeton University Press, 1972, p. 25.

11 This is very clear from some of the speeches of Cicero relating to the *interdictum quod vi aut clam*, namely the *Pro Tullio* and the *Pro Caecina*; see in this connection B. Frier, *The Rise of the Roman Jurists*, Princeton, Princeton University Press, 1985, and the review of this book by A. Watson in the *Michigan Law Review*, 85 (1987), pp. 1071–82.

12 See on this subject also R. A. Baumann, *Lawyers in Roman Republican Politics. A Study of Roman Jurists in their Political Setting, 316–82 BC*, Munich, Beck, 1983.

13 D. 35.1.73; on this matter, see M. Kaser, *Das römische Privatrecht* I, 2nd edition, Munich, Beck, 1971, p. 54.

14 Regarding this *cause célèbre*, see F. Wieacker, 'The Causa Curiana and Contemporary Roman Jurisprudence', in *The Irish Jurist*, new series, 2 (1967), pp. 151–64. See also J. W. Tellegen, 'Oratores, Iurisprudentes and the "Causa Curiana" ', in *RIDA*, 3rd series, 30 (1983), pp. 293–311 with a different and more convincing interpretation.

15 Cicero, *De oratore*, 2.142 tells us that Cato and Brutus used to mention

the names of the parties as well, but he is happy to say that this is no longer done.

16 For a reconstruction of the works of the republican jurists see O. Lenel, *Palingenesia iuris civilis*, 2 vols, Leipzig, Tauchniz, 1889 (reprinted Graz, Akademische Druck- und Verlagsanstalt, 1960), *passim*.

PART III THE PRINCIPATE (27 BC–284)

7 General outline

1 M. Cary and H. H. Scullard, *A History of Rome*, 3rd edition, London, Macmillan, 1975, pp. 331–450, *passim*.

2 A. N. Sherwin-White, *The Roman Citizenship*, 2nd edition, Oxford, Clarendon, 1973, pp. 221–394.

3 H. F. Jolowicz and B. Nicholas, *A Historical Introduction to the Study of Roman Law*, 3rd edition, Cambridge, Cambridge University Press, 1972, pp. 350–2.

4 R. P. Saller, *Personal Patronage under the Early Empire*, Cambridge, Cambridge University Press, 1982.

5 See R. Syme, *The Augustan Aristocracy*, Oxford, Clarendon, 1986. He describes how the old nobility, renascent after years of civil war, went down in the embrace of the dynasty, itself from the outset an aristocratic nexus (text from jacket).

6 However, as from the second century senators from the provinces were obliged to invest one quarter of their capital in property in Italy, so in a formal sense the senate could still be regarded as the organ of the Roman and Italian aristocracy even if it consisted mainly of persons from the provinces.

7 Regarding the transport of food to Rome, see A. J. B. Sirks, *Food for Rome*, Amsterdam, Gieben, 1991. On the functioning of Rome as a city, see O. F. Robinson, *Ancient Rome: City Planning and Administration*, London and New York, Routledge, 1992.

8 Cary and Scullard, ibid., pp. 377–82.

9 According to P. A. Brunt, 'Publicani in the Principate' in *Roman Imperial Themes*, Oxford, Clarendon, 1990, pp. 354–432.

8 The state

1 Cary and Scullard, ibid., pp. 283–312. The most famous book on this subject is undoubtedly by R. Syme, *The Roman Revolution*, Oxford, Clarendon, 1939, who considers Augustus as the corrupter and destroyer of the republic. K. Raaflaub and M. Tohler (eds), *Between Republic and Empire*, Berkeley, Los Angeles and Oxford, University of California Press, 1990, try to give a more balanced and up-to-date account of Augustus and his principate.

2 This had been done by other leaders before him and was in fact a variation of the traditional *clientela*-relationship.

3 Cary and Scullard, ibid., pp. 315–30.

4 Regarding the steady detachment of the emperor from the republican

institutions of the city of Rome, see F. Millar, *The Emperor in the Roman World*, Ithaca, New York, Cornell University Press, 1977, *passim*. For a biographical survey of the Roman emperors, see M. Grant, *The Roman Emperors. A Biographical Guide to the Rulers of Imperial Rome 31 BC–476 AD*, New York, Scribner, 1985.
5 See R. J. A. Talbert, *The Senate of Imperial Rome*, Princeton, Princeton University Press, 1984.
6 See Jolowicz and Nicholas, ibid., pp. 326–40.
7 It now became customary not to appoint the two consuls for a whole year but to replace them once or several times within the year by other so-called *suffecti*; the first consulate of the year, however, remained the most important one, because the year was still referred to by the name of the first two consuls.
8 Cary and Scullard, ibid., pp. 338–9, 448–9, and 492–3.

9 The law

1 Jolowicz and Nicholas, ibid., pp. 353–420; see also *ANRW* II, 13 (1980), 14 (1982) and 15 (1976) containing essays on a variety of aspects of classical Roman law.
2 It is certain that they stipulated that all unmarried men aged between 25 and 60 and all unmarried women aged between 20 and 50 were more or less excluded from bequests made via wills and legacies: they could only inherit from next-of-kin; they were also forbidden to attend games organised by the government. People who were married but had no children could only receive half of what was left to them in a will. On the other hand, people who had children were favoured in various ways. In addition, these laws stipulated that members of the senatorial aristocracy could not legally marry manumitted women, i.e. former slaves.
3 According to Gaius, *Inst.* 1.157 and U. E. 11.8; see on this subject J. F. Gardner, *Women in Roman Law and Society*, London and Sydney, Routledge, 1986, pp. 14–20.
4 The *oratio Severi* stipulates that any (invalid) gift to a husband/wife becomes valid when the donor dies, unless the latter has cancelled the gift.
5 Tacitus, *Annales*, 14.42–45 describes how in the year 61 the city prefect Pedanius Secundus had been murdered by one of his 400 slaves and how the jurist Gaius Cassius pleaded successfully in the senate for full application of this senatorial decree. The *SC Silanianum* was still applied even at the beginning of the second century; cf. Pliny the Younger, *Epistula*, 3.14 on the murder of Larcius Macedo and *Epistula*, 8.14 on the death of Afranius Dexter.
6 Cf. D. 16.1.2.1. See on this subject Gardner, ibid., pp. 75–6 and 234–5; on p. 234 Gardner erroneously suggests that the praetor could moderate the effect of the *SC Velleianum* by granting an exception to the creditor. This cannot, however, be correct because the creditor was a plaintiff and could not be granted an exception. It was the woman who was

granted an exception when she had acted contrary to the *SC Velleianum* and was sued by her creditor for the money.

7 The *SC Tertullianum* under Hadrian improved the successory position of the mother with regard to the inheritance of her child; the *SC Orfitianum* (of 178) declared that children were the first to succeed to the estate of their mother. S Dixon, *The Roman Mother*, London and Sydney, Croom Helm, 1988, pp. 52–5 explains that these decrees only formalized an existing practice.

8 Cf. Ulp. D. 29.1.1. By the end of the principate most of the formalities relating to the making of a valid will were dropped so there was no longer any justification for the continued existence of soldiers' wills as a special category. See on soldiers' wills in the time of Diocletian, O. E. Tellegen-Couperus, *Testamentary Succession in the Constitutions of Diocletian*, Zutphen, Terra, 1982, pp. 44–8.

9 For the development of criminal law in that period see also the recent monograph by B. Santalucia, *Diritto e processo penale nell'antica Roma*, Milan, Giuffrè, 1989, pp. 91–133 with sources and bibliography.

10 For instance, he declares in the constitution in which he proclaimed the Digest (const. *Tanta*, 18) that the senate gave Emperor Hadrian and his successors the task of adjusting the edict when necessary, but according to the Greek version of this constitution Hadrian entrusted the task to the magistrates.

11 We can, however, make some assumptions. First, the task assigned to Julian must have related not only to the edict of the praetor *urbanus*, as is mentioned in the sources, but also to the edict of the praetor *peregrinus* and that of the curule aediles; otherwise these magistrates would have retained a greater degree of freedom than the praetor *urbanus*. What is certain is that Julian introduced one new clause, in the area of the law of succession; since the juridical literature of the time refers to this clause as *nova clausula Juliani* it is probable that Julian did not add many new clauses. Finally, it is unlikely that Julian significantly altered or adapted the system and the terminology of the edict – although this is difficult to demonstrate.

12 O. Lenel, *Das Edictum perpetuum. Ein Versuch seiner Wiederherstellung*, 3rd edition, Leipzig, Tauchnitz, 1927 (reprinted Aalen, Scientia, 1956).

13 In certain cases they could refuse to deal with a case of appeal, for instance when the accused appealed against the verdict in order to delay its execution whereas the verdict was based on his own confession; in the Middle Ages this rule (*confessus non appellat*) again became valid law in continental Europe.

14 In one letter (*Epistula*, 4.9) he explains how he found the arguments for his speech; it is striking that he exactly followed the rules laid down by his tutor, Quintilian. Perhaps it should be mentioned that Pliny has no collection of opinions to his name, so he is not regarded as a jurist.

15 The subject has been dealt with since 1678, but the first monograph is by H. E. Dirksen, *Beiträge zur Kunde des römischen Rechts. Erste Abhandlung: Ueber die Schulen der römischen Juristen*, Leipzig, Duncker & Humblot, 1825. The most recent monograph on this subject

NOTES

is by G. L. Falchi, *Le controversie tra Sabiniani e Proculiani*, Milan, Giuffrè, 1981 with bibliography.

16 Most recently F. Wieacker, 'Respondere ex auctoritate principis', in J. A. Ankum, J. E. Spruit and F. B. J. Wubbe (eds), *Satura Roberto Feenstra Oblata*, Fribourg, Switzerland, Fribourg University Press, 1985, pp. 71–94 with sources and bibliography.

17 J. W. Tellegen, 'Gaius Cassius and the Schola Cassiana in Pliny's Letter 7, 24, 8', in *SZ* 105 (1988), pp. 263–311, particularly pp. 278–87.

18 Vespasian, for example, wrote a letter to the Vanacini in Corsica telling them he had written to his procurator and had sent his surveyor to solve the controversy between them and the Mariani about the boundary between their land; cf. S. Riccobono (ed.), *FIRA* I, Leges, 2nd edition, Florence, Barbèra, 1968, pp. 419–20.

19 See E. Posner, *Archives in the Ancient World*, Cambridge, Mass., Harvard University Press, 1972, pp. 192–205. The rescripts were not collected until the end of the third century.

20 B. Kübler, *Geschichte des römischen Rechts*, Leipzig, Dreichertschen Verlagsbuchhandlung, 1927 (reprinted Aalen, Scientia, 1979), pp. 424–33, particularly p. 428. D. Liebs, 'Rechtsschulen und Rechtsunterricht im Prinzipat', in *ANRW* II, 15 (1976), pp. 197–286 distinguishes between elementary and higher education in law, and assumes that the latter was given by the jurists in the law-schools. However, there are no sources to prove this hypothesis.

21 We shall discuss the way in which the Digest was compiled in Part IV.

22 O. Lenel, *Palingenesia iuris civilis*, 2 vols, Leipzig, Tauchnitz, 1889 (reprinted Graz, Akademische Druck- und Verlagsanstalt, 1960, with a supplement by L. E. Sierl).

23 Regarding classical Roman law, see M. Kaser, *Das römische Privatrecht* I, 2nd edition, Munich, Beck, 1971; see also W. W. Buckland and P. Stein, *A Text-Book of Roman Law from Augustus to Justinian*, 3rd edition, Cambridge, Cambridge University Press, 1963, reprinted with corrections and an addition to the bibliography, 1975.

24 Cf. H. L. W. Nelson, *Uberlieferung, Aufbau und Stil von Gai Institutiones*, Leiden, Brill, 1981, p. 78.

25 See in particular W. Kunkel, *Herkunft und soziale Stellung der römischen Juristen*, 2nd edition, Graz, Vienna and Cologne, Böhlau, 1967; see also R. Syme, 'Fiction about Roman Jurists', in *SZ* 97 (1980), pp. 78–104. Since the publication of *ANRW* II, 15 (1976), which contains essays on the jurists Celsus, Julian, African, Pomponius, Gaius, Papinian, Paul and Ulpian, a few new monographs have been published; they will be mentioned with the jurists whom they concern.

26 Cf. R. Astolfi, *I libri tres iuris civilis di Sabino*, Padua, Cedam, 1983.

27 Cf. B. Eckhard, *Iavoleni Epistulae*, Berlin, Duncker & Humblot, 1978; U. Manthe, *Die Libri ex Cassio des Iavolenus Priscus*, Berlin, Duncker & Humblot, 1982.

28 Cf. T. Honoré, *Ulpian*, Oxford, Clarendon, 1982.

PART IV THE DOMINATE (284–565)

10 General outline

1 The standard work on this part of Roman history is by A. H. M. Jones, *The Later Roman Empire*, 2 vols, Oxford, Blackwell, 1964. See also the more recent book by M. Cary and H. H. Scullard, *A History of Rome*, 3rd edition, London, Macmillan, 1975, pp. 507–58 with sources and bibliography.

2 For a well-nigh complete edition, see *Edictum Diocletiani et Collegarum de pretiis rerum venalium*, 2 vols, ed. M. Giacchero, Genoa, Istituto di storia antica e scienze ausiliarie, 1974.

3 Byzantium was a Greek city on the Bosporus; there Constantine founded a new city in 324 and named it Constantinople after himself. Nowadays Constantinople is known as Istanbul.

4 H. F. Jolowicz and B. Nicholas, *Historical Introduction to the Study of Roman Law*, 3rd edition, Cambridge, Cambridge University Press, 1972, pp. 433–8.

5 Diocletian introduced as tax units the *iugum* (literally, yoke, meaning the quantity of land that could be cultivated by one man and support his household) and the *caput* (literally, head, meaning one man). However, the criteria for fixing the amount of *iugum* or *caput* payable varied from place to place. Concerning the imperial census, see T. D. Barnes, *The New Empire of Diocletian and Constantine*, Cambridge, Mass., and London, Harvard University Press, 1982, pp. 226–37; regarding this and the other economic measures of Diocletian see also S. Williams, *Diocletian and the Roman Recovery*, London, Batsford, 1985, pp. 115–39.

6 The *navicularii* were organised in *collegia*, in other words in associations set up by the emperors on behalf of the *fiscus*. In the provinces the *collegia* had existed since the first century, while in Rome they had existed since the third century. Because initially membership of a *collegium* had been financially very attractive, sons often succeeded their fathers; in the second century, when the *collegia* began to lose their lucrative character, membership became compulsory and from the third century it even became hereditary. *Collegia* of this kind were also set up, for instance, for artisans like potters, carpenters, blacksmiths and weavers and for millers, bakers and butchers.

11 The state

1 See Williams, ibid., pp. 41–114.

2 This abdication is almost unique in Roman history; it can only be compared to the retirement of Sulla in 79 BC. Diocletian retired to his palace at Split on the Dalmatian coast, which was built like a military fort. Parts of this palace can still be seen today.

3 On the emperors between 284 and 337, see Barnes, ibid., pp. 3–87.

4 See Barnes, ibid., pp. 91–191.

5 Regarding the relationship between the Christian church and the

emperors, see F. Millar, *The Emperor in the Roman World*, Ithaca, New York, Cornell University Press, 1977, pp. 551–607. Concerning the relationship between Christianity on the one hand and the Roman state and pagan religions on the other hand, see numerous articles in *ANRW* II 23, 1 (1979) and 2 (1980), and 25, 1 (1982), 2 (1984) and 3 (1985).

6 The definitive separation of the Greek Orthodox church from the Roman Catholic church did not take place until 1054.

12 The law

1 The qualification is from F. Schulz, *History of Roman Legal Science*, 2nd edition, Oxford, Oxford University Press, 1953, pp. 262–4. Concerning the law of this period see also M. Kaser, *Das römische Privatrecht* II, 2nd edition, Munich, Beck, 1974; Jolowicz and Nicholas, ibid., pp. 439–515, and W. W. Buckland and P. Stein, *A Text-Book of Roman Law from Augustus to Justinian*, 3rd edition, Cambridge, Cambridge University Press, 1963, reprinted with corrections and an addition to the bibliography, 1975.

2 The rescripts were granted in the name of the emperor, but they were actually prepared by the head of the chancery *a libellis*. T. Honoré, *Emperors and Lawyers*, London, Duckworth, 1981, has studied the style of about 2000 rescripts dating from 193 to 305 and has tried to identify at least twenty lawyers who headed this chancery.

3 For instance G. E. 2.1.2 mentions 'obligationes de diversis contractibus scriptae' (written obligations stemming from various contracts) among the incorporeal things, whereas Gaius himself in that connection had mentioned 'obligationes quoquo modo contractae' (obligations incurred in whatever way), cf. *Inst.* 2.14.

4 For numerous examples see E. Levy, *West Roman Vulgar Law, the Law of Property*, Philadelphia, American Philosophical Society, 1951, pp. 22–3 and 64–6.

5 The standard work on this subject is still M. Kaser, *Das römische Zivilprozessrecht*, Munich, Beck, 1966, pp. 410–529.

6 Cf. B. Santalucia, *Diritto e processo penale nell'antica Roma*, Milan, Giuffrè, pp. 135–51 with sources and bibliography.

7 H. L. W. Nelson, *Überlieferung, Aufbau und Stil von Gai Institutiones* Leiden, Brill, 1981, pp. 80–96.

8 *Theodosiani libri XVI cum constitutionibus Sirmondianis*, ed. Th. Mommsen, Berlin, Weidmann, 1904 (reprinted Dublin and Zürich, 1971).

9 Cf. A. H. M. Jones, op.cit., pp. 269–302, who emphasises the first two ambitions.

10 Regarding the life of Tribonian, see T. Honoré, *Tribonian*, London, Duckworth, 1978, pp. 40–69.

11 Concerning the legislation of Justinian see also the recent work of N. van der Wal and J. H. A. Lokin, *Historiae iuris graeco-romani delineatio*, Groningen, Forsten, 1985, pp. 31–8 with literature.

12 F. Bluhme, 'Die Ordnung der Fragmente in den Pandektentiteln', *Zeits-*

chrift für geschichtliche Rechtswissenschaft 4 (1820), pp. 257–472, reprinted in *Labeo* 6 (1960), pp. 50–96, 235–77, 368–404.

13 Largely through a numerical and statistical analysis Honoré, op. cit., pp. 139–86 has tried to extend and complete the work of Bluhme. However, his theory has been refuted convincingly by D. Osler, 'The Compilation of Justinian's Digest', *SZ* 102 (1985), pp. 129–84.

14 The fundamental work on this subject is by M. Kaser, *Zur Methodologie der römischen Rechtsquellenforschung*, Vienna, Cologne and Graz, Böhlau, 1972.

15 For instance, the word *mancipatio* has been automatically altered into *traditio* by the compilers. Because the effects of the *mancipatio* differed from those of the *traditio* and because the compilers did not adapt these effects, this alteration is usually easy to recognise.

16 Cf. E. A. Lowe, 'Greek Symptoms in a Sixth-Century Greek Manuscript of St Augustine and in a Group of Latin Legal Manuscripts', in *Didascaliae, Studies in Honor of A. M. Albareda*, New York, Rosenthal, 1961, pp. 277–89 (= L. Bieler (ed.), *Palaeographical Papers, 1907–1965* II, Oxford, Clarendon, 1972, pp. 466–75).

17 A photographic copy of the *codex Florentinus* has been published recently, namely *Justiniani Augusti Pandectarum codex Florentinus*, 2 vols, eds A. Corbino and B. Santalucia, Florence, Olschki, 1988.

18 *Digesta Iustiniani Augusti*, eds Th. Mommsen and P. Krüger, 2 vols, Berlin, Weidmann, 1868–70 (reprinted 1962–3); this is the so-called *editio maior* which includes an extensive critical apparatus. Commonly the *editio minor* or *-stereotypa* is used: *Iustiniani Digesta*, eds Th. Mommsen and P. Krüger, Corpus Iuris Civilis I (pars 2a), 16th edition, Berlin, Weidmann, 1954 (reprinted Dublin and Zürich, 1973). An English translation has been published recently, cf. *The Digest of Justinian*. Latin text ed. by Th. Mommsen with the aid of P. Krüger, English translation edited by A. Watson, 4 vols, Philadelphia, Penn., University of Pennsylvania Press, 1985.

19 *Iustiniani Institutiones*, ed. P. Krüger, Corpus Iuris Civilis I (pars 1a), Berlin, Weidmann, 1872. The Institutes have also been translated into English recently, cf. *Justinian's Institutes*, translated with an introduction by P. B. H. Birks and G. MacLeod, Ithaca, New York, Cornell University Press, 1987.

20 It is clear that Tribonian c.s. removed constitutions because the Law of Citations is not included in the revised Code. We know, however, from a papyrus containing the index to the first Code that this law had been included in the first Code.

21 *Codex Iustinianus*, ed. P. Krüger, Berlin, Weidmann, 1877. This is the *editio maior* with critical apparatus and introduction. For the *editio stereotypa* see *Codex Iustinianus*, ed. P. Krüger, Corpus Iuris Civilis II, 11th edition, Berlin, Weidmann, 1954 (reprinted Dublin and Zürich, 1970).

22 *Novellae*, eds R. Schöll and G. Kroll, Corpus Iuris Civilis III, 6th edition, Berlin, Weidmann, 1954.

BIBLIOGRAPHY

Baumann, R. A., *Lawyers in Roman Republican Politics, A Study of Roman Jurists in their Political Setting, 316–82 BC*, Munich, Beck, 1971.

Buckland, W. W. and Stein, P., *A Text-Book of Roman Law from Augustus to Justinian*, 3rd edition, Cambridge, Cambridge University Press, 1963, reprinted with corrections and an addition to the bibliography, 1975.

Cary, M. and Scullard, H. H., *A History of Rome*, 3rd edition, London, Macmillan, 1975.

Ferenczy, E., *From the Patrician State to the Patricio-Plebeian State*, Amsterdam, Hakkert, 1976.

Frier, B., *The Rise of the Roman Jurists*, Princeton, Princeton University Press, 1985.

Gardner, J., *Women in Roman Law and Society*, London and Sydney, Croom Helm, 1986.

Jolowicz, H. F. and Nicholas, B., *Historical Introduction to the Study of Roman Law*, 3rd edition, Cambridge, Cambridge University Press, 1972.

Honoré, T., *Tribonian*, London, Duckworth, 1978.

Honoré, T., *Emperors and Lawyers*, London, Duckworth, 1981.

Jones, A.H.M., *The Later Roman Empire*, 2 vols, Oxford, Blackwell, 1964.

Jones, A.H.M., *The Criminal Courts of the Roman Republic and Principate*, Oxford, Blackwell, 1972.

Kaser, M., *Das römische Zivilprozessrecht*, Munich, Beck, 1966.

Kaser, M., *Das römische Privatrecht*, 2 vols, 2nd edition, Munich, Beck, 1971–4.

Kaser, M., *Zur Methodologie der römischen Rechtsquellenforschung*, Vienna, Cologne and Graz, Böhlau, 1972.

Kennedy, G., *The Art of Rhetoric in the Roman World* (300 BC-AD 300), Princeton, Princeton University Press, 1972.

Kunkel, W., *Herkunft und soziale Stellung der römischen Juristen*, 2nd edition, Graz, Vienna and Cologne, Böhlau, 1967.

Levy, E., *West Roman Vulgar Law, the Law of Property*, Philadelphia, American Philosophical Society, 1951.

Liebs, D., 'Rechtsschulen und Rechtsunterricht im Prinzipat', in *ANRW* II, 15 (1976), pp. 197–286.

Millar, F., *The Emperor in the Roman World*, Ithaca, New York, Cornell University Press, 1977.

Mommsen, Th., *Römisches Staatsrecht* I, Leipzig, Duncker & Humblot, 1887 (reprinted Graz, Akademische Druck- und Verlaganstalt, 1971).

Mommsen, Th., *Römisches Strafrecht*, Leipzig, Duncker & Humblot, 1899 (reprinted Graz, Akademische Druck- und Verlaganstalt, 1955, and Darmstadt, Wissenschäftliche Buchgesellschaft, 1961).

Nelson, H. L. W., *Überlieferung, Aufbau und Stil von Gai Institutiones*, Leiden, Brill, 1981.

Robinson, O. F., *Ancient Rome: City Planning and Administration*, London and New York, Routledge, 1992.

Santalucia, B., *Diritto e processo penale nell'antica Roma*, Milan, Giuffrè, 1989.

Schulz, F., *History of Roman Legal Science*, Oxford, Clarendon, 1946.

Sherwin-White, A. N., *The Roman Citizenship*, 2nd edition, Oxford, Clarendon, 1973.

Sirks, A. J. B., *Food for Rome*, Amsterdam, Gieben, 1991.

Strachan-Davidson, J. L., *Problems of the Roman Criminal Law* I, Oxford, Clarendon, 1912.

Syme, R., *The Roman Revolution*, Oxford, Clarendon, 1939.

Talbert, R. J. A., *The Senate of Imperial Rome*, Princeton, Princeton University Press, 1984.

Tellegen, J. W., *The Law of Succession in the Letters of Pliny the Younger* I, Zutphen, Terra, 1982.

Tellegen, J. W., 'Gaius Cassius and the Schola Cassiana in Pliny's Letter 7, 24, 8', in *SZ* 105 (1988), pp. 263–311.

Tellegen-Couperus, O. E., *Testamentary Succession in the Constitutions of Diocletian*, Zutphen, Terra, 1982.

Treggiari, S., *Roman Freedmen during the Republic*, Oxford, Clarendon, 1969.

Van der Wal, N. and Lokin, J. H. A., *Historiae iuris graeco-romani delineatio*, Groningen, Forsten, 1985.

Watson, A., *Law Making in the Roman Republic*, Oxford, Clarendon, 1974.

Watson, A., *Rome of the XII Tables*, Princeton, Princeton University Press, 1975.

Wenger, L., *Die Quellen des römischen Rechts*, Vienna, Holzhausen, 1953.

Westbrook, R., 'The Nature and Origins of the Twelve Tables', in *SZ* 105 (1988), pp. 74–121.

Wieacker, F., *Römische Rechtsgeschichte* I, Munich, Beck, 1988.

Williams, S., *Diocletian and the Roman Recovery*, London, Batsford, 1985.

INDEX

172

GALATIANS

ROMANS

Frank Stagg

KNOX PREACHING GUIDES

John H. Hayes, Editor

HE1325

John Knox Press

ATLANTA

Library of Congress Cataloging in Publication Data

Stagg, Frank, 1911-
   Galatians/Romans.

   (Knox preaching guides)
   Bibliography: p.
   1. Bible. N.T. Galatians—Criticism, interpretation, etc. 2. Bible. N.T. Romans—Criticism, interpretation, etc. 3. Bible. N.T. Galatians—Homiletical use. 4. Bible. N.T. Romans—Homiletical use. I. Title. II. Series.
BS2685.2.S7   227'.106   79-92066
ISBN 0-8042-3238-5

© copyright John Knox Press 1980
10 9 8 7 6 5 4 3 2 1
Printed in the United States of America
John Knox Press
Atlanta, Georgia 30365

Contents

ROMANS

GALATIANS

Introduction

No military commander likes to find himself in a situation where he must fight on two fronts at the same time, but for the Christian "soldier" that kind of warfare is normal. Galatians speaks directly to this problem, for Paul found himself having to fight on two fronts: against the legalism which robs us of our God-given freedom and against the permissiveness which undermines our morality. On the one hand, legalists were trying to "Judaize" (2:14) the Galatians by imposing circumcision upon them. To Paul this amounted to turning from God's grace to human works and surrendering the freedom of the gospel for bondage to the Mosaic Law. On another front, there were people within the church who interpreted freedom in Christ as freedom from all law, moral as well as ritual. This attitude was known as "antinomian" (rejecting *nomos*, Greek for "law"). It is also referred to today as "libertine," turning liberty into license. "Permissiveness" is yet another term for it.

How can one be both free and responsible? How can the preacher proclaim the gospel as both the word of freedom and the word of responsibility? These issues are at the heart of what Galatians is about. Christ sets us free, and we must resist all bondage. The freedom Christ gives does not relieve us of moral or ethical obligation. In fact, being "in Christ" puts us under the heaviest possible demand. The demands of faith, love, acceptance, and commitment within the family of God are heavier than the demands of circumcision, kosher foods, sabbaths, and the like. Legalism is appealing because it seems to give us a fail-safe escape from sin and impiety, with measurable results. Libertinism is appealing, because it seems to let us "have our cake and eat it too." Legalism is deceptive because it only regulates the outward life with no necessary corrective to the inner life of thought, feeling, or intention. Libertinism is deceptive, because it is "cheap grace," all gift and no demand, a new label for an old unchanged product.

The perennial problem for us is how to combine freedom and responsibility. Life itself is gift, whether natural life received in physical birth or the higher life received as the gift of God's redeeming grace. Life also is a responsibility. One of my friends put it this way: "I am not responsible for being here; but being here, I am responsible." That is it! Much of the NT, including Galatians, is concerned with showing how "in Christ" we are called to live in awesome freedom with its correspondingly awesome responsibility. This takes us to the heart of where people must struggle for meaningful existence today and always. Galatians should provide preaching today with a wealth of insight for leading Christians into the art of living in both freedom and responsibility. One sermon subject here could be, "Does Christ Rid Us of Tension?"

Galatians is as relevant today as when first written. True we are not concerned with circumcision as a religious rite, but the issues Paul had to face are perennial in essence. There is always the threat of turning religion into a set of outward rules (creedal belief, ritual forms, social patterns, or whatever), and there is always the threat of the undisciplined life of permissiveness in the name of freedom. Religion tends to fall off on one side or the other. The real test is how to avoid both errors. How can we live in open goodness without ostentation, and how can we live in freedom without license? Preaching today should make this clear both as to theory and practice.

Most important for understanding Galatians are occasion and purpose behind the letter. F. C. Baur (1831) contended that Paul's opponents were Jewish Christians from Jerusalem (Judaizers) bent upon forcing the Mosaic Law, at least circumcision, upon Gentile converts, holding this to be necessary to salvation and/or fellowship. For him, legalism was the central problem. Wilhelm Luetgert (1919) saw Paul as fighting on two fronts, not only against the Judaizers but also against some ultra-Pauline Christians who saw themselves as "spiritual" (pneumatic) and thus free from all law, moral as well as ritual. These are characterized as Libertine and Antinomian or permissive. Currently Walter Schmithals contends that Paul fought on a single front, not against Baur's Judaizers but against Gnostics, people who made a sharp distinction between the material which they saw as inherently evil and the spiritual which they saw as the only good.

Probably the best approach today is to see two basic problems, legalism and license, without trying to determine the precise shape of those holding these positions. Instead of two parties, there may have been only a strange mixture of both motives in the same people. It is not uncommon to find legalistic people ("law and order" people) to be immoral. What matters for us are the two ideas, not the precise identity of Paul's opponents. The opponents are gone, but the ideas are yet with us. A sermon subject here could be "An Unchanging Issue in Changing Times."

Paul's Greeting and Opening Statement
(Galatians 1:1–10)

Greetings (1:1–5)

Paul lost no time in declaring who he was, whose he was, and the origin and nature of the Gospel which he was commissioned to preach. For him these foundations to his self image were not negotiable. Although willing and able to give and take in the interest of Christian harmony (see 1 Cor 9:12, 19–23), there were for Paul some things so primary that he would not compromise them, whatever the cost. He was willing on occasion to surrender personal privilege or to live together with others in a measure of disagreement, but he was unwilling to buy acceptance at just any price. He was open to counsel but refused to surrender his integrity by submitting to any council of men. Ultimately, he answered to God and not his peers (he rejected the idea of superiors). Using Paul as an example, a suggested sermon subject could be: "An Uncompromising Gospel in a Compromising Age."

This context gives occasion for a sermon on the subject "The Importance of Knowing Who You Are." What was Paul's self image? He saw himself as "Paul, apostle, not from men nor through any man but through Jesus Christ and God the Father who raised him from the dead" (v. 1). His commission was from God, and he was answerable to God. This was the "bottom line" in his fight with Legalists (Judaizers) and Libertines (v. 10). The Legalists especially tried to discredit Paul by scorning him as a "Johnny-come-lately" who preached only a second-hand gospel which he had gotten from the "real apostles" at Jerusalem, like Peter and James the brother of Jesus. Paul's angry reply was that he was "no man's man." He belonged to God as he had come to know him in the risen Christ.

There is another sermon here: "Whose are You?" (1:1). Paul declared that he was "no man's man," but he did not imply that he was "his own man." He belonged to God. To whom do we belong? Of course, this theme may be presented in paradox; for in a real sense we belong to one another as well as to God. We are debtors to all people, and all have claim upon us, just as we have legitimate claims upon ourselves. Ultimately, we belong to God, not to other people or to self. These claims need not be competitive. The options are not so limited that we must be either "lone rangers/rangerettes" or "yes persons." We can be our own selves, in community and under God.

Whose are we? We belong to the one/ones we serve. In the OT the true prophet and the false prophet were distinguished at precisely this point. The true prophet spoke for God, whether this pleased or displeased the power figures or power structures of his time: the king or whomever. The false prophet was the "Court Chaplain" who shaped his message to suit the king. For whom do we speak today? There is always the temptation to "preach another gospel," suited to the political, economic, or religious power structures of our times. Galatians reminds us that the true Gospel is "not from men nor by any man" and not to be shaped to accommodate any power structure, security, or convenience.

Another sermon could be preached on "The Question of Authority" (1:1). Paul's letters and journeys show that he wanted to be understood and to understand. He wanted to get along with his fellow followers of Christ. Paul never reflects the attitude, "I couldn't care less." He was not a "lone ranger" but rather very sensitive to the feelings of others. On the other hand, he refused to grant ultimate authority to the apostles at Jerusalem, to councils, or to any human court (see I Cor 4:1–5). It is a function of the human mind to judge (measure, weigh, approve or disapprove), but we are fallible in our limited knowledge and in our vulnerability to prejudice and bias. Further, we have not been appointed to "the bench." Only God has the knowledge and integrity to make a final judgment, and fortunately it is before him that we stand or fall. We know God best in Jesus Christ. Even Scripture is to be understood in terms of the manner and teaching of Jesus. No isolated proof text is to be given absolute or ultimate authority over us—even it must be understood in the light of Him who said, "Ye have heard it said . . . but I say unto you."

Yet another sermon lurks in 1:3–5, "Gift and Demand." The sermon could be entitled: "The Nature of Salvation." God's promise is "grace and peace." Grace is God's favor, free, freeing, and inexhaustible. Peace to Paul would be *shalom* in Hebrew. *Shalom* is well-being under the rule of God, order but God's order, not the world's "law and order." In the world "law and order" usually turn out to be some power figure or group making laws for other people and ordering their lives. God's order is not partisan, and it is not tyranny. It is freedom and responsible existence under God's control. It is at the same time "deliverance from this present evil age" (v. 4). This is authentic "Liberation Theology," not by brute force (deplored yet acceptable as a last resort in much "Liberation Theology"), but by the power at work in Him who gave himself for us. The power of redeeming love is the power in true liberation theology. Deliverance is gift, yet it is costly demand for Christ and for us (see 2:19–20).

The Non-negotiable Gospel (1:6–10)

Paul did not pretend to conceal his astonishment at the ease with which the Galatians had let themselves be taken in by "another *(heteron)* gospel" which was not really "another *(allo)* gospel." What they were accepting was no gospel at all. It was bad news, not good news. It was bondage and not freedom. They were regressing, not progressing. The so-called righteousness which they now were seeking through circumcision was not real righteousness. It was salvation achieved by one's own "do-it-yourself kit." It was superficial, dependent upon cutting off a piece of foreskin with a knife. Is there any wonder that Paul said, "I wonder!" It is amazing that anyone could think that salvation or fellowship should depend upon an external rite like circumcision or keeping the days on a religious calendar (4:8–11). Imagine being lost and going to Hell for want of a pocket knife! If we think the Galatians foolish, what about us? What about exclusion from salvation or table fellowship (Communion!) for a shortage of a liquid made up of two parts of hydrogen and one part of oxygen, commonly called water? Is this a *reductio ad absurdum?* Paul thought it was absurd to swap grace for law, dependence upon the Spirit for trust in cultic acts.

A sermon timely anytime is one on the subject, "No Other Gospel" on "The Non-negotiable Gospel" (1:6–7). Any "gospel" bound to works of the Law is an anomaly. It has an inbuilt contradiction. It is like dry water or cool fire. Circumcision is not a problem in our churches today, but legalism keeps on appearing in various shapes. Theologizing is proper as we try to articulate our faith and experience, but a hardened creed imposed by some on others is slavery, not freedom. It is a brittle skin long since having lost its wine, yet many confessional groups continue to be torn apart by theological controversy. Ritual acts may express or even induce and cultivate Christian experience, but when they become ends in themselves they are counter-productive, just another form of idolatry. The authentic Gospel sometimes is supplanted by Culture Religion, the church merely reflecting the values and patterns of society. Civil Religion is another substitute for "gospel," where God and country are barely distinguished from one another. Of course, a constant threat in another direction is religion without demand, the permissiveness of the Libertine. Wherever there is anything authentic—like the Gospel of Jesus Christ—there is the counterfeit. Sermon subject: "Accept No Substitutes."

Paul's Apostleship and Gospel
(Galatians 1:11–2:21)

Paul's credibility as to his gospel was tied up with his being recognized as an apostle. He defended his apostleship in terms of his independence of the apostles at Jerusalem (1:11–24), in terms of his acceptance as a peer by the Twelve (2:1–10), and his having publicly to reprimand Peter at Antioch because of the latter's inconsistency (2:11–14). In 2:15–21 Paul sets forth the heart of his gospel.

Independence of the Twelve (1:11–24)

By gospel Paul seemingly meant not just factual data but perspective and meaning. Surely he must have gained information from Peter and others about the events which concerned Jesus (1:18–19; 1 Cor 15:3–7). His understanding of the gospel he owed not to his peers but to God. Especially does Paul have in mind the implications of the gospel of grace as the foundation to his understanding of freedom from the Mosaic Law and also for his recognition that "in Christ there is not any Jew and Greek, bond and free, male and female" (3:28). This is what he received "by revelation." Peter and James were too provincial to have helped him here. It was nothing short of his encounter with the risen Christ which opened his eyes to who Christ is and who people really are (see 2 Cor 5:16). Saul of Tarsus heard Stephen and was enraged, yet later he shared the stance for which Stephen gave his life. He met Jesus Christ and gained new understanding of God and of all humanity, seeing that being persons was more significant than ethnic, legal, or sexual difference. This was a part of the gospel which came to him from above.

Paul's purpose in 1:11–24 is to show that through the formative period of his Christian life he had very little contact with the Christian community at Jerusalem, including the apostles. His first encounter with them was hostile, persecuting God's church and devastating it (v. 13). His earliest Christian life was in Damascus and Arabia, not Jerusalem (v.

17). It was some years before he met any of the apostles and then was with them but briefly, remaining unknown by face to most of the churches in Judea (vv. 18–24). His point is that he had come to his understanding of the gospel apart from being instructed by those in Jerusalem or Judea.

I would suggest a sermon here on "Revelation" (1:12). Revelation is God's giving knowledge of himself, not propositions. Revelation is God's self-disclosure, not just historical facts or theology. God is our Savior, God whom we meet directly in Jesus Christ. We are not saved by theology (see Ja 2:19, where even the demons can recite the Shema). Good theology is better than bad theology, but neither can save us. Theology as an end in itself is a form of idolatry. Saving knowledge is knowing God personally (Jn 17:3), not qualifying as a theologian, a truth forgotten in heresy hunts. God's fullest self-disclosure is in Jesus Christ, and in him all values and perspectives and teachings are to be tested. We must hear him, not just one another. We must hear him, but this does not mean that it must be in isolation or in a vacuum. We best hear in community, yet we must hear with our own ears. This could be gathered into a sermon on the subject "The Nature of Revelation" with these points: (1) It is personal—not propositional. (2) It is redemptive—not restrictive. (3) It is in community—not isolation.

In 1:13–14 Paul's point is that the formative period of his Christian understanding came before he had more than a marginal relationship with the apostles at Jerusalem. For a time he was their bitter opponent, persecuting the church. He was then a zealot for his "patriarchal traditions" in Judaism. He was proud of his "roots" and saw Jesus as a threat to his way of life. At the heart of this was his "God and country" commitment, with its exclusion of "sinners of the Gentiles" (2:15). Pride in one's "roots" can be a very wholesome thing, but it also can take a negative turn as fierce as the "Nordic" pride by which Hitler and his Nazis killed 6,000,000 Jews for no better reason than that they were Jews and not Nordic. Unfortunately, no ethnic, racial, or religious group is immune to the partisan pride which persecutes. Paul confessed to such misguided "zeal." A sermon could follow here on the subject, "The Piety that Persecutes" or "The Dangers of Civil Religion" (1:13–14). Religion is capable of bringing out the best

or the worst in us. The whole Judeo/Christian tradition is
marked by its persecuted and persecutors, its prophets and
bigots, those willing to give life and those willing to take life.
Some of the bitterest fighting today is intramural, with the
Christian "army" shooting its own soldiers.

On a happier side, out of v. 16 arises the text, "To reveal
his son in me." Paul makes special reference to preaching the
gospel to the Gentiles, but the text allows two ideas: articulat-
ing the gospel and embodying the gospel. Paul preached
Christ as overcoming the estrangement between people as
widely separated as Jews and Gentiles, but nothing spoke so
eloquently as his entering into full fellowship with non-Jews,
even to eating with them (see 2:12). Paul earned the right to
preach that "in Christ there is no Jew and Greek" so soon as he
accepted table fellowship in the home of the Philippian (Roman) jailor (Acts 16:34). One of the most significant books of
recent years is John A. T. Robinson's *On Being the Church in
the World* (London: SCM Press, 1960), in which he rightly
makes the point that the major mission of the church in the
world is *to be* the church. Only then are what it says and does
really significant. Being has priority over doing and saying.
There can be doing and saying without being, and this is
sham. Words and deeds may express what we are in Christ,
and thus Christ is revealed in us.

Yet another sermon may arise out of v. 23, "Rectifying the
Past." Paul preached the faith he once tried to destroy. He affirmed the people (especially Gentiles) whom he once despised. "Born again" religion is credible only when it
produces a new quality of existence. "Conversion" is credible
only when one acknowledges his wrongs and seeks to rectify
damage done. Simply to move from penitentiary to pulpit
with no retraction of "dirty trick" letters or public apology to
persons wronged is mere self-serving. Paul practiced what
John the Baptist called "fruits worthy of repentance."

Acceptance by the Twelve (2:1–10)

Paul's independence of the Twelve did not imply indifference toward them. He sought and gained their recognition of
his mission to the Gentiles. He made one visit to Jerusalem to
get acquainted with the apostles there (1:18) and a later visit
to seek agreement regarding the gospel and to correlate their

ministries to Jew and Gentile. Paul did this at the risk of being considered subordinate to the apostles at Jerusalem. He maintained his own independence and the integrity of his apostleship, and he resisted all pressures to compromise the gospel by letting Titus be forced into accepting circumcision.

There is a call for preaching today which would "clear the air" with respect to contemporary "Judaizing" as Paul did for the Galatians. The Judaizers were self-appointed monitors of other people's orthopraxy. They saw themselves as defenders of "the truth." Paul branded them as spies, and spying is fatal to fellowship. He saw them not as doing but undoing the liberating work of Jesus. He saw them not as defenders of the truth but a hindrance to it. A sermon could be preached here on "Gospel Defender or Hinderer?" What was at issue was not words but integrity, freedom, and personhood. What about a sermon here on "The Truth of the Gospel"? Develop it not in terms of verbalizing a creed in the name of "orthodoxy." Show how the good news is hindered by the "pseudo-brethren" who try to impose their little systems on everyone else: creedal, ritual, mores, or whatever. To give in to their coercion does not "appease" them; it only further inflates the ego which demands yet more victims to a slavery called freedom.

"Peers but not Superiors" may capture in sermon another truth for the Church. Paul was plainly irked by any "hierarchical" tendencies within the church. Twice he refers to "those seeming" or "those seeming to be pillars," (vv. 6, 9), and made little effort to conceal his impatience with the whole idea of "Mr. Bigs" in the church. Paul did not look down upon little people and he did not look up to "big" people. One only is the rightful Lord of the church. All the rest of us are rightfully peers with no place for superiors. This does not mean that we are equally gifted, equally influential, or equally responsible. It does not exclude differing roles within the church. We are equally precious, and each has equal right to being himself or herself. Individuality was preserved in the equal recognition of the mission of James, Peter, and John to the Jews and, on the other hand, the mission of Barnabas and Paul to the Gentiles. Colleagueship was preserved to the extent that each recognized the right of the other to be and the right of the other to minister in terms of his gifts and vocational direction.

Galatians offers rich source material for a sermon on "The Right Hand of Fellowship (koinonia)" (v. 9). In the very next paragraph (2:11– 14), Paul describes a sharp confrontation within the church as it gathered in Antioch; and here Paul writes about shaking hands with this very "opponent." Were the sequence the reverse, it would make a better case: a quarrel and a handshake. As it is narrated, it was a handshake and a quarrel. There is no hint in 2:11– 14 that the confrontation there broke fellowship between Paul and Peter, as sharp as it was. In any event, there is need within the church for the quality of fellowship *(koinonia)* as to make it possible for both: handshake and dispute; dispute and handshake. When we really accept one another, there is room for open difference as at Antioch. We can debate ideas, issues, and practices without rejecting one another as persons in Christ. In fact, the more fully we accept one another in love and respect, the freer we become to openly debate our differences. Suggested sermon subjects are: "Disagreement with Honor" or "Holding the Truth in Love."

Correcting Peter at Antioch (2:11 –14)

The church in Antioch of Syria was an early center of fellowship overcoming the barriers between Jew and Gentile. It was at Antioch that followers of Jesus were first called "Christians" (Acts 11:26), probably because it was there that their oneness in Christ was seen to lift them above their ethnic or cultic differences. It is this background and the importance of the issue to Paul which explains the feeling reflected in vv. 11– 14.

F. C. Baur more than a century ago saw the church as polarized between Peter and Paul, but a far stronger case could be made for the polarization centering in James (the brother of Jesus) and Paul. Peter was caught in the cross-fire between James and Paul. Peter is accused of "hypocrisy" (v. 13) or inconsistency (v. 14). Peter knew better than to discriminate against uncircumcised converts. He faltered in the presence of "certain ones from James" (v. 12). He had been eating with these Gentile converts until the coming of some from James created an incident. Peter's withdrawal from table fellowship influenced even Barnabas to withdraw also. Paul was furious at this discrimination. He stood up to Peter and condemned him to his face (not behind his back) before the church.

Poor translation of v. 14 has obscured for many readers the real force of Paul's position. It should read: "But when I saw that they were not walking upright toward the truth of the gospel . . ." The Greek preposition is *pros*, "toward." A break in table fellowship is a blow at the essence of the gospel. In this act of separation, Peter was walking away from and not toward the truth of the gospel. The truth of the gospel is not to be found down the road of exclusion, separation, discrimination. To deny another's salvation or to deny full fellowship is to turn away from the truth of the gospel. This speaks directly to the whole issue of segregation and also to the issue of "closed communion." In some way, most confessional groups have excluded Christians not satisfying their codes as to ordination, baptism, or such. Paul's indictment of "Judaizing" (v. 14) falls properly upon all elevation of cultic values above human values, and no one taught this so powerfully as Jesus (see Mk 3:35).

Crucified with Christ (2:15– 21)

There are at least three major movements within this paragraph: we are made righteous in Christ and not through the law (vv. 15– 16); righteousness is real and not indulgence in the same old life (vv. 17– 18); and we are being made righteous through the abiding in us of the Christ with whom we have both been "crucified" and raised to new life (vv. 19– 21). These ideas could be preached under the subject "Right Thinking About Righteousness." The points in the sermon could be: (1) Righteousness is granted in Christ and not ourselves. (2) Righteousness is new character, not new bookkeeping. (3) Righteousness derives its power from the indwelling Christ.

V. 15 distinguishes between the two major divisions of humanity Paul first knew: "Jews" and "Gentile sinners." Of course Paul no longer upholds the position he once held, even though here he repeats the old terms in order to pose the problem. The whole letter shows that he now rejects the idea that ethnic heritage or ceremonial rites are valid criteria for the family of God (3:28). Neither Jew nor Gentile is "justified" by

the "works of the law." The Greek terms usually rendered
"justify" or "justification" are built upon a root meaning "uprightness." Paul is not dealing with a forensic (legal) idea
here. He is talking about real righteousness. His contention is
that neither Jew nor Gentile is counted righteous or made
righteous by complying with the Mosaic laws. Both standing
with God and a new quality of existence characterized by uprightness come from God. One finds new standing with God
and new kind of existence by trusting in the trustworthiness of
God, by faith in the faithfulness of God. Faith is openness to
God—to receive him into one's life as a saving presence. Being
Jew or Gentile, circumcised or uncircumcised, has nothing
necessarily to do with whether one is open to God's saving
presence or not.

God's grace is not cheap. Salvation is not indulgence. In
vv. 17–18 Paul rejects the idea that since saving is God's work
we may go on in sin (more of this later in Galatians and Romans). Christ is not a minister of sin (v. 17). Christ did not
come to destroy the law but to rescue its heart and to enflesh
its intention (Matt 5:17–20). God does not just "count righteous" ones who are not righteous. He accepts the sinner when
the sinner trusts him, but God's work in the sinner is that of
making him actually righteous. To sin willfully is to be a
transgressor (v. 18) even if in the name of "justification by
faith."

In preaching, the example of physician and patient may
illustrate two sides of salvation: acceptance and therapy. The
physician/patient relationship is a matter of mutual trust,
acceptance, and commitment, not awaiting the patient's cure
or improvement. But the purpose of the physician/patient relationship is health. Jesus becomes our physician at the point
of our consent, and that settles that. But Jesus becomes our
physician with a view to curing us of our sins. "Justification"
is all of this: new relationship and new kind of existence.

"I live, yet not I" (v. 20). To understand this paradox is to
understand the heart of Paul's theology of salvation. From beginning to end, salvation for him is God's work; yet it is never
imposed. God's initiative and saving power never override
human freedom. Saving faith is not reflex action; it is willing
response to divine calling. When God saves a person, it is not
like a mechanic fixing a motor. God saves us not by manipu-

lating us but by awakening in us the faith which is openness to his grace, openness to his saving presence within our lives.

Paul saw the discontinuity between his life outside Christ and his new life in Christ as so radical that he used model upon model (analogy) to articulate it. One model was that of crucifixion: "With Christ I have been crucified!" Of course, this was not literally so, else Paul would not have been around to write Galatians. He did mean it most seriously. He did not say, "I got tired of the old man and slew him." He did not say that Christ did it without his consent. Paul's faith was a submission to Christ in which Christ began to put to death the old egocentric Saul of Tarsus and to create a new man instead. Paul is not talking about some "transactional atonement" by which Paul died with Christ at Golgotha. The old Saul was very much alive long after Golgotha. It was first on the Damascus road that Paul was "crucified" with Christ. The Cross is saving, but only as existential—only as it penetrates the life of faith and changes its character and direction. Christ does not save by substituting for us but by entering into us. He does not send us to the bench so he can play the game for us; he leaves us in the game and in union with us plays it to a different effect. A sermon here could be entitled "Life after Death Now."

Works of Law or Obedience of Faith
(Galatians 3:1–4:31)

In the middle chapters of Galatians, Paul draws a sharp contrast between two mutually exclusive understandings of the gospel, and picks up what he had in mind in 1:6–7, "another (*heteron*-different) gospel, which is not another (*allo*-another of the same kind)." A number of key words mark the contrast: works of the law vs. the obedience of faith; spirit vs. flesh; slaves vs. sons. Paul sees salvation as the free gift of God's grace, in no sense our achievement in righteousness. Paul by no means holds to salvation without righteousness; rather he contends for a real righteousness brought about as God's achievement in those who trust him.

The Righteous Shall Live Out of Faith (3:1– 14)

Paul built much of his theology of salvation upon Habakkuk 2:4 (3:11; Rom 1:17). The Hebrew text reads, "The upright one shall live by his faithfulness." It is not clear whether "his" refers to God or "the upright one." The Greek translation removed the ambiguity: "The upright one shall live by my faithfulness" (God's faithfulness). Paul's Greek sentence may be rendered, "The upright one shall live out of faith." The Greek word *pistis* includes two related ideas: faith and faithfulness (cf. Rom 3:3). Probably Paul's meaning is best captured in paraphrase: "The upright (righteous) person lives by faith in the faithfulness of God (trust in the trustworthiness of God)." God's faithfulness awakens us to faith in him, and righteousness is what God brings about when we live out of his own goodness. For preaching today, the Word of God from this passage is this: The really righteous person is the one who has the faith to dare to live by trusting in the faithfulness of God. Out of the relationship of mutual trust flows a new quality of existence characterized by uprightness.

"Who bewitched you?" (v. 1). To exchange faith in God for

faith in circumcision and the like was to Paul nothing short of "brainless." Twice (vv. 1, 3) Paul calls the Galatians "foolish" (*anoetos*-senseless or brainless). They were acting as though under a spell, "bewitched." They had been taken in by the very kind of piety which crucified Jesus, that which made more of sabbath, purification rites, kosher foods, etc. than of human beings (see Mk 3:4, 6). Why look for salvation out of the kind of "piety" which crucified Jesus Christ? By the "hearing of faith" they had been in touch with him who could supply "the Spirit and the energizing of power" (v. 5). The Spirit of God could penetrate their own existence and work powerfully from within them. To turn from this to a set of cultic rites was an almost incredible act of folly. There is a sermon here: "On Being Led Down the Garden Path."

Having begun "in spirit" they were trying to complete their salvation "in flesh" (v. 3). No English dictionary can show what Paul meant by spirit and flesh. Paul's meaning is to be found contextually. By spirit he meant the whole self under redemption (5:22–23). By flesh he meant any or all of self apart from redemption (5:19–21). In this usage "spirit" does not mean ghostly, nor does "flesh" mean literal flesh. Any aspect of us can be "spirit" or "flesh," depending upon whether submissive to God or not. Any religious effort to save oneself is "flesh," mere human striving. To live by faith, drawing life from the goodness of God, is "spirit."

By saying that Christ became a curse for us (v. 13) Paul did not imply all the transactional ideas which atonement theories have read into the text. God did not punish Jesus as a substitute for us. God did not curse Jesus. Jesus was cursed by sinful men and treated like an accursed man. Jesus endured the curse as he offered the world a new kind of existence. He was opposed chiefly by the piety which gave cultic rites priority over human beings. Jesus refused to be personally enslaved to "the law," and he offered to free us from it (Mk 2:27–28). He came under the curse of piety and world as he sought to save us, and in him we may be freed from "the curse of the law."

It is well for us in preaching from Galatians to avoid any implication that legalism (or libertinism) is especially a Jewish problem. Jesus was a Jew, and he drew heavily from Jewish, prophetic tradition and perspective. Paul was a Jew.

Every religious community has its prophets and its bigots. Legalism takes many shapes and colors, and no religion is immune to it.

The Law and the Promise (3:15–20)

Paul's main point here is that God made a covenant with Abraham 430 years before the Law was given to Moses and the Law does not cancel the covenant. This was a covenant given out of God's grace (v. 18), and it anticipated the inclusion of the nations in its provisions (Gen 12:3; 18:18). In Genesis the phrase "to thy seed" obviously refers in the collective sense to all Abraham's "children" but Paul in rabbinical fashion (which he concedes in saying that he is speaking "humanly") fixes attention on the singular form of "seed' and refers it to Christ. He thus finds the fulfillment of the covenant with Abraham to be realized in Christ. Abraham's true children are all people who are "in Christ" (3:26–29). For preaching today, basic direction may be found from the fact that both the OT and the NT represent God as always being in the saving business and that there has never been a time when salvation did not depend upon God's grace received by man's faith. In Christ, God is extending and intensifying what he did for Abraham and promised all nations. A sermon subject here could be "Grace Always" or "Grace From the Beginning."

"Why then the Law?" (v. 19). Paul insisted that the Law was added (God was already saving people) because of transgressions, and that it was only provisional, until Christ came. Further, the Law served to show up human failing but could not of itself supply the power for overcoming sins. Yet more, in Christ we have direct access to God, from whom comes our salvation. For a second time within this paragraph, Paul drew from his rabbinical background, this time using the tradition that God gave the Law to Moses through the mediation of angels. In this rabbinical tradition (which is not found in the OT), Moses stood between mankind and angels (plural), but Christ links us directly to God, with no need for a "go between." Moses was the "go between" between angels and mankind (according to rabbinic tradition), but God is One and needs no "go between"; he does his own speaking. A sermon lurks here on "Nothing Between." Christ is not "another God"; Christ is Immanuel (God with us). Christ is God himself addressing us and saving us directly, not dependent upon mediation of angels or the Mosaic Law. God saved before Moses and God saves now directly and personally. The name "Jesus" is from Hebrew and means "JHWH Savior" (Matt 1:21). Preaching today needs to do a better job in affirming what is not less emphatic in the NT than in the OT: God is one God. This undercuts such ideas as that a kind Jesus saves us from an angry God. Here Paul affirms that in Jesus Christ (JHWH Savior) God himself comes to us, giving us direct access to his presence and his salvation (see Frank Stagg, *The Holy Spirit Today* [Nashville: Broadman, 1973], chapter 1).

Not Slaves but Children of God (3:21–4:7)

This generation should be able to understand that righteousness is not assured by "law and order." Hitler offered his followers "order, security, and prosperity." He enslaved people and devastated moral, ethical, and personal values. Our own country in the seventies went through an era of "law and order" only to learn that corruption permeated the very system which proclaimed law and order. Uprightness must be first an inner condition, a reality only when God is admitted as a saving Presence deep within one's existence.

"Baptized into Christ" (v. 27). Having rejected circumcision as a saving rite, does Paul now substitute water baptism as a saving rite? If so, the whole argument is one of "tweedle dum, tweedle dee!" Surely Paul is not swapping one rite for another. He does use "baptism" as a model or an analogy for union with Christ. He could speak of baptism in a literal sense or metaphorically. Jesus spoke of a "baptism" which both he and his followers must endure, and he obviously was talking about "the cross" and not simply immersion in the Jordan River (Mk 10:38; Lk 12:50). Paul could make a distinction between circumcision "in flesh" and circumcision "not made with hands" (see Col 2:11; Eph 2:11). He needed to do this, because some claimed that literal circumcision was necessary for salvation and/or table fellowship. Presumably no one was claiming for water baptism what the Judaizers claimed for circumcision, else Paul would have needed to distinguish between "baptism in flesh, made by hands" and "baptism not made with hands."

In Galatians Paul means more than "baptized into

water"; he means being joined personally to Christ. Becoming a child of God is not through a ceremonial rite; it is by "putting on Christ." To be "in Christ" makes irrelevant the whole matter of whether one is Jew or Greek, slave or free person, male or female (v. 28). Ethnic, cultic, legal, and sexual distinctions are realities in the world, and they have their significance there; but "in Christ" it is irrelevant to make such distinctions to apply. We are in Christ and we are "children of Abraham" by faith. Greeks, slaves, and women are as much children of God and heirs of God as are Jews, free persons, and males.

Preaching today cannot be responsible if it neglects the implications of any part of Paul's claim that in Christ there is "not any Jew and Greek, bond and free, male and female." The church today is almost exclusively Gentile, so we are not about to neglect the claim for "Jew and Greek." After nearly two thousand years we are about to commit ourselves to erasing within the church the world's distinction between slaves and free persons. We are just now beginning to put on the agenda of the church the issue of woman and the church. It is not just a question of recognizing the full personhood of woman (freedom, rights, and responsibilities), but of ceasing to apply sexual distinction where "in Christ" it does not apply. Paul here does not restrict his "no male and female" to salvation; it rightly applies to all that is meant by being "in Christ." That the church moved in another direction, with increasing discrimination against slaves and women, does not invalidate the truth of verses 26–29 (see Evelyn and Frank Stagg, *Woman in The World of Jesus*, Philadelphia, Westminster, 1978).

"Abba, Father" (4:6). The language remains male-oriented despite the liberating vision of vv. 26–29. Most language is male-oriented, that fact itself reflecting how deep discrimination has run against woman. In Paul's world, "father" served as a model for God. It is not to be forgotten that the first creation narrative (Gen 1:27–2:4a) has it that "male and female" were created together in the image of God. God is neither male nor female, but he is such that both male and female find likeness in him. Paul's point is that it is God unto whom we cry out, not unto the Law. We cry out to him as a child does to a parent. Paul chides anyone who will accept bondage to the Law in place of the freedom and fulfillment offered us as children of God.

Preaching today not only has the problem of avoiding chauvinistic implications in the traditional reference toward God as "Father," but it also has the problem posed for children who know a father only in negative terms, including neglect or abuse. Traditional models and terms are serviceable or not, depending on what they communicate to the people addressed. Here as elsewhere, preaching may require "fresh skins" if it is to preserve the "wine" of the gospel. What about a sermon on "Woman in the World of Jesus" and/or one on "Jesus in the World of Woman"?

Paul's Concern for the Galatians (4:8–20)

In this section Paul made two basic pleas: first, that they not aba don their freedom in Christ for slavery to such little things as a religious calendar, a return to a form of idolatry which would mean that all Paul's work was wasted (vv. 8–11); and second, that they not turn from him, a longtime and trusted friend, to some newcomers now courting them for their own advantage (vv. 12–20).

Paul reminded the Galatians that they once worshipped what were not gods in their own right, only made so by their worshippers (v. 8). Now they were in danger of turning to a new set of unnatural gods or man-made gods, being enslaved to a religious calendar with its "days, months, seasons, and years" (v. 10). What made this flirtation with a new form of idolatry so startling was that it came after they had come to know God by whom already they had been known (v. 9). Paul had reason to say, "I fear you," (v. 11), for the unpredictable will of mankind is frightening. What Paul saw among the Galatians is not isolated, for mankind has a sad record of tending to choose the phony over the genuine, in religion as in life generally.

"Knowing God, rather being known by God" (v. 9). Here is the heart of salvation (see Jn 17:3). Knowledge here is not that of a subject knowing an object like a fact; it is that of a subject knowing a subject, a knower knowing a knower, a person knowing a person. We are not saved by this or that or by knowing or believing this or that. We are saved by God and only as we know him in direct, personal encounter. Paul first

said, "knowing God" and then backed up to put it in better
perspective: "rather being known by God." Just as we are able
to love God because he first loved us (1 Jn 4:10, 19), so we are
able to know God because he knows us before we know him.
Saving knowledge takes place where God and we meet in the
openness of trust and love, each vulnerable to the other and
each open to the gifts of the other. Remember that we can
bless God who first blesses us. Neither idols nor cultic rites
can know us or love us or save us. Why then swap the true and
living God for such gods as circumcision, calendars, and the
like? A sermon here on "Saving Knowledge" or "Our Knowledge of God" could expose the current gods by which our people are tempted and point them to the heart of what the NT
means by salvation.

"Have I become your enemy speaking the truth to you?"
(v. 16). Paul saw his Judaizing opponents as courting the Galatians not for the Galatians' sake but for their own self-serving
ends. The ministry is an open field for egocentrics willing to
exploit the masses for money, power, or fame. Just listen to ra-
dio or watch the manipulators or "the electronic church" rake
in their millions of dollars per year. They know how to appeal
to fear, prejudice, and the mania for the feeling of security.
Obscurantism, fail-safe "faith," short cuts to health or wealth,
and whatnot are marketable to a gullible public. Barnum and
Bailey built a circus on their claim that "there's a sucker born
every minute." Nowhere are people more easily taken in than
in religion.

"Speaking the truth" renders a Greek term which could
as well be rendered "being true." Paul was true to the Galatians and he spoke the truth to them. He was compelled to face
the astonishing fact that he may be or could become "their enemy" by being true to them. Paul refused to preach only what
was the price of acceptance. Here is where preachers and
preaching must be tested. What about a sermon here on: "The
Cost of Truth?"

Paul reminded the Galatians that it was because of his
sickness that he first preached to them (v. 13). Paul was a man
of faith and piety, but this did not exempt him from sickness.
Many good people suffer serious illnesses, and preaching
should help them see that there is no necessary implication of
guilt in this. "Faith healers" are cruel when they make inno-

cent people feel guilty because they are sick or impaired. Many good people today are not only hurting because of physical illness or impairment, but they are hurting at an even deeper level as they feel or are made to feel guilty. A sermon speaking to their needs might be developed on the subject "Good People Get Sick Too."

Apparently Paul was sick enough that he could not move on to more distant fields, so he preached where he was when his sickness overtook him. His sickness was such that the Galatians could have found him loathsome. There is a hint here that he may have had an eye infection (v. 15), a disease which often had loathsome outward effects. Whatever the nature of the sickness, the Galatians were true to Paul when he needed them and their help. Instead of despising him in his "weakness of the flesh," they received him as "an angel of God" or "messenger of God" (the Greek work means either, a human or heavenly messenger). They received him "as Christ Jesus." This can mean that they received him the way they would have received Christ or even as though he were Christ, reminiscent of Christ's word, "In that ye did it unto one of these . . ." (Matt 25:40; see Phlm 17). This is the *koinonia* (fellowship) which belongs to the essence of the Christian calling. Why trade such a relationship with Paul for a cheap romance with those who court them but whose intentions are not for their good (v. 17)? People need help today in sorting out the many preachers who bid for their following, and especially for their money. A sermon on "The Marks of Authentic Leadership" would help. Special attention might be given to the threat of "the electronic church."

"Until Christ be formed in you" (v. 19). Salvation is more than observing cultic rites; it is having Christ formed within one's being. Christ's kind of existence is to displace our former kind of existence. Salvation is not a matter of ritual performance, creedal confession, or hitch-hiking on divine transactions (cf. the artificiality of much preached under the name of "atonement"; see later on Rom 5:11). Salvation means nothing less than Christ's penetration of our deepest inner self to transform it. Paul's metaphors or logistics of pregnancy may be a bit strange, but his deep concern is clear. He will be suffering "birth pangs" for them until they "become pregnant with Christ!" His anguish for them is like that of a mother suffering birth pangs as she tries to bring forth her child. His goal is that they undergo the birth pangs in which Christ is formed within them. Analogies aside, Paul wants them to be like Jesus Christ (see Rom 8:29).

Lessons from Hagar and Sarah (4:21–31)

Paul took from Genesis the story of Hagar and Sarah and gave it an allegorical interpretation, plainly acknowledging what he was doing (v. 24). Abraham's wife Sarah was barren until given her child Isaac late in life, while Abraham's concubine, Hagar, bore her child, Ishmael, to Abraham long before Isaac's birth. Sarah was a free woman and Hagar a slave. The Israel of God is traced through Sarah and not Hagar. Paul concludes that we are children of Sarah, thus free, and not children of Hagar, thus slaves. In his allegorizing of the story, Paul links the Mosaic Law with Hagar and God's promise to Abraham with Sarah. We thus are children of promise, with salvation as the gift of God. We are children of freedom and not slavery (to the Law).

Paul's clearest or most convincing writing is seldom in his illustrations. His point is usually clear apart from his illustrations. Paul employed the allegorical method less than much of the ancient world: pagan, Jewish, and Christian. His unyielding stand for Christian freedom is secure in Galatians, apart from the allegory of Sarah and Hagar. We are under a covenant of promise and not of law. We live by faith out of the goodness of God and not by satisfying the requirements of the Mosaic law.

V. 27 quotes Is 54:1, and it is difficult. Apparent in Paul's application, the woman who "never had children," who "never felt the pangs of childbirth," and who "was deserted" is Sarah *before* she bore Isaac and when all seemed hopeless. As it turned out, she had "more children than the woman living with the husband," i.e., Hagar. The lines are difficult, but Paul's application is clear. We are children of God as the result of his promise, like Isaac. We are not children of Hagar, and we are not children of bondage to the Law. Sarah's true children, and there are many, are those who have faith in God, whatever their ethnic or cultic background.

Paul makes the further point that just as the son of the free woman was persecuted by the son of the slave woman

(Isaac persecuted by Ishmael and Jacob by Esau), so it is now. God's children born of God's Spirit are persecuted by the legalist whose highest allegiance is to the Law. Just see who has persecuted whom throughout Christian history! In the world, legally free people have persecuted slaves. In religion, persecution comes usually by slaves to some creedal stereotype, ceremonial rite, or code of culture. Jesus is crucified, Stephen is stoned, and Tyndale is burned at the stake—by what kind of religious people? They are legalists all! A sermon could be built upon this record. The subject could be: "The Legacy of Legalism," with such points as: (1) It denies us freedom. (2) It blinds us to grace. (3) It "sanctifies" our inhumanity.

Freedom and Responsibility
(Galatians 5:1–6:10)

In chapter 5 Paul fights on two fronts, rejecting legalism and also the permissiveness which tries to pass for freedom. He holds freedom in Christ to be non-negotiable, and he holds that freedom must be exercised responsibly. The outcome is to be in terms of the "fruit of the Spirit" and not "the works of the flesh." Contextually, he leaves no doubt as to what this means. In chapter 6 Paul pleads for mutual acceptance within the church, with members supportive of one another in the burdens of life. He takes some parting shots at his legalistic opponents and calls for a clean break between church and world under the claims of the cross of Jesus Christ.

The Call to Freedom (5:1–15)

V. 1 sounds redundant—for freedom Christ freed us—until we reflect on our disposition to surrender freedom about as fast as we claim it. We like the idea of freedom, but we are frightened by the cost of it and wearied by the burden of it. The Galatians were not alone in the ease with which they gave up the hard-won freedom achieved by Christ. Paul's reminder is not redundant: For freedom Christ freed us! Bondage to Law, Mosaic or otherwise, is a constant threat.

Freedom is lost and religion becomes bondage when we become preoccupied with ceremonial rites which once were fresh skins for new wine but now are only brittle skins, when we simply repeat creeds which once articulated another's faith, or when we confuse some culture's codes with moral/ethical responsibility. The Galatians were about to settle for circumcision and a religious calendar in place of the freedom Christ won for them. What about a sermon on "The Practice of Freedom"? Attention could be given to receiving it gratefully, exercising it responsibly, and preserving it faithfully.

"You are fallen away from grace!" (v. 4). This is the heart of Paul's warning. These are difficult words for those holding to "eternal security" or "once saved always saved." Is that the issue? Conditioned as we are by theological debate, "fallen from grace" usually implies something like moral lapse, settled indifference, or renunciation of Christ. This does not remotely approach the Galatian problem against which Paul spoke out in terms of being "rendered inoperative from Christ" and "fallen away from grace."

Those described as "fallen from grace" were intensely zealous people who were trying to achieve righteousness through such cultic laws as circumcision and religious calendars. In turning to themselves they thereby were turning from Christ. In turning to their "works" they thereby were turning from grace. One cannot have it both ways: human merit and divine grace. If salvation is our achievement, it is not God's gift. Those who "fall from grace" are those who trust in their own compliance with the Law as the means to salvation or maturity in salvation. Paul is not discussing "eternal security" or "apostasy"; he is discussing the ground and nature of salvation. A "gospel" of human works is no gospel at all (1:6–7). To Paul it is an "either . . . or"—Law or Grace. A sermon here could boldly bear Paul's caption: "Fallen Away from Grace." It could be developed as any turning from basic dependence upon the goodness and grace of God to the presumption of one's own goodness or achievement as foundational to life.

"Out of faith we await the hope of righteousness" (v. 5). Paul does not concede a corner on righteousness to his Judaizing opponents. He is as intensely interested in righteousness as anyone. The requirement of righteousness is not the issue, for both sides affirm that. Paul differs from the legalists in understanding the nature and the source of righteousness. He has no respect for a contrived righteousness, either by observing superficial rules or by settling for "forensic" (bookkeeping or make-believe) righteousness. By righteousness he means moral/ethical/personal integrity. This belongs necessarily to salvation, but it is God's achievement in those who trust him, not man's achievement by satisfying religious laws. Man cannot "lift himself by his bootstraps," but God can make righteous anyone who looks to God for help. Those who hunger for righteousness are filled (Matt 5:6). A sermon may follow on the subject: "Goodness as Evidence of Grace."

"Faith working through love" (v. 6). What a sermon topic!

This can mean our faith energized by God's love or our faith expressing itself in love for other people. Probably the latter is intended, but either meaning fits the context. Faith itself is response to God's loving presence and action. We have a part in it, for it is response (we are response-able). Faith is not a package unloaded on us; it is our action. On the other hand it is response, implying a prior action, that of God. Faith then is something in us energized by God's love. Faith also is to use its energy in loving other people. By contrast, neither circumcision nor uncircumcision has strength for anything. They can create neither faith nor love.

"You were running well; who cut in on you?" (v. 7). Paul hits hard in vv. 7– 12. Using the analogy of a foot race, he describes the Galatians as running well until someone cut in on them, blocking them out so as "not to obey the truth." The whole idea of salvation by observing religious rites is against the truth. Anticipating that the Galatians might say, "Paul, you are making too big a thing of this," Paul reminds them that a little leaven (yeast) leavens the whole lump. Circumcision implies more, the whole package! It is the beginning of an endless road, calling for more and more "Brownie points." Laying the heaviest blame on the Judaizers who were talking the Galatians into accepting circumcision, Paul put aside all nice talk and said bluntly, "I wish that those upsetting you would castrate themselves" (v. 12). There is a play on words between their "cutting in" (*enkopsen*) in v. 7 and Paul's wish that they "cut off" (*apokopsontai*) the whole thing in v. 12. If a little cutting helps (circumcision) why not a complete job? There are alternate interpretations to this verse, but this probably is Paul's meaning.

"Through love serve one another" (v. 13). The call to such love is in the context of freedom. The Galatians are not to understand freedom as license to satisfy their own "flesh." By "flesh" Paul can refer to sensuality or to any disposition or action outside the will of God. "Flesh" is self apart from God or apart from redemption. Freedom is not for self-serving. Rather freedom is to be exercised in serving "one another" in love (*agape*). This does not exclude but rather includes "self-serving" in the best sense. The command is: "You shall love your neighbor as yourself." Authentic love excludes none, neither God, neighbor, nor self. We are so bound up with one another (God, neighbor, and self) that to love one is to love all and to exclude one is to exclude all. Thus, freedom is not to be confused with permissiveness; and neither is it to be used selfishly. It is not freedom to "bite and devour" one another; it is freedom to serve one another out of love. There are many facets (faces) to love and its serving. What about a sermon on "Love's Many Faces" or "The Love That Serves"?

The Works of Flesh and the Fruit of Spirit (5:16–26)

Flesh and spirit, as seen above, must be understood as Paul used the terms, not as they may be defined in an English dictionary. Words have usage, not inherent or permanent meaning. Paul sometimes uses "flesh" in a material sense; here the term is used metaphorically or ethically. Flesh stands for any or all of personhood outside redemption. "Flesh" is a person apart from God. The opposite term is "spirit," but this does not imply something ghostly. "Spirit" for Paul may refer to any aspect of personhood under redemption, related to God. To live "according to flesh" does not have a special reference to sensuality, although that may be included. Spirituality for Paul does not imply otherworldliness. The whole self in its historical, bodily existence may be "spiritual." For Paul the contrast between "flesh" and "spirit" is not like that of the Gnostics to whom the material as such is evil and the good is non-material (i.e., soul or spirit).

"The works of the flesh" (vv. 19–21). Only five of the things listed as "works of the flesh" are sensual, ten being non-sensual. Both types are equally "flesh." In fact, the fifteen examples (not exhaustive) fall into four classes: sensuality, magic, self-assertion, and revelry. Envy and jealousy are just as much "flesh" as are fornication and drunkenness. We are not naturally corrupt, but any aspect of personhood can be corrupted: feeling, thinking, will, action, or whatever. Any or all of personhood may be redeemed and under God be "spiritual." The ugly list here, not exhaustive, includes sexual immorality, idolatry, sorcery, anti-social feelings and vices, impiety, drunkenness, and revelry.

It is clear here that Paul was concerned to refute more than the empty claims of legalism. In disowning the hollow victories of life only outwardly regulated by cultic laws, Paul was careful not to play into the hands of the permissiveness of the libertines or antinomians. Salvation has its moral/ethical and its personal/social demands. Those practicing "the works of the flesh" will not inherit (gift) "the kingdom of God." In fact, as they practice these works they show that they are not now living under the claims of the kingdom of God. The kingdom of God is the sovereign rule of God. It means that God is king. One cannot have it both ways—God as king and yet these "works of the flesh" as king.

"The fruit of the Spirit" (vv. 22–23). True spirituality is not otherworldliness. It is a different quality of existence brought about within us and affecting the outward manner of life. The list given here contains nothing exotic or bizarre, as in much that passes for "spirituality." Pagan notions of spirituality gravitated toward "ecstasy" (standing outside oneself, or the "soul" escaping the body). Escape from bodily limits, as in some angelic speech, was the ideal of pagan spirituality. For Paul this is not so. True spirituality occurs in one's historical and bodily existence (see Rom 12:1–2). Love (*agape*), joy, peace (*shalom* in Hebrew, is well-being under the rule of God), patience, kindness, goodness, faith (*pistis* means faith or fidelity), gentleness, and self-control are the basic marks of spirituality. These cannot be produced by any system of law; and where they characterize human life, there is no need for laws. This is not to imply that in the world there is no need for laws; it is to say that it is in the absence of "the fruit of the Spirit" that laws become necessary. Laws are never equal to the task of bringing order out of chaos. Laws are "stop-gap" measures; the hope for the desired quality of existence is the transforming presence of God in human life.

"Those of Christ Jesus crucify the flesh with its passions and selfish desires" (v. 24). The core of all sin is egocentricity: self-serving and self-assertion. The Cross of Christ becomes saving not in an automatic sense but only as it penetrates our existence and reverses our self-centeredness into the servanthood which seeks God's glory and the good of other people. Crucifying the "flesh" is basically God's achievement, but it is never accomplished without our consent. Here, contrary to his usual manner, Paul speaks of our crucifying the old selfish way (see 2:20 with the passive voice: "I have been crucified with/in Christ").

Preaching on "The Works of the Flesh" enables one to deal both with the messy sins which are almost universally scorned (yet practiced) and the more "respectable" yet more deadly sins of the flesh like envy, jealousy, pride, prejudice, etc. Preaching on "The Fruit of the Spirit" enables one to expose the false or superficial "spirituality" of popular religion and to set forth the true spirituality which is moral/ethical/ personal—and bodily/historical! In these word studies related to the works of the flesh and the fruit of the Spirit there is enough preaching material for a whole season.

Bearing One Another's Burdens (6:1–10)

There is deliberate tension here: we are to bear one another's burdens (v. 2), yet each is to bear his/her own burden (v. 5). Two different Greek words are used, possibly implying that some burdens are of such nature that they may be shared, while others are so personal and individual that one person cannot take over for another. Probably the tension is to be understood another way: one should always be ready to get under another's burden, but one should not be disposed to unload upon another. Of course, these are not fixed rules, and no rule applies in every case. What is important is the willingness to share in burden bearing and also the willingness to bear one's own burden. Sometimes we wrong ourselves as well as others by refusal to accept the help of others. This withdrawal may imply lack of trust or love; it may be a way of shutting another out of one's life. On the other hand, to dump our burdens upon others too readily may be selfish or irresponsible.

We suggest a sermon here on the subject: "What to Do with Life's Burdens." The sermon could deal with burdens which one must bear for oneself, burdens which one must help one's neighbor bear, and the burdens which are to be cast upon the Lord.

Especially are "the spiritual," i.e., the strong or mature, to bear the burdens of the weak. Good people can be "overtaken"; they can fail. There are no fail-safe children of God. It is when they fail that they most need the support of the community. To "set another right" is a proper ministry, but it is dangerous as to motive or result. The restorer needs to be on guard as to his/her own life. Motives may be ulterior, and one qualifies to get "the speck" out of the other's eye only when willing to submit to the removal of "the beam" from his/her own eye (Matt 7:5).

"What one sows is what one reaps" (v. 7). As in physical nature, so in human nature and life, there are laws which work impartially. We become what we give ourselves to, whether "flesh" or "spirit." Just as self-centeredness is the essence of "flesh," so the love which seeks the good of others is the essence of "spirit." It is our business to bring about good for all people, beginning within the family of faith but not stopping there. There is place here for a sermon on "The Law of the Spiritual Harvest."

Summation and Concluding Words
(6:11–18)

No set of religious laws can make such heavy claim upon us as does the Cross. It calls for the radical self-denial (out of which comes the truest self-affirmation). Paul is content to have one boast alone—the Cross of Jesus Christ. Out of this "crucifixion" comes a "new creation" (v. 15). Strangely enough, we live only by dying.

As one bearing literal scars from stonings and beatings, as well as the "stigma" of one viewed by his own people as apostate, he made no pretense of concealing his impatience with his legalistic opponents. In effect he said, "Get off my back" (v. 17). Turning from this, he closed the letter on a positive note, praying for the grace of the Lord Jesus Christ upon ones whom he called "brothers."

Bibliography

Three old commentaries on Galatians remain classics in the field. These do the spade work, dealing with background, critical problems, and exegesis from the Greek text, but much of their findings are accessible to one without Greek. Most thorough is Ernest De Witt Burton, *A Critical Commentary on the Epistle to the Galatians* (New York: Charles Scribner's Sons, 1921). Detailed exegesis and argument for the "North Galatian" theory is offered by J. B. Lightfoot, *Saint Paul's Epistle to the Galatians* (New York: Macmillan, 1890, Zondervan reprint, 1957). Noted for rich historical background and the "South Galatian" theory is W. M. Ramsay's *A Historical Commentary on St. Paul's Epistle to the Galatians* (London: Hodder and Stoughton, 1899; Baker reprint, 1965).

Among the more recent commentaries on Galatians are three in particular which are highly serviceable for the pastor. John A. Allan, *The Epistle of Paul the Apostle to the Galatians* (London: SCM Press, 1951), offers a brief exegesis for the general reader, with some helpful essays on Pauline terms and ideas. No one matches A. M. Hunter in bringing the best findings of critical scholarship to the general reader. His commentary on Galatians appears along with those on Ephesians, Philippians, and Colossians in volume 22 of *The Layman's Bible Commentary* (Atlanta: John Knox Press, 1959). Readable and relevant is William Neil's *The Letter of Paul to the Galatians* (New. York: Cambridge University Press, 1967). A concise package tailored for pastors is *Review and Expositor* (Fall 1972), "The Letter to the Galatians" (2825 Lexington Road; Louisville, KY 40206).

ROMANS

Introduction

Decisions, decisions! That's an old story and a continuing one for most of us. Paul was no exception to the rule, and never did he make a more significant decision than when he wrote Romans. During a winter at Corinth (Acts 20:1–3) he made a monentous decision with which he had struggled for at least some months. This issue was: Should he go directly to Spain by way of Roman or turn back to Jerusalem with an offering between Jewish and Gentile Christians (1 Cor 16:1–4;2 Cor 8–9; Rom 15:22–33). The claims of Jerusalem won out over those from Rome and Spain, for Paul settled for a letter to the Romans and made a trip to Jerusalem. If we understand what entered into that decision we will have a major key to understanding what Romans is about.

Spain or Jerusalem? A new mission in the far West or pastoral problems back at the home base for Christianity? That was Paul's dilemma. The missionary felt compelled to postpone indefinitely the most ambitious mission he ever dreamed of so that he could go back to Jerusalem and try to get Jews and Gentiles to accept one another. As a pastor, does this bring to your mind some agonizing decisions which you have been compelled to make? What "Jerusalem" have you been forced to place ahead of "Spain"? To put the question another way, How much does what goes on in the local church (or the larger church) have to do with world missions? Can our outreach be any better than what we are at home?

A sermon here could follow on the subject, "First Things First." It could be developed something like this: (1) The Cause before Self. Paul subordinated personal desire to the needs of the church. (2) Church Unity before Outreach. A divided church has no message for a broken world. (3) Self-giving before Substance. The gift without the giver is bare.

What kind of book is Romans to you? Do you think mostly of theology when you think of Romans? The letter is full of theology, some of it very difficult; but Paul did not write it for speculative reasons. The letter was written to deal with a problem which was splitting the church and jeopardizing missionary outreach. It was the problem of getting along with one another. In this case it had to do with the relationship between Jews and Gentiles (Paul calls Gentiles "Greeks"). The feeling between these two groups was so strong that it was carried over even into the church. Paul sensed that this problem struck at the very heart of the gospel. For him it was pointless to go to Spain with a reconciling gospel if behind him was an unreconciled church, split between Jews and Gentiles.

Romans is theological throughout, but its theology is down-to-earth. It is geared to the question of Jews and Gentiles under God—both in judgment and in salvation. It affirms that God is righteous in his dealing with both Jews and Gentiles. He judges each fairly. He offers salvation to each on terms within the competence of each. That is what Romans is about. Since the issues of life remain basically the same, Romans can speak to us today just as it intended to do long ago when Paul wrote it.

Although the Jew-Gentile relationship dominates the whole of Romans, there are many other related issues: sin, salvation, security, freedom, responsibility, moral integrity, ethical responsibility, inner struggles between impulses toward good and impulses toward evil, basic relationships in the family, in the church, in the workaday world, and in public (civil) life. In this commentary we will look at these issues as Paul treats them, with special attention to what they may mean to our own personal existence and as to how they may serve others through preaching.

To get our bearings, let us observe that Romans was written from Corinth around A.D. 55 (that's about as close as we can pin-point it) just following the Corinthian letters. We can be fairly certain about this through help from Acts and especially by tracing Paul's agonizing over the "collection" for the saints at Jerusalem. He wondered whether he could entrust its delivery to a committee or whether he personally should make the trip (1 Cor 16:1 – 4) so as to implement its ultimate goal. This goal was to get Jewish Christians to accept the Gentiles as well as their money (Rom 15:30 – 32) just as he had sought to get Gentiles to give not only their money but themselves (2 Cor 8 – 9). During the winter in Greece, presumably Corinth (Acts 20:1 – 3), he reached his decision to go personally to Jerusalem with the collection. He did this despite the warnings of his best friends (Acts 20:36 – 38; 21:12 – 14), and despite his eagerness to be on his way to Spain by way of Rome (Rom 15:22 – 25). He undertook this ominous trip to Jerusalem because of an inner compulsion. This was something he had to do for the sake of the unity of the church and the integrity of the Gospel. Romans was written out of this agony. It speaks to us today in terms of our own "Jerusalem before Spain" situations.

It is not likely that Paul wrote from an outline, but there is a traceable movement of thought throughout Romans. It begins with an elaborate greeting, probably anticipating the extreme importance of the issues to be pursued (1:1 – 7). Next Paul introduces the matter of his deep desire to visit Rome, with no hint at this point as to another claim which will delay such a visit (1:8 – 15). The theme of God's righteousness with its universal reference (Jew and Greek) follows in 1:16 – 17. Much of the letter will be a spelling out of the fact of God's being righteous in judgment and salvation, with respect to Jew and Greek (i.e., Gentile).

The section 1:18 – 3:20 paints a very dark picture, that of the universality of sin: its origin, nature, pervasion of all human life, and its results. Taken alone, this is a most dismal picture, seemingly negative throughout. But this passage does not stand alone in Romans. It is the dark foil against which Paul presents the righteousness of God expressed positively in salvation (3:21 – 8:39). This section falls into two parts, one dealing with salvation as a new standing with God, made pos-

sible out of the sheer grace of God (3:21 – 4:25). The other side
of salvation is shown to be a new kind of existence made possible by this new standing (5:1 – 8:39). Salvation is gift, and a
good gift. It is God's work, and it is good work. It is by grace,
but not by cheap grace. It is liberty for good but not license for
evil.

Chapters 9 – 11 come to the heart of Paul's concern, the
Jew and Gentile under God and in relationship with one another. This is the issue which turned Paul back to Jerusalem
and which delayed his dream of a mission to Spain by way of
Rome. This is a hard section, but its basic intention is clear
enough. In chapter 9 Paul argues that the Jew can be lost. In
chapter 10 he shows why: the refusal to respond to God's overture. In chapter 11 he argues that the Gentile too can be lost
and the two can yet be saved.

In 12:1 – 15:13 Paul spells out how the righteousness of
God is to penetrate our existence in our individual lives as
well as in our many relationships: family, church, community, state, etc. In 15:14 – 32 Paul finally "lets down his hair" or
bares his heart, speaking explicitly and movingly about his
commitment to a mission to Jerusalem, one which could fail
but which he trusts will succeed. He begs the Romans for their
prayerful support to the end that he be delivered from "the
disobedient ones" in Jerusalem and that his "mission" become acceptable to "the saints." Chapter 16 stands to itself,
concerned with personal greetings, unusually tender in appre-
ciation and expectation, with special significance for us today
as we reassess the role of woman in the church.

Paul's Greeting and Opening Statement
(Romans 1:1-17)

Greetings (1:1-7)

A man under claim—that is how Paul introduced himself to the Christians in Rome. He saw himself as *slave* of Christ Jesus, an *apostle* by calling, and one set apart for the *gospel* of God. That was his self-image. It implied his accountability to God first and last, ultimately to none other than God. It implied mission to the world and to the church.

Slave of Christ Jesus. A *slave* in the Roman Empire was the property of his master, with no legal rights of his own. Under Roman law, the master had total claim upon his slave. Paul, a free citizen, would have chafed under such a dehumanizing system; but he proudly yielded as slave to Christ. Paul found not only security as a slave of Christ but also freedom and fulfillment. Christ freed him from every other bondage (Gal 4:7; 5:1). Each one of us lives under some claim, consciously or not. We have no option of living under no master (cf. Matt 6:24). Through the "bondage" which is really freedom and fulfillment, Christ offers freedom from the slavery which robs us of our humanity. *Christ*, like the Hebrew Messiah, means "anointed." He is God's anointed, anointed to rule. Only God has the right to ultimate and absolute claim upon us, and his claim confronts us most directly and fully in his Anointed, Christ Jesus. *Jesus* is the Greek form for the Hebrew name Joshua, which means "JHWH Savior." Christ Jesus is God himself come to us in a genuine human life, claiming us fully as his own. He is our Savior only by becoming our Lord. Though created in the likeness of God and commissioned to rule over the rest of creation (Gen 1:26 – 2:3), we were created to be under God. Our true fulfillment is to be *under* God, *with* one another as persons, and *over* the rest of creation.

A called apostle. "Called" is an adjective in the Greek text,

not a verb. The same adjective is found in v. 7, *called saints.*
Our basic calling is to discipleship. All are "called" in this
sense. This is our basic vocation (calling). We are called to
faith (trust) in God as we meet him in Christ Jesus, thus finding acceptance and a new kind of existence as God's gift of
grace to us. There are further callings to various ministries,
one being that of *apostle.* The apostles were people "sent" or
commissioned to witness to Christ Jesus, with special attention to his resurrection (Acts 1:21–22; 1 Cor 9:1). Calling
stresses God's initiative in our salvation and ministry. Initiative always is with God, not us. He calls and we answer. He
calls but does not coerce. Our humanity is preserved in our being called, for we are given the awesome option of saying yes
or no even to God (see 1:18–32). *Saints* are people "set apart"
by God and unto God. All God's people are saints, the term being used by Paul for all people under redemption. We are
saints though yet sinners, sinners who are being saved (see 1
Cor 1:18).

Separated unto the gospel of God. The gospel is the good
news from God and about God. The gospel of God is also the
gospel of his son (1:1, 9; see also Mk 1:1, 14). Some theology
seems to imply: "Now there is good news and bad news; the
good news is Jesus but the bad news is God." Instead, Jesus is
the good news from God and about God. God is like Jesus
Christ. He is God come to save us. He is Immanuel, "God with
us." Paul saw God as one (Rom 3:30); and he could refer to
"the Spirit of God" (8:9), "the Spirit of Christ" (8:9), "Christ"
(8:10), and "the Spirit of the one raising Jesus" (8:11) as the
same divine presence. Hence the good news of Jesus Christ is
"the gospel of God."

There is a sermon here on "Self Image." Before one is able
to minister to others one must have a healthy self-image. This
is not to be confused with selfishness or "navel gazing." There
is a self-affirmation which is not vain or selfish. There is a self-
affirmation which is the reverse side of self-denial. Like Paul
we can see ourselves as belonging to Christ, under his total
claim, yet called to discipleship and commissioned to the high
privilege of proclaiming the good news from and about God.
We can be bound yet free, "slaves" yet fulfilled. Paul wrote
this letter to Rome and set out to Jerusalem seeking the understanding and support of Christians in both cities, but

Christ Jesus had the final claim upon him—not even the church! Put in question form, a sermon subject could be, "How Do You View Yourself?" This could be answered in terms of identity (who and whose you are) and purpose (one's sense of vocation).

There are sermons here on vocation. All of us are called to faith and salvation. All are called to enroll in the school of Christ. Discipleship is to come under Christ's discipline: his lordship and teaching. All of us are called to ministry, although ministering roles differ widely (see 12:4–8). Some are called to special leadership roles as "equipping ministers" (see Eph 4:12), but all are called to some ministry.

Shalom. Absolute Lordship does not degrade us; it is our fulfillment. Where there is the "obedience which arises out of faith" (v. 5), we have "peace" (v. 7). To Paul as a Jew "peace" meant *"shalom,"* well-being under the sovereign care of God. *Grace* is God's favor, his goodness out of which we live. Peace is the quality of existence afforded us under his sovereign care. It is not a matter of the good Jesus saving us from a hostile Father; grace and peace come from the God who likewise is our Father, and it comes from God through our Lord Jesus Christ.

The opening paragraph of Romans is rich in texts out of which significant sermons should grow. First of all, God! If we miss it here, the rest is hopeless. The oneness of God is not compromised in Romans, and we dare not compromise it. Neither do we have to obscure the doctrine of God by using a lot of jargon which neither we nor our people understand. Christ Jesus is our clearest and fullest picture of God. God is like Jesus. There is good news from God and about God, and Christ Jesus is that good news. The gospel of Jesus Christ is the gospel of God (see Mk 1:1, 14).

In preaching the oneness of God known to us variously as Father, Son, and Holy Spirit (as well as Creator, Revealer, Judge, Shepherd, Savior, Comforter, and otherwise) a good "model" drawn from everyday life will help. In truth, all the above terms are models. God is not literally anyone of these, but these models help us understand who he is and what he is like. I have found in preaching that the personal model communicates best. Person may not be an adequate model, but it is the best we have. We know God as we know a person. We know him relationally, only as we relate. We relate in many roles, capacities, and situations. My wife knows me as husband, my children as father, and my parents knew me as son. You know me as a writer. I am not many; I am one. I am not part son, part husband, part father, and part writer. I am each in my wholeness. I am encountered and known variously, but I am one. God is like that. He is one, yet we know him in many ways. We know him only as we relate. We know him only partially (relatively), never fully, just as we know no one fully, not even ourselves.

A clear doctrine of God seen in his oneness will help overcome the fallacy of an angry Father appeased by a loving Son. It will overcome the shallow spirituality which sees the Holy Spirit as a separate God, or separate part of God, more "spiritual" than Father or Son. It gives a solid foundation for a unified and healthy humanity, for only if God is one is there hope that we be holistic as individuals and live in unity as his people. A fragmented God cannot give wholeness to broken humanity.

The good news about God is good news to those who have the trust that obeys (v. 5). He offers grace and peace. Grace is the new ground God gives us upon which to stand (acceptance and reconciliation), and it is the new power out of which we live. Peace is God's order, not tyranny or coercion but well-being under God's rule. This is not for Jews only but for "all the Gentiles" as well (v. 5). All of us may be "called ones of Jesus Christ" and "ones beloved of God" (vv. 6– 7). The oneness of God means that there may be the oneness of humankind, Jew and Gentile. Remember that Jesus grounded the love commandment in the oneness of God (Mk 12:29– 34). Romans is concerned with oneness of Jew and Gentile in Christ. Were there two or more gods or were God divided, there would be no hope for a fragmented world. God is one God, and his grace and peace are intended for all people. God has entered history in one who is truly human, so God's grace and peace are readily available to all people.

A suggested subject here is, "How Should We View God?" Possible development could be: (1) As one—not three. (2) As one who is like Jesus—in character. (3) As one who is on our side—redemptively. (4) As one who would make us one—not divide us. This is good news!

Paul's Desire to Visit Rome (1:8–15)

Not until chapter 15 does Paul tell the Romans that he has decided in favor of Jerusalem rather than Rome, but this early in the letter he begins to lay the groundwork for it. He will close the letter with an agonizing appeal to the Romans to give him prayerful support in his ominous mission to Jerusalem, but from the outset he wants them to know how much he yearns to visit them. Actually he will seek their support in two directions: in a mission to Jerusalem and then to Spain (15:22–32). Although he intends to make these heavy demands upon the Romans, he does not intend just to use them. No self-respecting person wants to be used. He has great esteem for them and affection for them. He feels that he has something to offer them but also to receive from them. Paul maintains a careful balance between giving and receiving. He begins with the promise of "some spiritual gift" which he may impart (v. 11), but he immediately puts this in better focus by proposing a mutual benefit as their faith and his meet (v. 12).

What a sermon lurks here! Paul's self-image is positive. For all the greatness and fame of the church at Rome, Paul has no doubt but that he has something for their further enrichment. He has no intention of going to Rome "hat in hand" as a mere suppliant. On the other hand, Paul has respect for the Romans as seen here and in chapter 15. They have something for his personal enrichment as well as for the support of his missions to Jerusalem and Spain. Although it is not until later that he used the beautiful expression "having koinonia in the matter of giving and receiving" (Phil 4:15), that is what is implied already in Romans. True koinonia must work both ways: in giving and receiving. Paul was secure enough to offer help and to accept help from the Romans. Here is a model for us today. You might entitle a sermon: "Koinonia in Giving and Receiving" and demonstrate it from Romans. Such a sermon could be a catalyst for the salvage, renewal, or enrichment of many who hear you preach.

"I am debtor!" Paul already has received; he is under obligation to give. Paul acknowledged debt to Greeks and barbarians (cultured and uncultured Gentiles from a Greek perspective), to the wise and unwise (probably the same groups under a different stereotype). For Paul to acknowledge debt to Gentiles, cultured or uncultured, was to have come a long way from the pride of Saul of Tarsus. By debtor he clearly meant that he owed it to them to preach the gospel to them, for this is explicit in v. 15. But more seems to be intended. Paul had drawn heavily upon the Gentiles. The Greek language in which he wrote Romans was of Gentile origin. The roads he travelled were Roman roads. Greek and Roman cultures had influenced him in many ways, for no man is an island and no ethnic or religious group is an island. Jew, Greek, Roman, and those called barbarian all lived in such dependence upon one another that there was giving and receiving whether conscious or not, intended or not.

Paul was a debtor in a double sense: he benefited from the larger world of which he was a part, and he had been entrusted with a gospel designed for all people. Here is a sermon for us all. It might be entitled, "No Islands Among Us." There are no "self-made men" or "self-made women." There are none who can rightly boast that they are "beholden of nobody." We are all debtors not only to God but to all the people who have a part in producing or preparing the food we eat, the gadgets we use, the language we speak, the books we read, the protection we count on, etc. We will see more of this in Rom 13, with respect to our debt to the civil order and in Rom 14 with respect to individuals about us. We have a special debt with respect to the gospel, the good news about the one God and from the one God and intended for Jew and Gentile.

Suggested Subject: "How Do You View Others?" It could be developed thus: (1) As persons from whom you receive. (2) As persons to whom you can contribute. (3) As persons of such worth that Christ died for them.

The Power of the Gospel (1:16–17)

When I began preaching as a lad of 19 years I was very shy, and this gave me no reason to challenge the popular understanding of Paul's claim not to be "ashamed" of the Gospel. I thought that he meant that he was not embarrassed to get up and preach. Through the years I have come to what probably is a better understanding of Paul's intention. There is no hint anywhere that Paul was ever timid or shy. He seems always to have "come on strong," before his conversion and after. Saul of Tarsus was a proud man, and it was a shattering experience when his encounter with the living Christ compelled him to abandon positions which he had so zealously defended and turn to one whom he had scorned. Paul lets us in on something of that trauma in passages like Gal 1:23; 1 Cor 15:9; Phil 3:2–11; 1 Tim 1:12–17.

The shame which Paul now does not fear is that of disappointment. He once was put to shame by having found that many of his most cherished treasures had to be discarded as not "gains" but "loss" (Phil 3:7). He had known the shattering experience of that moment of truth when he came to see that one whom he had despised was his rightful Lord and that the people whom he had persecuted were his brothers and sisters in the family of God. He had been wrong about the Gentiles, wrong about circumcision, wrong about true righteousness, and wrong about much of which he had been most confident and outspoken. It was a trauma to have to confess that he had been wrong in a zeal so strong that it was expressed in persecuting the very people with whom he now identified (Gal 1:13). It is most difficult to admit wrong—to oneself and to the public. What about our willingness as preachers to admit that we have been wrong? Sermons here may well attend to this need—our admitting to our people that we many times have been wrong and helping them through this same trauma.

Sermons are needed, too, on the side of confidence, as "A Gospel Which Produces What It Promises." It can reconcile a sinner to God. It can reconcile people as far apart as Jews and Gentiles. It can reverse the course of a life, from self-destruction to fulfillment.

One might ask Paul: Since you confess that you were wrong before, how do you know that you are not wrong now about the gospel? Of course, we can be wrong a second time and many times; and the fact that we have been wrong in the past should temper our present manner. Life is not fail-safe for us fallible humans. However, the very fact of facing one's moment of truth and enduring the trauma of having to reverse one's course should be a plus and not a minus. Paul could be wrong a second time, but his confidence is in the compelling force of that Presence which turned him about. His former "treasures" were largely handed down to him; his faith now and his gospel have become his through an agony which has yielded a tested and chastened faith.

Paul is now confident that the Gospel which he preaches is dependable. He will not be put to shame again by preaching what must be discarded. The Gospel is indeed God's power to save anyone who will trust, Jew or Greek (=Gentile). The faith for which he once had fought was a borrowed one. He had carried theological luggage which others had placed in his hands. He had defended a tradition into which he had been born. This is not to say that one's heritage is necessarily wrong. It can be profoundly right. However, authentic faith must be one's own, not borrowed. Positively, it was nothing less than Paul's encounter with the risen Christ which turned him around. Paul's confidence in the Gospel he preached was based not simply on tradition or logic but upon his personal experience of Christ. The faith he now held was not one he had sought but one he had resisted. His faith was not an extension of his bias or prejudice; it was one which overcame positions to which he had tried to cling.

"The just shall live by faith!" Drawing upon Habakkuk 2:4, Paul found in this text the heart of the Gospel he proclaims in Romans. Our problem is in capturing its full intention. A paraphrase may do it best: "The righteous person is the one who lives by faith in the faithfulness of God." Righteousness is not a human achievement. Righteousness is not the product of a series of religious acts: circumcision, food laws, Sabbath observance, etc. True righteousness is a kind of existence which only God can bring about in a human life. The righteous person lives out of the goodness of God. Life itself is the gift of God's grace (6:23). Love, joy, peace, patience, kindness, goodness, faith/faithfulness, self-control, and the like are the fruit of God's Spirit (Gal 5:22).

An ad has it that the test of a good tire is "where the rubber meets the road." Paul has it that to live in true righteousness is a reality where the faith of mankind meets the faithfulness of God. That is the saving Gospel. God is righteous and we may become righteous. God is trustworthy, so we may confidently trust him. God is faithful, so we may have faith in him. Faith is more than theology, more than believing this or that. Saving faith is the openness to God which admits him into one's life as a saving presence. That probably is what Paul means by "from faith unto faith" (v. 17). God has faith in us before we have faith in him. We have no hesitation to accept the truth that God loves us. Do we believe that he trusts us? Does not creation itself imply that? God trusted us enough to make us capable of trusting or distrusting him, loving or hating him. God made himself vulnerable to our hurting him. Faith always is vulnerable. To trust is to risk being hurt. From faith unto faith is our faith responding to God's prior faith in us.

But there is more. The Greek word for faith (*pistis*) clearly means "faithfulness" in 3:3. God's righteousness begins to take shape in us when our faith responds to his faithfulness: from faithfulness of God to faith on our part. Of course, just as God both exercises faith in us and remains faithful to us, we are called to faith and faithfulness. God's faith in us and faithfulness to us should awaken in us the faith which is faithful: from the faith that is faithful (God's) to the faith that is faithful (ours).

"From Faith unto Faith" is sufficiently rich in sound exegetical possibilities for such sermonic developments as: faith from start to finish, from faith to greater faith (qualitative as well as quantitative), from God's faith in us to our faith in him, from faith to faithfulness. A sermon could be preached on the subject, "How Do You View Saving Faith?" It could be developed thus: (1) It must be your own, not borrowed. (2) It must be personal trust, not just theology. (3) It must be a journey, not just a destination.

God's Righteousness
in Judgment
(Romans 1:18–3:20)

The Wrath of God (1:18–32)

Although the term *orge*, usually rendered wrath, appears about thirty times in the NT, only here is "the wrath of God" explicitly identified or characterized. Paul's usage must be found here, not read into the passage from elsewhere. What is said is plain enough, and what is omitted is significant. Just examine the passage. There is no reference to Adam or the Fall. There is no mention of Satan. There is no apocalyptic language. It is not that we have suppressed such references but that Paul makes no mention of them in what probably is his most profound, depth-analysis of sin: its origin, nature, and results.

This passage is a sermon in itself. Most "hell-fire and damnation" sermons on sin are shallow compared to this awesome passage. In brief, Paul sees "God's wrath" to be one expression of God's righteousness. Notice that the subject of 1:17 is "God's righteousness" and that of 1:18 is "God's wrath." Paul has not changed subjects, although there may seem to be an abrupt change. The overriding subject remains God's righteousness, and 1:18–32 traces one expression of that righteousness. It is because God is righteous that he delivers over to themselves (vv. 24, 26, 28) those who choose not to know him (vv. 21, 28). Because he is righteous, God does not take back our freedom of choice, even if we use it perversely and to our ruin. God so respects the creature made in his image that he will permit that one to exercise freedom even to the extremes described in this passage. Put one way, "the wrath of God" is the outworking of sin in a human life, the self-destruction which a sinner brings upon self. Put another way, "the wrath of God" is his faithfulness to us in respecting our freedom, turning us over to ourselves when we choose self against him. God makes himself knowable; he warns and pleads; but God does not coerce or impose himself upon us. In giving us the power to trust he thus gives us the power to distrust and destruct.

Let's see how Paul traces out this outworking of God's wrath. V. 18 puts the finger on the sore spot, mankind's suppressing or holding down the truth. This is not a matter of ignorance; it is wilful choice. What truth or reality? V. 19 pinpoints what it is that man suppresses: it is the knowledge of God. Mankind refused to know God. The knowledge alluded to here is not information about something but rather personal acquaintance. One kind of knowledge is that of a thing, a subject (person) having information about some thing. This is not saving knowledge. Another kind of knowledge is personal acquaintance, as when you "know" another person. This is the meeting of two subjects, not a subject and object. Salvation occurs only as God and we meet person to person. We cannot discover God but he can make himself knowable to us. God does this, but we yet can refuse to know him in a relationship of trust. Paul clearly affirms that God has from the beginning of the creation been engaged in making himself knowable through all that he has made or done (v. 19). Of course, Paul taught that it is in Jesus Christ that God comes personally and fully (2 Cor 5:19, Col 2:9), but he also taught that God shows something of himself in all creation and history.

Man's fateful choice is his refusal to know God for who he really is, the God worthy of our worship and gratitude (v. 21). Although Paul makes no explicit reference to Gen 3, he pictures each one who brings upon himself the wrath of God as repeating the sin of Adam: the assertion of self in the place of God. Man tends to worship the creature rather than the creator (v. 23). The creature man most worships is himself. His folly is the self-trust, self-love, and self-assertion which come at the price of keeping God out of any meaningful place in one's life. There is a proper affirmation of self and love of self (see Mk 12:31), but the self to be loved and affirmed is the one emerging in a relationship of trust with God, never apart from God or from other people.

A major dimension of "the wrath of God" is the damage one does to oneself in cutting oneself off from God. Paul puts it this way: "their senseless heart was darkened" (v. 21). In re-

jecting the light one does not put out the light but one does put
out one's sight. To refuse to know God can lead to one's not
being able to know him. One can self-destruct. We can erode
and destroy our God-given powers to see, hear, feel, and know
at the highest level. That is what Jesus taught when he healed
a man born blind only to be opposed by another kind of blind-
ness in the religious piety of his day (John 9). God's wrath is
not a matter of his hurling thunderbolts or arbitrary punishment in any way; it is God's allowing us to exercise the awesome power of freedom even when we so abuse it that we
deaden within ourselves our capacity for the higher life. That
is what Paul means by the wrath of God.

Three times Paul drives home the point: God gave them
over (vv. 24, 26, 28). To what? To whom? The context leaves no
room for doubt. God turned them over to their own stubborn
choices. "We have met the enemy and it is us!" The choice to
shut God out of one's life is a choice in the direction of ruin. It
is a choice for less and less. Seeking more, we get less. Paul
traces this in two directions: the breakdown of the individual
(vv. 24 – 27) and the breakup of the human family (vv. 28 – 32).
He illustrates the first result in terms of homosexuality,
though other examples could be traced. Created to be a full
person in relationship with God, some became only males and
females. Sexuality is a proper and significant aspect of our
God-given humanity, but when existence is reduced to being
only males and females, this is reductionism. Homosexuality
is one step further in the reductionism, where the male/fe-
male relationship designed in creation becomes male/male or
female/female. Salvation is fulfillment, not reduction. Salvation is God's work in enabling us to become fully human: in
relationship with God, with other persons, with ourselves,
and with all creation. The sin which begins with cutting God
out goes on to cut out more and more of what belongs
necessarily to true humanity.

Vv. 28 – 32 trace the wrath in another direction, in the
breakup of the community. Into the void left by the refusal to
know God is poured such ugly anti-social vices as envy, jealousy, greed, hate, slander, strife, etc. To see how negative and
ugly this list is, compare it with the fruit of the Spirit (Gal
5:22).

V. 28, with a play on words, is a basic key to our whole

passage: When they "proved" not to have God in their knowledge, God gave them over to an "unapproved" mind. Put another way, man put God to the test and "flunked" him, compelling God to give man over to the mind which really flunked in flunking God. This is not "impersonal" wrath. God is not thus represented as leaving creation to natural law. Paul means that God makes every provision for man's salvation, but God will not override man's freedom. In the final analysis, we make the choice of our own destiny. God is free enough to give us freedom, and he is righteous enough not to take it back when we use it against him and against ourselves. To override our freedom would not be our salvation but another form of our destruction. We may self-destruct but God does not destroy us.

Preaching should not hedge with respect to "The Wrath of God." Sermons should show that it is precisely because God respects our humanity (free and responsible) that he turns us over to our choosing when we insist. What about a sermon on "The Power to Self-destruct?" Another could be, "The Love That Lets Us Go," showing that God's love does not fail or forsake us, but it is a love which respects our freedom even if we use it to our ruin. Yet another subject could be "How Do You View Freedom?" It belongs necessarily to human existence. It may be used to one's ruin. Experienced in Christ it means life.

God's Righteousness in Judgment (2:1–16)

Paul makes two major points in this passage: (1) God is just (righteous) in judging any sinner and (2) God is impartial in judging sinners, in particular with respect to Jew and Gentile. In supporting the first point, Paul appeals to two factors: man's practice of judging other people (v. 1) and the fact of conscience, a sense of right and wrong found universally (v. 14). One of our favorite pastimes is that of criticizing one another. In the very act of judging another we acknowledge our ability to tell the difference between right and wrong or good and evil. This means that we are accountable. Paul warns that we do not escape being judged by turning it on others; rather we thus invite heavier judgment upon ourselves. Jesus warned against the folly of seeking to evade judgment by climbing upon the judge's bench (Matt 7:1– 6). What about a sermon here on "Who Judges the Judges?"

In a sermon today on judging, it is well to acknowledge that the *fact* of our judging is inescapable. There is no way to put our minds into neutral and not have value judgments about everyone and everything under our observation. It is normal for us to weigh, measure, and approve or disapprove what comes before us. The problem is not here. What we dare not forget are our limitations: fallible, biased, prejudiced, too hard on some and too easy on others, etc. Also, we dare not forget that though by nature we are endowed with the capacity to judge, we have not been appointed judges over one another. Paul's point is not that we should engage in no acts of judging but that we should face up to the implications of the fact that we do judge one another. It means above all that we thus leave ourselves open to being judged. God has the right to judge us, and only he has the knowledge and integrity sufficient for a final judgment upon anyone. There is room for a sermon here on "Bringing Judgment under Discipline" or "The Limits Within Which We Judge."

The fact of conscience is Paul's second major argument for the justice of God as he judges sinners. God does not hold one accountable beyond his competence. Responsibility is ability to respond. Paul saw that the Gentiles have by nature the power of discerning, even without the help of the Mosaic law (v. 14). In v. 15 he makes explicit reference to conscience. It does not follow that conscience is always right; in fact, conscience is no better guide than the light it has. Many sincere people do deplorable things in good conscience, as in the case of pagan mothers who have given their precious babies to the god they were taught to worship. Sincerity is good, but it is not enough. Paul's point is that conscience is a fact, and that God does not impose judgment upon people incapable of sensing right and wrong. A sermon here might follow on the subject, "The Implications of Conscience." Some implications are accountability and the need conscience has for both light and integrity.

The impartiality of God in judging Jew and Gentile is a major concern of this passage. Paul argues that God does not judge the Gentile by the Jew's advantage. He judges the Gentile in terms of the revelation he has and the conscience he has (vv. 9 – 16). Many of us are not comfortable with this doctrine. In fact we are less comfortable with it than is Scripture. We might do well to ponder this. Scripture sees God as having always been engaged in making himself knowable to people, forgiving their sins, and saving them. God may be reaching some people in ways unknown to us. It is not our proper function to make pronouncements upon this. It is well for us to respect Paul's point: God is righteous in judging people, Jew or Gentile. The greater the advantage, as with the Jew, the greater the accountability. On the other hand, the least advantaged are subject to such judgment as falls within their own limits or competence and advantage.

In any sermon today on this passage, people will be listening for the implication of this for missions. If God can reach Gentiles through what he is doing in all history and through their conscience, why engage in missions or evangelism? This question becomes more acute in light of the fact that to increase advantage is to increase accountability. Why not let good enough alone? But there is more to be said. Salvation is not just a matter of standing; it is a matter of condition. There is a quality of existence which Jesus Christ came to give us, and this enrichment of life is a vital part of what is to be offered in evangelism and missions. Surely, any new light carries with it new peril; but there is no significant life without risk. God himself took a calculated risk in creation, creating us with awesome potential for good and evil. Parents take calculated risk in bringing children into the world, for a child can be sick or healthy, highly gifted or retarded, and grow up to be beautiful or criminal. All meaningful life is with risk. So with missions. The preached gospel opens up the possibility of new dimensions for life; it does so at the calculated risk that those hearing may be worsened.

A sermon on "Missions and Risk" would open the way to the discussion of the many sides to this issue: the heightening of options for the enrichment of life, the accountability of advantage, and the risk in all creative life.

We often hear sermons on why there can be suffering in a world over which a good God supposedly rules, but Paul deals with a different though related problem in vv. 4–8, that of what may be interpreted as the softness of God. He warns against confusing God's patience with indifference. The forbearance and kindness of God intend to bring us to repentance; they do not imply God's indifference to evil (v.

4). To seemingly get away with sin for a time may lull one into the illusion that one can get away with it forever. V. 5 introduces again the matter of "wrath," with the reminder that in keeping with God's righteous judgment there is a day of wrath, i.e., a time of reckoning. This does not imply arbitrary punishment for sin but rather the fact that sin carries within itself its own penalties. This is not a light doctrine of sin. On the contrary, it is the most serious view possible. If punishment has to be from the outside, the problem is not in sin but in the enforcement officer. Sin is like cancer; it has within itself its destructive force. It is the presence of cancer, not its detection, which is the problem. So with sin. Our people need to have this understanding of sin, else they may suffer the illusion that it is enough to have a good God. The sinful act may be forgiven, but the reality of sin in a life calls for cure.

A sermon here could follow on the subject, "The Peril of Misreading the Goodness of God." It may be shown that human well-being is bound up with condition and not just standing. Sin produces its results even though the sinner is loved by God and good people.

What It Means to Be a Jew (2:17–3:8)

At this point Paul chides his fellow-Jews for priding themselves in the privileges of being Jews without due attention to the obligations belonging to privilege. In effect he asks them if they practice what they preach (2:17–23). Doctrine is like medicine; it must be taken. Medicine in a bottle with the stopper left in helps nobody. Doctrine embalmed in creeds does nothing for life. Only as embodied do doctrinal, moral, or ethical teachings achieve their goal. What about a sermon on the subject, "The Proof of the Pudding is in the Eating?"

V. 24 is devastating. God's name is dishonored in the world by those who claim to be his people but who disregard his requirements. The cause of Christ is hurt more by those of us who claim to be Christian yet go contrary to his teaching and example than by those attacking it from outside. The most subtle and damaging "atheism" is that of people who profess to believe in God but ignore his expressed will. Sermon suggestion: "Atheism Anonymous," showing that the deadliest atheism generally goes unnamed.

In 2:25– 29 Paul makes a clear distinction between outward conformity to some religious standard and inward conformity to the will of God. True circumcision is not something made by cutting off some skin with a knife; it is rather something which God does within one's "heart." A true "Jew" is not one who physically descends from a certain ethnic line; he/she is one who has inner qualities pleasing to God. One may outwardly satisfy the requirements of people, but what counts is to be found pleasing to God. Already in Gal 3:28 Paul had boldly declared that "in Christ" there is no Jew nor Gentile, bond nor free, male nor female. These differences are real, but they have no relevance to salvation or ministry for those whose new quality of existence is derived from their vital relationship with Jesus Christ.

What about preaching this today? Paul's distinction between outward conformity and inward quality—in terms of "circumcision" and "Jew"—can apply today to us and our religious experience. What about such practices as baptism and communion? Jesus spoke of a "baptism" and a "cup" which go far beyond literal baptism or communion (Mk 10:38). What he demanded of his disciples is not dispensable: enduring with him his "baptism" and drinking with him his "cup." Millions have experienced some form of water baptism and partaken of a ritual act of communion. Dare we take as radical a position with respect to such matters as Jesus or Paul did? Do we cling to "brittle skins" which long since have lost the "wine"? Dare we identify the family of God as Paul did in the verses before us—judged strictly in terms of inner qualities of personhood and not by creedal, cultic, ethnic, or other such secondary tests? Paul seems clearly to follow in the tradition of Jesus, who declared: "Whoever does the will of God is my brother and sister and mother" (Mk 3:35). Do we? Dare we preach accordingly? Forms, structures, creeds, and much else in religion may serve us, but they likewise are vulnerable to becoming "skins" without "wine." Failure to know the difference may enslave and impoverish the devout. Refusal to acknowledge the difference is a form of idolatry. It is the proper function of prophetic preaching to distinguish between "wine" and "skins." There is no easy check-list for either; sensitivity to the difference comes with a questing faith and a mind constantly being renewed (12:2).

The Universality of Sin (3:9–20)

Jew and Greek (Gentile) are in the same boat! Both are guilty before God. There is no meaningful future for either unless sin is honestly confessed. There is not one truly righteous person upon the earth (v. 10). Every boasting mouth must be stopped (v. 19). God has good news for mankind, but his first word to the proud or boasting sinner must be, "Shut up." With this is the companion word, "Listen." Sinners may talk with God and walk with God but only if they confess that he is right and they are wrong.

V. 9 repeats the argument: there is no ultimate difference between Jew and Gentile, for both are found guilty and stand under judgment for their sin. Paul then presents a catena (chain) of references from the OT, a devastating exposure of the extent and depth of human sin. Mankind as a whole is characterized by senseless self-seeking, turning away from God, neglect of goodness, speech filled with deceit and arrogance, inclination toward cruelty and destruction, strangers to peace, and lack of reverence for God. Man is most hopeless not because of his sins—as bad as they are—but because of his false pride and confidence in himself.

Karl Barth's commentary on Romans (1918) is probably the most powerful preaching on this passage known to us. He captured the Word of God behind the words in Romans. Only as we are willing to hear God's "No!" to all our sin and all our proud boasts as to our virtues or achievements is it possible to hear his "Yes!" We hear much today about "self-affirmation," but this is false if it is not first of all an honest admission of our guilt. We are all sinners, and to fail to include our sin in our self-affirmation is to falsify the self we intend to affirm. Paul's point is that God in his faithfulness to us is willing to affirm and save sinners, but he does not thus ignore the fact of our sins. No less than does God may we deny our sin and enjoy any meaningful self-affirmation. Let us hear God's "No" that we may hear his "Yes." That is Paul's gospel in Romans. A sermon here could be entitled, "Hearing God's No That We May Hear His Yes." Another topic might be, "Taking our Sins into Our Self-Affirmation." This is who we are, persons of worth yet persons in sin.

The Righteousness of God in Salvation
(Romans 3:21 – 8:39)

Upon working through 1:18 – 3:20 with a class once, a student voiced an understandable response: That's pretty negative isn't it? Taken alone, Paul's first major development is negative, but it is real. Not only so, but it is the foil against which the righteousness of God is best seen. It is the dark background against which salvation as the gift of God's grace is best seen. Just as God remains just (righteous) as he judges Jew and Gentile, so God remains just (righteous) when he saves sinners, Jew and Gentile. Salvation is his gift, not a human achievement (3:21 – 4:25). Salvation is a good gift, not mere indulgence (5 – 8). God's righteousness is seen in that he provides new standing for sinners who have forfeited their rights and by releasing his own power so as to bring about a new quality of life for those who trust him.

Salvation as New Standing with God (3:21–4:25)

This section will reassert the fact of sin, but its concern is to ascribe salvation to God's mighty work, mankind's part being to receive it by faith. God is the active giver, but man is not simply negative; faith itself is an active response to the initiative of God. Although salvation is gift, it is not imposed. It must be received, and only through the openness of faith as trust may it be received.

Righteousness through Faith (3:21–31)

"Apart from law" apparently means from the Law given through Moses. Paul's point in v. 21 is that God's righteousness is not tied to the Mosaic Law, and the Scriptures themselves attest to this. They show that God saved Abraham (a prime example) before the Law was given through Moses and before Abraham was circumcised. Salvation is rooted in the personhood of God himself, not in something secondary, even if it is as important as the Law of Moses.

Preaching at this point is urgent. Wherever did we get the idea that God's hands were tied until some event in history took place, even events so significant as the giving of the Law through Moses or the crucifixion of Jesus? The Bible clearly teaches that there has never been a time when God could not forgive sins and save sinners, conditioned only upon their willingness to hear him and trust him. There did not have to be some transaction by which God was appeased or satisfied before he could or would forgive sins and save sinners. This does not invalidate the Law or the Cross, but it compels a closer study of the whole matter in the Bible. God saved Abraham! That says it. What God has done further in terms of revelation and penetration into his world, as in the incarnation, is extension and intensification of what from the beginning he has been doing to save sinners.

"Through faith of Jesus Christ!" This is a close rendering of Paul's Greek in v. 21. Presumably he means that God's righteousness in saving us is manifested as we trust Jesus Christ. It is God himself whom we meet in Jesus Christ. To trust Jesus is to trust God. Greek syntax permits the idea that God's righteousness is manifested in the faith which Jesus Christ exercised. Already we have seen in 1:17 the possible meaning: God's righteousness is revealed "from faith unto faith," i.e., from his prior act of faith in us to the faith thus awakened in us. Whatever Paul's intention, God does trust us before we trust him. Creation itself was an act of faith, as God gave us such awesome freedom. God's supreme act of faith was when the Word became flesh and dwelt among us. Saving faith on our part is a radical commitment to the very God who from the first has trusted us and whose self-giving trust reached its highest point in Jesus Christ. A suggested sermon topic is "Trusting the God Who First Trusted Us."

"No distinction." Ethnic, cultic, or other distinctions of which world and religion tend to make so much fade into insignificance in the face of our common predicament, the fact of sin. Karl Barth said it eloquently throughout his commentary on Romans to this effect: when we speak of our "virtues" or "achievements" we are competitors; when we confess our sins we are brothers/sisters. He said more, for not only do we become rivals as we stress our merits but we cut ourselves off from our only hope of standing before God when we submit to him our "credentials." Only as we are willing to hear God's "No!" to all our pleading of our merits can we hear his "Nevertheless" and his "Yes." That is what this paragraph is saying. A sermon here could expose the many ways in which we obscure the fact of "No distinction" and falsely represent ourselves as excelling in virtue, thus "deserving" more reward. The sermon could show that we thus cut ourselves off from our only hope—salvation through the grace of God.

"Short of the Glory of God." This must imply the sinner's falling short of God's own goodness, but it may imply more. Sin is falling short of what we were created to be. We were created in the image of God, created to participate freely and responsibly in God's own life and work. How miserably short we have fallen of that. It is precisely this "reduction" which Paul traced in 1:18–32, the awful consequence of refusing to know God. Conversely, salvation is fulfillment, whatever else it is. Salvation is God's work of enabling us to become truly human—nothing more, nothing less, and nothing else. We are not God; we are not angels; we are not mere animals; we are created and redeemed to be truly human.

Suggested here is a sermon on "Salvation as Fulfillment" or "On Becoming Human." The sermon could show how we fall short of the humanity for which we were created, reduced in various ways by our sins or unrealized potential.

Another sermon might be preached on "Caught Short" (v.23). Here sin and human failure may be presented as falling short of the image of God and our own authentic existence. This is the identity question. Liberation Theology takes a different turn in much of the world, embracing the taking of life when seen as necessary. The NT has a doctrine of "Redemption" or Liberation," and it is through "blood," but it is in giving one's own blood and not in taking the other's.

Vv. 24–26 have a heavy concentration of difficult theological terms. We need not read into them all the meanings they have taken on in centuries of theologizing. This by no means implies that centuries of study have not clarified the terms; they have both clarified and obscured. It is when we construct a tight scheme of "transactional atonement" that we read into the passage more than the letter as a whole permits. God did not have to be appeased before he could or would save. Salvation is God's doing.

"Redemption" translates a Greek term which basically means "liberation." The emancipation of a slave by a purchase price is one expression of "redemption," and within limits it serves to indicate what salvation is like. Pressed unduly, this analogy misleads. Jesus did not pay off the Father, the Devil, or anyone else. He "paid" in the sense that to free is costly. Liberation always is costly. Our liberation is from our own disposition to self-destruct in our blind attempt to save ourselves. Paul uses the term twice in Romans, in 3:24 for liberation from the bondage of sin and in 8:23 for liberation from death and decay. Full "redemption" is liberation from all that enslaves, degrades, or defeats what we were created to be. What about a sermon on "Liberation in Christ: Its Nature, Cost, and Results"?

Hilasterion (v. 25) is rendered "propitiation" (KJV) or "expiation" (RSV), the latter more suited to Paul's usage than the former. This is the only occurrence of the term in Paul's writings, but in 1 John 4:10 it clearly refers to God's active work of overcoming or "expiating" sin, not to the passive idea that God is "propitiated" or appeased. The latter is a pagan idea. This expiation of sin is "in his own blood" or "by his own blood." In biblical thought the life is in the blood, and giving one's blood is giving one's life. God has always been "the crucified God," in the sense that he always has related sacrificially to his creation. His self-giving reached its ultimate expression or dimension in Jesus Christ. Jesus did not pay the Father. He is "JHWH Savior" come to us in a saving mission which cost him all that the incarnational event reflects. He paid dearly. He did not pay a collector. There is need for a sermon on "Jesus Paid It All," not with the traditional idea of paying off the Father but in the sense suggested above.

"Just and Justifier" (v. 26). How can God justify a sinner and remain just? That is the question. A sermon is suggested here under the title "How Can a Just God Justify Sinners?" The proper function of a court of justice is to acquit the innocent and convict the guilty. One answer is that God only "counts right" the one who really is wrong. That does not adequately represent Paul's intention. We have already seen that "justification" is richer in Pauline usage than that. It is "to count right" but also "to make right." Forgiveness is creative, in that it deals positively with sin so as to overcome it. Indulgence merely ignores it. "Just and one justifying" renders a Greek adjective and participle, each a cognate of the Greek term for "righteousness." God "right-wizes" the sinner. He not only gives the sinner acceptable standing, but he works within the sinner to bring about a new quality of life. That will be developed in chapters 5–8.

"If God is one" (v. 30). This probably echoes Deut 6:4, the *Shema* recited in every synagogue service. The oneness of God is at the foundation of Old and New Testaments. Paul is not uncertain about the oneness of God. The "if" is to challenge the readers to face up to the implications of monotheism. One God implies that all people are his creation and rightfully belong to him. In v. 23 he charged that all people have sinned and fallen short of the glory of God. There is no difference there. Now he applies the same principle to salvation. Jews and Gentiles are saved alike, on their part through faith. God is as much the God of Gentile as of Jew. In our Gentile-dominated world, we need to confess that God is God of the Jew as much as of the Gentile.

"Corollaries to Monotheism" is a sermon subject opening up a whole cluster of ideas. The oneness of God implies that all people are his creation. Paul extends this to show that all are properly his in redemption. He shows that salvation is open to all on the same basis, that of faith. Points in a sermon could be: (1) one human race, (2) one common plight, (3) one common hope.

The Example of Abraham (4:1–25)

As an uncontested progenitor in faith to Jew and Christian, Abraham was an excellent choice for Paul's purpose. The fact of his salvation is assumed, requiring only an inquiry into the ground for it. Paul argues that if Abraham was justified on the basis of his own works he could boast of his achievement, but this is not the case. Abraham trusted God and this was counted to him as (or unto) righteousness (Gen 15:6). He argues that the worker gets a wage, not as a favor (grace) but as what is owed him (v. 4). That was not the case with Abraham. His was the righteousness accounted to him because he trusted "the one justifying the ungodly" (v. 5). Paul does not pursue

here the other side of "justification," the new quality of life
brought about, concentrating here on the new standing received by trusting in God's grace.

Before or after circumcision? Paul's clincher is reached in
asking a question the answer to which was clear. Did God justify Abraham before or after his circumcision? Of course, it
was before as a comparison of Gen 15:6 and 17:10–11 dis-
closes. Could or would God save Abraham without circumcision? He did! There is not a hint here or elsewhere, as some
theology has it, that Abraham was saved "on credit." God did
not have to await some development in history any more than
he looked to circumcision or other works as conditions for salvation. God's will to save and power to save are within himself, not vested in cultic rites or historical events. In a sense,
Abraham was a "Gentile" (uncircumcised) when God saved
him. Paul concludes that Abraham received circumcision as a
"sign" or "seal" for the righteousness already having been received by faith. Abraham thus is "father" to both circumcised
and uncircumcised, Jew and Gentile. The test is faith, neither
"flesh" (v. 1) nor ceremonial rite (v. 10).

"Those following in the steps of faith" (v. 12). Paul not
only affirms the standing of the uncircumcised who share
Abraham's kind of faith, but he is careful to specify that those
circumcised must also participate in Abraham's faith to enjoy
his blessings with him. One may be saved with or without circumcision, but one cannot be saved without faith.

Sermons much needed today lurk throughout this passage. What about one on "God our Savior." God does not have
to go outside himself for his part in saving us. He needs only to
wait for our response in faith. For many people God has about
lost out to "Jesus" or "the Holy Spirit." Nothing that belongs
authentically to biblical teaching about Jesus or Holy Spirit
need be sacrificed. To be rejected are such understandings of
"atonement" which pit Father and Son against one another or
such pseudo-charismatic understanding as makes Holy Spirit
different from Jesus or God. I have spelled out my understanding of the biblical teaching here in the first chapter of my book
The Holy Spirit Today.

"Not through the Law"(v. 13). Here Paul goes beyond excluding circumcision as necessary to salvation; he excludes
"the Law" itself. Abraham was recognized as justified 29

years before he was circumcised (Gen 15:6, 17:10–11) and 430 years before the Law came through Moses (though Paul does not mention the 430 years here as in Gal 3:17). He repeats the basic argument with some modification, that if the inheritance of the world came to the adherents of the law instead of the promise of God, it would nullify faith and promise in favor of law and adherence. This is just another way of saying that salvation cannot be by our merit and God's grace at the same time. It is one or the other. Paul argues that it always has been by grace and never by human works. This holds for Abraham and his "children," whether these be circumcised or uncircumcised, under the law or not. Paul further holds that the law of itself can only bring "wrath," for it adds the dimension of responsibility without being able to supply the power for its observance. In v. 15 the word *parabasis* is introduced, stressing willful disobedience. There may be involuntary failure, but "transgression" carries the guilt of willful rejection of God's command.

"Life to the dead" (v. 17). Paul closes this section on God's righteousness in providing salvation as new standing by employing three exciting analogies: creation, birth, resurrection. What is it like when God saves a sinner? It is like calling being out of non-being (v. 17), like bringing forth Isaac from Sarah's barren womb (v. 19), and like raising Jesus from the dead (v. 24). This is what is meant by the "grace" out of which God justifies sinners from Abraham to us (v. 16). That is why it depends upon faith and not works on our part. All the ingredients for a powerful sermon are here on the surface of this passage: "Being out of Non-Being" or "The Miracle of Salvation."

V. 17 employs the striking expressions: "the things not being" and "/the things/ being." Creation is not explicit, but this may be implied. If so, this sees God as creating "being" out of "non-being." Possibly the expressions allude to what is explicit in context, the giving of a son to Abraham in his old age and Sarah in both her old age and barrennesss of womb. When God saves a sinner, Jew or Gentile, it is like creating something out of nothing and like giving a child to a couple unable of themselves to produce the child. The final analogy is to the resurrection of Jesus. When God saves a sinner it is by the very power which raised Jesus from the dead. Salvation is a mira-

cle! It is the creative act of God, out of his grace, in keeping
with his promise, and conditioned only upon the faith which
is trust or openness to receive what already God wants to give.
"Over against whom—he believed—God" (v. 17). The adverb *katenanti* basically means "opposite" or "over against."
Paul pictures Abraham as facing God or standing in his presence. This is not incidental. Abraham's radical faith in God
was awakened as he met God personally, as he stood in his
presence. His saving faith was in God, not in anything detach-
able from God. He believed that God had within himself the
will and the power to keep his promises. Even when it seemed
that all hope for a son with Sarah was gone, he yet clung to
hope in what seemed to be hopeless. He trusted God. That is
the faith to which Paul calls his readers.

In addition to the sermon ideas thus far suggested, two
further sermons could be developed thus: "Cursed Be the Ties
that Bind." (1) The ties of sin—universal and beyond human
power to correct. (2) The ties of special privilege, when the
privilege which could be exercised creatively becomes a fetter. (3) The ties of theological misconceptions, as when the
ideas of God, cross, salvation, righteousness, etc. are distort-
ed. Another sermon, "Blest Be the God Who Saves." (1) He
saves because it is his nature. (2) He saves because of our predicament. (3) He saves for an exalted purpose—to enable us to
achieve our humanity.

Salvation as a New Quality of Life (5:1–8:39)

In Rom 5– 8 Paul answers the question raised in 3:26.
How can God justify sinners and yet remain just? If God only
counts righteous those who actually are not righteous, this is
indulgence. It would be like issuing a certificate of health to a
person dying of a terminal disease. It would be like a judge
"fixing" a ticket for a traffic violation. God does not do such.
He receives into full standing the sinner who trusts him, but
in the new relationship are the motives and resources for a
new life. This is Paul's answer to legalists who scorn salvation
without "works." It is Paul's answer to libertines who see salvation by grace as gift without demand, a license to continue
the old life without its penalties.

In chapter 5 Paul introduces the new life in Christ, con-
trasted with the old in Adam. In chapter 6 he refutes the liber-

tine stance that grace is license to sin. In chapter 7 he probes the depths of the competing impulses to good and evil within us. In chapter 8 he traces the victorious life in Christ, from no condemnation to no separation.

Peace with God (5:1–11)

What Paul means by peace is closely related to what he means by reconciliation (vv. 10, 11). Peace does not mean primarily a subjective feeling, although that may follow. What is meant is a right relationship with God. He has overcome the enmity between us and has changed us from his enemies to his friends. Peace as reconciliation with God is not something which comes in addition to justification; it is something belonging to justification itself. When God justifies a sinner, he enters into a personal relationship with the sinner. A human judge may hear a case and justify (or condemn) a plaintiff without becoming personally involved. If he acquits the plaintiff he does not necessarily become his friend, and if he convicts him he does not necessarily become his enemy. If fact, human courts are supposed to be "courts of law" and not "courts of persons," lest in the latter case there be bias or prejudice. However, God is never an indifferent judge. A part of his justifying the sinner is in bringing about a new relationship between himself and the sinner and thus a new quality of life in the sinner. Peace with God is reconciliation with God. This opens the way to peace with oneself and peace with one's situation.

The term "reconciliation" appears first in Paul's writings in 2 Cor 5:18–21. A divided church in Corinth is reminded that "in Christ" God was engaged in the business of reconciling the world to himself. If we are "in Christ," that is our business. Peacemaking is our business. It is in peacemaking that we show ourselves to be the children of God (Matt 5:9). Romans was written as a part of a major effort, along with a gift of money from Gentile churches to Jewish Christians in Jerusalem, to bring about a solidarity between Jews and Gentiles, especially between Jewish and Gentile Christians. Rom 5:1–11, then, is at the heart of the letter's concern. Here Paul stresses peace or reconciliation with God. This is the foundation to the appeal for friendship between people alienated from one another.

Only once does the KJV employ the term "atonement" in the NT, and that is in Rom 5:11 where *katallage* is rendered "atonement"; everywhere else the term is rendered "reconciliation." By "atonement," the KJV meant "reconciliation." Etymology is not always significant in understanding the meaning of a word, but here it is. "Atonement" originally meant "at-one-mind." The Latin "mens" is behind the suffix "ment," and denotes "mind" in the sense of attitude or disposition. Atonement in this sense is God's work of bringing us into "one mind" with himself. Although another Greek word is used in Phil 2:5, the idea is the same: "Have among yourselves the mind which, indeed, you do have in Christ Jesus." The hope that we be reconciled to one another rests in our being reconciled to God. We are to be made "at one" with God. Strictly speaking, God atones sinners. He makes them "at one" with himself. He converts sinners from enemies into friends. God is the active agent, not the passive object in effecting what may be termed peace, reconciliation, or atonement.

The stage is set for a sermon on "God's Peace." A world torn by wars and threatened by nuclear destruction as well as people everywhere frantically seeking "peace of mind" form a part of this setting. Paul is not talking about peace as commonly understood in the world. God's peace holds out hope for peace with oneself and peace with other people, but it means first of all being reconciled to God. Only there does our true identity begin to be recovered, with far-reaching implications for peace with self and others as well as with God.

"We exult in our troubles" (v. 3). Can Paul mean this? He had plenty of troubles when he wrote Romans. Surely Paul was no sadist craving suffering for its own sake. He does not say that sufferings as such are good or that they come from God. He holds that finding ourselves surrounded by sufferings, we yet may exult, knowing what God can do with these factors in our lives (see 8:28–30). Even these adverse or hostile forces and factors may be made to serve the ultimate "hope," our being made into the likeness of God. This hope will not disappoint, for God's love has been poured out into our existence (v. 5). Outward circumstances remain the same, including the sufferings; but a new dynamic is at work within God's love. Salvation is not a transaction worked outside us; it is something which God accomplishes within our existence. A sermon here is suggested on the subject, "How Troubles Can Be Made To Work for Us."

"God ... Holy Spirit ... Christ" (vv. 4–8). Paul affirmed the oneness of God (3:30), and he also used terms which led eventually to a formal doctrine of "Trinity." It is significant that here Paul ascribes the same love and its reconciling effect to "God," "Holy Spirit," and "Christ." The same divine presence is inferred throughout (see 8:9–11 for a striking interchange of terms). The one and only God is seen under various terms and roles, but he is not three or one divided into three. V. 8 is especially significant. Here Paul declares that it is God's love which is shown in the death of Christ. There is no implication that a loving Son did something to open new options to an alienated Father. Salvation is God's work, out of his love and grace, and its reality may be set forth in terms of Holy Spirit (v. 5) or Christ (v. 8). Preaching need not apologize for making clear what the NT, including Romans, explicitly affirms.

A sermon here is much needed, showing the Cross as an expression of God's love, not as a means for overcoming something in God. Romans is in agreement with John 3:16. God has always been like he was at Golgotha. The love which in creation made us free and God vulnerable was there embodied in Jesus at the Cross.

"Reconciled to God by the death of his Son" (v. 10). Out of context this is a prooftext for a theory of transactional atonement: the Son dying to appease an angry Father. In context this is excluded. Reconciliation is not a one-way street; God is not only active agent, but he is affected. For Paul the problem causing the alienation between humanity and God is in mankind and the cure must be there. We are to be reconciled *to God*. Reconciliation is bound up with "the death of his Son." At the Cross two ways meet, one the way of self giving and the other the way of taking. God's kind of existence is one of love, with the disposition to serve the true interests of the other, whatever the cost. God has always been like that, and this is why he always has been able to save. He has always been the crucified God. It was only when God came into the world in the person of Jesus that he could be crucified physically. The radical self-giving of God, evident since the creation, came to

its ultimate expression in the death of Jesus Christ. Man's egocentric way, which is his self-destruction, is overcome in the
direct encounter with God, whose way is that of self-giving
love. It is "at the Cross" or "through the blood" that God saves
sinners.

"Saved by his life" (v. 10). Out of context this can be used
to depreciate the Cross. Paul has not forgotten what he has
just written. We are not saved by a dead Christ but by one living and present. "In his life" may better translate the Greek.
Only in direct union with the living Christ can his life become
ours. In 6:3 – 11 Paul will show that we can enter the saving
life of Jesus Christ only by meeting him in his death. In a real
sense we must be crucified with him to live with him. The
point is that we are not saved by some distant transaction, not
even by "Salvation History." We are saved by none other than
a Savior, and he is the living God, uniquely present in Jesus
Christ. Our "boast" is in God, and it is "through our
Lord Jesus Christ" that we have received "atonement/
reconciliation."

Adam and Christ (5:12–21)

Paul saw the one under salvation as "in Christ." That implied being in the church, the body of Christ as well as having
entered into a personal relationship with Jesus Christ. This is
the theme of 1 Cor 12:12 – 31 and is resumed in Rom 12:4. The
opposite of being "in Christ" is to be "in Adam." Paul never
sees the individual believer as strictly isolated; in fact, he
rules this out as impossible (14:7 – 8). One is a part of those
headed up by Adam or by Christ. In Adam is death; in Christ is
life. Since one is in Christ only by consent, it would seem that
one is in Adam only by consent. Paul's declaration that all
mankind is guilty and his affirmation of God as righteous support this. Romans seems clearly to teach that the state of being in Adam is not a matter of imposition but of consent or
default. Apart from his/her own will, one is not lost in Adam
or saved in Christ.

A sermon here might be entitled "In Adam or in Christ."
An alternate subject might be "Choosing our Roots." Due to
Alex Haley many are interested in their family roots. We cannot choose our natural family roots but we can choose to belong to Adam or to Christ. In Adam are disobedience, sin,

defeat, death. In Christ are obedience, righteousness, victory, life.

"Inasmuch as all sinned" (v. 12). To be off course at the point of departure, however slight, means that the target can be missed by a wide margin. So it has been with historic interpretations of this verse. The Latin Vulgate contains a fourth century mistranslation of the Greek phrase *eph ho* as *en quo* ("in whom"). Neither Greek usage nor context warrants this rendering, and the theological consequences have been a disaster. All die "in as much" as all sinned; all do not die in one who died. Paul's point is that sin results in death, from Adam to us. One sinned and he died; all die because all sin. This got changed in translation to an entirely different thing: one sinned and he died; all died because one sinned. A more recent fallacy is that all of us died on Good Friday and all of us were raised on Easter! Says who? What evidence? Did Hitler die on Good Friday and was he raised on Easter? If so, it wasn't worth the effort. This is "transactionalism," and it corresponds neither to the intention of Romans nor to reality. Death spread *(dielthen)* to all people because all sinned *(hemarton)*. To hold that the Greek aorist tense used in this verse requires a singular action is totally to misunderstand the grammar. The aorist permits the rendering, "because all sinned" or "because all sin" (timeless).

By "death" Paul means the ruin which results from separation from God, falling short of his glory. It is not warranted to conclude from this passage that physical death itself results from sin. Such theology is embarrassed by fossil remains which demonstrate the existence of death millions of years ago. Life and death in Paul's usage have to do with the quality of existence (either in Christ or in Adam) not with the state of physiological animation (alive or deceased).

In vv. 13–14 Paul makes a distinction between sin as failure or falling short *(hamartia)* and the guilt of willful rebellion *(parabasis)*. The former word in some contexts takes on the connotation of guilt, but here it seems to serve another purpose. Adam's sin was not one of ignorance but of deliberate disobedience. The Mosaic Law heightens advantage and thus accountability and guilt where it is disobeyed. One can miss the way without choosing to. Such a one is without guilt but still misses the way. A little child is not guilty of suicide in drinking poison, yet the drink is fatal. An adult knowingly drinking poison is both dead and guilty. This is the distinction Paul is making, still defending his overriding theme that God is righteous. God does not hold one responsible for what is beyond one's competence. However, condition is reality, whatever the cause. Paul's further point is that just as Adam chose a course not imposed upon him, so did Christ.

Paul's argument in v. 15, might lead one to reply, "Then we have little chance, the cards are stacked against us." Paul will not have this. He argues that "in Christ" we have gained much more than has been lost "in Adam." It is true that we come into a world where history and circumstance seem to shove us inevitably toward wrong. This added to an impulse deep within us (the inclination was there before it was activated) seems to imply little hope. We will see more of this in chapter 7. Paul yet maintains the point that in Christ we have more than enough to turn the battle toward victory and against defeat (chapter 8).

The term for "gift" in v. 15 is *charisma*, the gift of God's grace *(charis)*. The resources from God's grace which we know in Christ (joined to him and his people) are more than sufficient for all the demands life puts upon us. Paul also makes the point that Christ's role is infinitely harder than Adam's. Adam came into a simple situation and started a chain-reaction in the wrong direction. Christ came into a situation of ruin and had the task of redeeming it. One match can start a fire, but it may take an army of workers to put it out. One child can start an epidemic, but it may take all that the medical profession knows to stop it. Adam and Christ are not peers in any sense. They remain the options before us. We choose "death" or "life" as we choose to be "in Adam" or "in Christ."

At surface reading vv. 18–19 may seem to teach that all of us were really lost when Adam sinned. If so, the universalists are correct in seeing that all were saved in the one obedient act of Christ, for the passage is as supportive of universal salvation as universal damnation. Paul means neither. Had he believed that all were made righteous automatically by one act of obedience on the part of Christ, his whole mission and the agony expressed in Romans would be pointless. The writer of Romans, the man who felt compelled to go to Spain by way of Jerusalem, did not believe that all were safely within the fold. The passage makes sense and is consistent with the letter as a whole.

Adam through one act of disobedience opened the floodgates to universal disobedience. Christ stands at the head of another disposition and pattern, that of obedience. Paul admittedly leaves himself open to being interpreted as saying that all are automatically lost in Adam and all automatically saved in Christ. His clarity at the latter point through his actions and writings as a whole excludes the latter. The two stand or fall together in vv. 14–15. More help comes from his adverbs: "just as" and "thus." We are saved in Christ the way we are lost in Adam, by commitment to the one or the other.

"Where sin abounded . . . grace superabounded" (v. 20). In returning to the point introduced in v. 15, Paul becomes clearer. God's grace is greater than all our sin. God is just in his dealing with us, for he has not left us in a battle which must be lost. Sin means death, and it hits us with all the force implied by that solidarity of history and humanity called "Adam." But there is more than enough power available to us in the grace of God than required for the victory over sin. Grace does not come to us in the abstract; it comes in person, in Christ Jesus.

"That grace might reign through righteousness" (v. 21) captures much of what Romans has to say. Grace is not cheap. It is no less concerned with righteousness than is the law. The difference is that it can achieve where law fails. As seen already, grace does not come in the abstract. It is through Jesus Christ our Lord. Jesus Christ is the grace of God in person. Jesus confronts us with the claims of Lord, and only as he becomes our Lord can he become our Savior. Again Paul has answered the legalist's fear of anarchy and the libertine's dream of gift without demand. Here is Paul's answer to the perennial need for personal fulfillment in responsible freedom. Here should be the makings of a sermon on "The Triumph of Grace." It comes in the person of Jesus, not in the abstract, and this is its assurance of power. It is firm in its demand for righteousness. It is neither libertine nor legalistic.

Grace No License to Continuing in Sin (6:1–7:6)

In 6:1 Paul poses the libertine question and then answers it through three analogies. Under grace one may not continue in sin, for one has died to the old life and been raised to a new one (6:2– 11); under grace one has a new master (6:12– 23); and under grace one has a new spouse (7:1– 6). Analogies do not prove the correctness of a position, but they illustrate and illuminate. Through these three analogies Paul stresses the radical discontinuity between the old life outside Christ and the new life in Christ. In 7:7– 25 he will return to the problem of indwelling sin, but first he totally rejects the libertine position that under grace one is free from demand. Under grace and in Christ one has a new relationship and standing, and one is called to a new quality of life suited to the new self one is becoming, the new master one serves, and the new spouse to whom one is now married. Living in a world familiar with "law and order," moral and ethical breakdown and permissiveness, the preacher has rich material here for giving hearers help on the problem of the paradox of the continuity of temptation extending from the old life into the new and the radical discontinuity between the old self outside Christ and the new self in Christ. This is not "playing in a theological sandbox"; this is life as we meet it daily.

Either one sermon or a series of three sermons could be developed on the three analogies Paul employs: "A New Self in Christ," "A New Master in Christ" and "A New Spouse in Christ." Content may be drawn from our discussion of these topics. Preaching must offer an alternative to moral laxity, and it must not be a return to Puritan codes. It must be "in Christ," where one comes to know what it is to live under a new master and to become a new self.

A New Self in Christ (6:2– 11)

Paul appeals to his readers to see the anomaly of having "died to sin" yet living on in the same (v. 2). If the initiation rite of baptism stands for anything, it means the death and burial of the old self and the raising up of a new self in Christ. Just as in 1 Cor 12:12 a divided church was reminded that to be "baptized into Christ" was to be baptized into his one body, thus excluding exclusion of one another in Christ, so now Paul reminds the libertine that to be "baptized into Christ" means to be baptized into his death. We are "saved by his life" (5:10), but only by joining him in his death do we enter into his stream of life. For Jesus Friday came before Sun-

day (Cross before Resurrection), and this holds for his followers. Paul almost becomes redundant throughout this passage,
but the issue was that urgent to him in the face of the libertine
threat. We were "buried together with him" in baptism and
raised to walk in "newness of life" (v. 4). Our very being has
been united with Christ's being both in a death like his and in
a resurrection like his (v. 5). V. 5 may refer to a future resurrection of the body, but in all probability Paul is referring to
the "resurrection" experienced already by one in Christ. The
"old self" has been crucified with Christ, and the new self lives
under new claim, not under the claims of sin and death (v. 6).
Paul does not say that "the old self" crucifies itself; he has no
"do it yourself kit" equal to this. One needs help from outside
oneself, and a person "in Christ" has had that help. Neither is
the "old self" crucified without its consent. At the point of a
faith-commitment the old self received the help and is "crucified with Christ." Throughout vv. 5–8 there is a strong eschatological reference, pointing to the future resurrection; but it
is cited in order to drive home the demand upon us now to live
in keeping with the full resurrection which awaits us. Para-
doxically, we await resurrection (bodily), yet already we have
been raised to newness of life. Just as Christ's resurrection
gave him freedom from the lordship of death (v. 10), so the do-
minion of sin is broken for one who is in Christ. We are to have
a new self image: We are to see ourselves as "dead people" so
far as sin is concerned and as "living people" who live "unto
God in Christ Jesus" (v. 11).

A New Master in Christ (6:12–23)

Vv. 12–14 are transitional between the analogy of the
change from death to life and the analogy of the change of
masters, from law to grace or from sin to righteousness.
Though Paul holds firm to the discontinuity between the old
self and the new, he recognizes the ongoing struggle with sin.
Vv. 12–13 are a call to action, a call to commitment. One is
not to let sin rule in one's "mortal body." Paul sees us as more
than bodies, but he also addresses us in our bodily existence,
not as "souls." He maintains a holistic view of personhood, including body but more. Note the interchange between "your
bodies" (v. 12), "your members," and "yourselves" (v. 13). We
are to present ourselves to God, in the service of righteous-

ness, not to sin. Although Paul issues a call to commitment (vv. 12 – 13), he also states what is both command and assurance: "Sin shall not rule over you, for you are not under law but under grace" (v. 14). Thus Paul not only rejects the libertine idea of grace as license to sin; but he turns it around, holding that sin can reign under law but not under grace. Remember that grace does not come as an abstraction; it comes in the person of Christ, and in Christ are the resources to break the tyranny of sin.

In v. 17, Paul speaks of "the type of teaching to which you were delivered." What a striking perspective! Normally we think of teaching delivered to us, not we to it. Especially in theological controversy, we see ourselves as the custodians of truth to be defended at all costs. Here Paul sees us in the custody of the teaching. We are to be in its hands and not it in our hands. We do not so much study it as that it studies us. As one delivered to the teaching, we are to obey it "from the heart." Paul does not explain what he means by "type of teaching," but presumably it has to do with the claims upon us under grace to give ourselves to righteousness as we live responsibly in freedom. This perspective is missed in "the Battle of the Bible," an old fight which keeps turning up with variations in many confessional groups.

A sermon here could put it in perspective, obedience to the teaching and not the arrogance of escapism of self-appointment to the protector role. That is, for preachers and laymen alike, our proper role is to yield ourselves to the claims of the Bible upon us, not to appoint ourselves as defenders of the Bible. It appeals to our vanity to "'protect" the Bible, and this offers us a seeming yet false escape from its heavy demands.

Some of these points may be gathered under the topic, "Setting the Record Straight." (1) There is an alternative to the Way of Adam—the inclination toward sin is great, but defeat is not inevitable. (2) The resources of grace are greater than the demands of Law—no room for moral laxity. (3) The truth controls us, we do not control it. These could be developed as three separate sermons in a series.

"The wages of sin ... the *charisma* of God" (v. 23). Although Paul has employed the analogy drawn from slavery, it is not to be pushed unduly. Masters do not pay wages to their slaves, but sin does pay wages in terms of death. Sin may be overt rebellion, but always it is failure, falling short of the glory of God, our being in the image of God. On the other hand, "eternal life" is not a wage paid for work but the "free gift" of God. Paul's word for "free gift" is *charisma*. Eternal life itself is charisma! Preaching needs to correct the gross abuse to which the term "charisma" has been subjected, both in the secular world and in the church. The secular world retains at least one truth, "charisma" is gift. Beyond that it does not parallel the NT in what it sees as charisma. Religious ideas of "charismatic" as something exotic or other-worldly distort the term's meaning in the NT. Anything which we have by God's grace is "charisma" or "charismatic." All people— without exception—who have drawn upon God's grace have charisma (see further in 12:6– 8).

Significant also is the fact that the *"charisma* of God" comes to us "in Christ Jesus our Lord." Nothing is said of the Holy Spirit. That does not imply that charisma is unrelated to Holy Spirit, but it does caution against the popular idea that charisma has more to do with the Holy Spirit than with Jesus Christ or God. Again, tritheism is invalid. Charisma is any gift of grace, whether thought of in terms of God, Christ, or Holy Spirit. Eternal life, that quality of existence known under the lordship of Christ, is the primary "charismatic" gift.

On another front there is preaching needed from this perspective. Because of much of our heritage, sometimes called "the Puritan Work Ethic," many people do not see worth in themselves. Only as they achieve do they "amount to anything." This robs many people of a valid and wholesome self-image, and it is especially problematic to older people who by incapacity or forced retirement feel that since they no longer "produce," life has no meaning. Although the burden of our passage in Romans is a call to responsible living in the service of God and righteousness, there also is the lesson that life itself is gift. We do not have to earn the right to be or the right to remain in the world. Preaching needs to keep a proper balance between the call to righteousness and service and the assurance that all of us have our being and our right to be as *charisma*. Preaching needs to give special attention to people whose worth has not been adequately affirmed: among them minority groups, women, and older people.

A New Spouse in Christ (7:1-6)

Already we have observed that Paul's illustrations are not without problems. Often we understand the illustration because we already understand the point he wants to make. The analogy itself is clear enough, for death frees the living spouse to remarry. Paul has it that "we died to the law" therefore we may rightly be joined to Christ as our new spouse. Logic would have it that since we died, the law now has the right to acquire a new spouse. Of course, Paul's interpreter is to try to sense his intention, not to be overly concerned with pressing the logic of his analogy. In truth, this is a principle essential to all communication. Intention and meaning are never in a one-to-one relationship with the audio or visual symbols we call words and language. Words have usage, and models or analogies have usage. Meaning is not inherent in language, else we could have only one word for each referent. To understand another, we must want to understand. We must be open to the intention behind the expression. See what I mean? Even as I write this, I am appealing to you to grasp what I am trying to say. Many of our tensions and conflicts in the home, in church, at work, and between nations arise out of misunderstanding. One reason is that we abuse language, especially when we apply some "logic" to what another says which fails to be sensitive to his/her intention. What we "overhear" (intention and motive) is often nearer the truth than what we "hear" (the literal words). We must evaluate all that we hear by what we overhear. A sermon here on "Hearing and Overhearing One Another" might make this point, demonstrating that our problem is not in understanding Paul's intention if we try, but to do so we must go beyond the naked words.

There is another problem lurking in this analogy, and it reflects a male-orientation which is both ancient and yet still with us. All through the analogy it is "the law of the husband" and terms upon which a woman is or is not an "adulteress." Again, we need not indict Paul as being deliberately chauvinistic, but at the least the analogy reflects a man's world. Preaching today cannot rightly neglect the urgency of reassessing the whole issue of woman—and all persons.

"That we may bear fruit to God" (v. 4) continues the answer to the libertine threat. Salvation is to issue in "fruit to

God." Contextually this means a righteous life. Although Paul speaks here of responsibility, it is not viewed as basically a human achievement. The fruit does not come by divine imposition or by human initiative. Paul writes, "Ye were put to death," not "you killed the old self." The point is that our "marriage" is no longer to the law but to Christ. From this union should come "fruit" unto God. "Fruit" is never used in the NT for "making another Christian." It refers to our becoming truly Christian. When the marriage is that between "flesh" and law, the "fruit" is "death" (v. 5). By "flesh" Paul means the old self apart from Christ. That he did not mean literal flesh, in a physical sense, is conclusive from the wording, "When you were in the flesh." He was not writing to ghosts. His audience or readers were still embodied in physical flesh. As in Gal 5:19, "flesh" usually refers to the unregenerate life outside of Christ. Sin has to do with the whole self (mind, will, feelings, body, etc.), and righteousness likewise has to do with the whole self: how we think, how we feel (our emotions), how we behave, how we relate to God, to self, to other people, and to the material world. Preaching needs to spell this out.

The Impulses toward Good and Evil (7:7–25)

Here if anywhere Paul speaks to our existence. This depth analysis of our melancholy, doing evil we despise and failing in good which we intend, surely describes our common humanity. This is neither a Jewish nor a Gentile problem; it is a human problem. There is a surd (an absurdity) which seems to run through our existence, with competing impulses toward good and evil. The drive toward survival is so strong that Darwin could build a strong case for "the survival of the fittest." What Darwin missed is the opposite drive alongside that to survive, the sacrificial principle in which the weak survive because the strong assume the protective role, as when a mother bird protects her young. It is not only among the birds and animals that we see "nature red in tooth and claw" yet also moved by the impulse to protect and serve, but we see these opposite impulses within ourselves. We give life and take life. We grasp and we share. We gravitate to what we despise. We reach out for the elusive good which we esteem. Paul is not alone in crying out, "Wretched man am I, who will deliver me from this body of death" (v. 24)? Such wretched persons are all about us, and they await help. The pulpit should be one source of help, and Paul leads the way here. Here if anywhere we should be able to preach from Romans on such themes as: "Our Melancholy," "The Absurdity within Us," "The Civil War within Us," or "Impulse Toward Both Good and Evil."

From his rabbinical background Paul may draw upon the idea that within each person there is the *yetzer hatov* (impulse toward good) and the *yetzer hara* (impulse toward evil), but he does not see these two as equally representing who we are. In spite of all the agony and despair in the passage, it has a sound basis for optimism. Paul identifies with the impulse toward good as who he really is, seeing the contrary impulse toward evil as some alien intrusion. This is not "passing the buck," for he acknowledges the "I" behind each impulse, but his basic will is toward good. He does not say, "the evil which I wish" or "the good which I wish not." He says, "the evil which I wish not" and "the good which I wish." In a sense this is a divided will; in another sense it is a failure in a will which both despises the evil and aspires toward the good. Paul's point throughout is that he needs help, and law itself is not a sufficient help. It sometimes only aggravates the matter, as it awakens him to options which he fails to manage. He needs help, and only "in Christ Jesus" does he find it sufficient.

"Is the law sin?" (v. 7). Paul rejects this position. To him the law was from God and it intended good. The law is not evil, but in heightening advantage it can heighten evil and guilt. Something in us rebels at restraint, and the command not to covet may itself trigger the impulse toward it (v. 7). In part this probably reflects the image of God within us which wants more—to be God. Alongside overt idolatry is the subtle idolatry within us, our impulse to rule, sometimes so strong that we are willing "to rule or ruin." However it is to be explained, Paul surely understood us as well as himself in seeing that the law tends to be counterproductive. We break it sometimes simply because it is there. Paul saw the goal of the Mosaic law as life, but in his case it resulted in death (v. 10). The law is "holy and righteous and good" in itself, but it becomes a "base of operations" for evil (vv. 11–12).

Paul speaks of sin almost as though it were an entity separate from himself, an alien and enemy having invaded his person (vv. 13, 17, 20, 23). At the same time he is acknowledging his guilt; it is his sin. It is a paradox. He could have said, "I, yet not I." Sin within us is to be owned and disowned. Sin occurs in us only by our wills, yet sin can be through a failure of will. Paul does almost objectify or personify sin, but he does not intend thus to exonerate himself or pass the buck. Interestingly, he does not allude to Satan or "the Fall" here. He does not charge his plight to his genes or society. He affirms no ultimate determinism, whatever forces or factors may be at work. The will is concerned with the outcome. He cries out for reinforcement to a will which is battered by other forces and tends to fail. He needs more than that something to be done for him; something must be done within him.

Preachers need to help their people at this point—this "caughtness" experienced by us all. First of all, help them to admit it as a fact of life. Help them to see that they are not alone or exceptional. Next, help them to see that one cannot win this battle alone. Then help them see that "in Christ" there is sufficient help. To be "in Christ" is to be related to Jesus Christ in the fellowship of his people—the church as the body of Christ. With the help of Christ and his people we can break out of this "caughtness," this bondage suffered by a battered will: A sermon topic here could be "The Power to Cope."

"I am carnal" (v. 14). We have seen already that for Paul "flesh" usually referred to the whole self outside redemption, with no special reference to the literal flesh or sensuality. Envy and jealousy are "flesh" as much as are drunkeness and adultery. The "I" who fights the losing battle under law, who suffers the anguish of frustrated will, is the "carnal I." That is the self trying to go it alone. This becomes clearer in v. 25, where "I myself" stands in sharp contrast to "in Christ" (8:1). For preaching today, "secular" may communicate Paul's idea better than "carnal." Secularity is trying to close the circle of reality (secular is Latin for cycle) without reference to God. Paul acknowledges that the "ego" cannot achieve its own destiny unaided, and chapter 8 exultantly proclaims its source of help.

"I don't know what I am doing!" (v. 15). What a confession! Paul confesses that he does not make sense to himself. There is an absurdity running through his existence. He keeps repeating the anomaly of not practicing what he wills but rather doing what he hates and wills not. It is not so much a

divided will as a failure in will; the will toward good is there
but the achievement is not (v. 18). The law (of Moses) is good,
and he agrees that it is suited *(kalos)* to his needs (v. 16). He
finds within himself a "law" wishing to do good (v. 21), but he
finds also another "law" within himself opposing "the law of
his mind" and taking him captive to "the law of sin" within
himself (v. 23). To what does all this add up? It confesses competing impulses, unresolved tensions, and a gap between the
self he wants to be and the self he knows himself to be. The
preacher does not have to search for relevance here. Little
children, young people, and adults know this painful experience. They need help. They need to know that they are normal
human beings in having these inner struggles. They need to
know where and how to find help.

"Wretched man am I" (v. 24). S. O. S.! Paul sends out the
distress signal. More, he cries out for someone to rescue him.
Rescue from what? From sin. Even more, it is rescue from
himself that is called for. The forces and factors which are en-
slaving him and destroying him are at work through as well as
against his will. He is not simply an object manipulated; he is
a person yielding. One may say that a motor yields to a
mechanic, but this overstates the case. The motor is passive,
sharing in no decisions. The sinner is not a motor; the sinner is
active agent. Paul participates in the self-ruin he describes.
Preaching should help people understand this "Dark Night of
the Soul."

"This body of death" (v. 24) is best understood along with
"the body of sin" (6:6), and "the body of flesh" (Col 2:11) and
in contrast with "the body of Christ" (7:4; 12:5; 1 Cor 12:27;
Col 2:17). Although an individual distinct from all others, one
is never alone but always bound up with others (14:7). Paul
can use "body" in this larger sense. Clearly, those under redemption are in "the body of Christ." Those apart from Christ
are "in Adam" or in "the body of flesh," "the body of sin," "the
body of death." The wretched man described in chapter 7 is
the man who tries to go it alone, but he is not alone. Outside
Christ he is caught up in a solidarity bigger than himself, and
it is a solidarity oriented toward death. The world of which we
are a part is more than we can cope with alone, with the absurd and wretched results Paul painfully describes.

V. 25 is transitional between 7:7 – 24 and 8:1 – 39. Unfortunately, the chapter divisions we inherited from Stephen Langton (1229) somewhat obscure the continuity of Paul's development. The deliverance acknowledged in 7:25 is spelled out in chapter 8. A key phrase in v. 25 is "I myself." Left to himself, Paul is torn between a "mind" which serves the law of God and the "flesh" which serves the law of sin. As created, apart from redemption, there is something within man which is aware of a higher claim, as Paul described in his discussion of the "conscience" found in all people (2:14 – 16). Something within us already acknowledges "the law of God." But left to our own resources, "I myself," the battle is lost to "the law of sin." It is not enough to be "flesh," the secular man without God.

"Thanks" in Greek is "grace" *(charis)*. "Thanks to God" is "Grace from God." By God's grace—Thanks to God—there is deliverance from the wretchedness in chapter 7 as from the wrath in chapter 1. It is not apart from our will, but it is not a possibility apart from God's grace. A sermon subject here is, "Where Can I Go but to the Lord?" We must include self and include law, but we must look beyond self and beyond law.

"Through Jesus Christ our Lord" (v. 25). Again, grace comes not as an abstraction but in person. We are delivered only by a deliverer, saved only by a savior. Under the Lordship of God's Anointed (Christ-Anointed to reign) we come to know him who is Jesus (JHWH Savior). Chapter 8 shows us what it is to be "in Christ," delivered from the frustration and death of remaining only "I myself."

Victory over Sin in Christ Jesus (8:1–17)

Rom 8 is a celebration, and it begins with a sense of release from the heavy burden of guilt and frustration marking 7:7 – 25. In Christ one does not have to live under condemnation. This is not libertine euphoria; this is the release of one whose sins are confessed and forgiven. When God justifies the sinner that settles it, and no one is to reopen the matter (v. 33). The call to repentance belongs inescapably to preaching; but for many who live daily under the burden of guilt (whether real or imagined), the good news is that "in Christ Jesus" the judgment has been lifted. Salvation begins with acknowledging our sins and accepting God's forgiveness. Preaching here can help people see that when they have gotten right with

God, they should be right with themselves—at peace with themselves.

"God in the flesh . . . condemned sin" (v. 3). This probably captures the thrust of v. 3. "In the flesh" may refer to sin, "flesh" thus standing for the self apart from God. Clearly it is God who "condemned sin," and it was through his Son whom he sent "in the likeness of sinful flesh and because of sin." The idea probably is that what the law could not do God could and did, and he did it in the sphere of flesh. God came into his world, penetrating it even to the extent of flesh, and there he had the victory over "sin and death" which we had failed to win. God in Christ won the victory over sin and death precisely where we needed a victory and had known defeat. Now we "in Christ" participate in the same victory. No longer do we live under "the law of sin and death" but under the new "law of the life-giving spirit" (v. 1).

"The righteous demands of the law fulfilled in us" (v. 4). This is an answer to both legalism and antinomian libertinism. In the law are non-negotiable demands. The intention in grace is not to waive these but to meet them. Jesus did not come to destroy the law or the prophets but to fulfill, to incarnate the intention of the law in his own person and in us awaken new motive und supply new power for meeting these demands (see Matt 5:17 – 48). Paul is not thinking simply about God's righteousness being observed in Jesus; righteousness is likewise his purpose for us—"in us who walk not according to flesh but according to spirit."

"Not in flesh but in spirit" (v. 9). Paul was not addressing disembodied spirits when he wrote this. His readers were bodily people living in Rome, but they were not "in flesh." Usage here is abundantly clear. "In flesh" is the same as "I myself." Apart from God we are "flesh." The whole self and all its striving, including its religious striving, is "flesh" apart from God. The faith which admits him as a liberating and transforming presence into our existence and us into his existence changes us from "flesh" to "spirit." This is not to become ghostly or otherworldly. It means a new dimension in our historical, bodily existence. The intense personal relationship is the essence of what is described as "in you" or "you in," whether the terminology for God be Spirit, Holy Spirit, Spirit of God, or Christ. This newness of life already being enjoyed anticipates a yet fuller dimension when the body itself shall be raised as Christ was raised (v. 11; see vv. 18– 25).

What determines our being "in spirit" and not "in flesh"? Paul's answer is clear. We/you are spirit and not flesh if "the Spirit of God dwells in you," "if anyone has the Spirit of Christ," "if Christ is in you," "if the Spirit of the one raising Jesus from the dead dwells in you" (vv. 9– 11). Obviously, there is no concern for one precise way of saying it. We are spirit and not flesh on condition of a personal relationship with God, however termed, as close and real as mutual indwelling. It is out of this personal relationship made possible by God's grace and by trust on both sides that salvation begins: both new standing and new quality of life. Its character is righteousness and not sin. Its end is life and not death. Freed from the threat of condemnation, we now may turn to the business of life.

Many have claimed to belong to some exclusive group and thus achieved status as "the children of God" (v. 16). For some the conditions necessarily exclude others, as when determined by circumstances of birth, ethnic or otherwise. Others lay claim to this distinction on grounds of cultic compliance or because of some other human merit or work. Paul recognizes, as did Jesus, that some but not all are "the children of God"; but neither Jesus nor Paul grounded it on anything like ethnic identity, ritual compliance, creedal excellence, or arbitrary election. It is a relationship of mutual trust (acceptance and commitment), and it is seen in the quality of life issuing from the relationship. "We are the children of God" can be a proud and selfish boast. Seeing ourselves as children of God can be salutary, a good self-image without pride or prejudice. We see *who* we are when we see *whose* we are. To know that we have the right to look to God and say, "Abba, Father!" means that we do not have to possess the spirit of a slave (slavery is not hard work but work without choice or participation in its fruits) or to live in fear. Being God's children means security, worth, dignity, meaning, future. We are heirs of God and joint-heirs with Christ. That means that we suffer with him and thus will share his "glory" (v. 17). What follows describes this "glory."

Preaching here should clarify what it means to be "Children of God." To be exposed as false are all accidental distinctions (ethnic, racial, etc.) and all superficial distinctions (our easy achievements in cultic rites, creedal confessions, or proud behavior). Show, as outlined above, what makes us truly God's children—the faith which admits him meaningfully into our lives. Show that being God's children is reflected in the life thus produced.

Our people need help on the identity question. Some need to be disabused of grandiose and unfounded ideas about themselves. Many need to have a better self-image. A wholesome self-image must correspond to reality, as we take into our self-affirmation both the negative and the positive, our sins and our redemption. Preaching here can help people see what it is to be a child of God: not just "sons" but "children," women included. By "adoption" in the sense that God chooses that we be his. Unlike adoption as generally practiced, the choice rests likewise with the child; we are not God's children by any understanding of election which negates human will. A slave enters only partially into the sufferings or glory of his master; the children of God enter into both sufferings and glory as can be done only within a family.

The Redemption of the Body (8:18–25)

Immortality of soul was enough for Plato and countless others before and after him; it is not enough for Paul. The idea of "soul" as the essential self with "body" as only its temporal residence, its prison or tomb, is pagan and not biblical. This dualism sees all reality as either "spirit" or "matter." To this view spirit is good and matter is evil. Paul's "dualism," as we have just seen, is moral: good and evil. Paul uses the terms "flesh" and "spirit," but not in the way Plato and others did. Although pagan "dualism" invaded Jewish and Christian thought, it has no secure basis in the Bible. Gen 2:7 is basic, where "man" (generic for the human being) was created out of the dust of the earth and became "a living soul" (a self) when God breathed into him the breath of life. To use modern terms, we are psychosomatic. We are holistic; constituted of many aspects (body with its senses, feeling, reason, will, a moral sense, social, etc.); and at the same time one indivisible self. (See my book, *Polarities of Man's Existence in Biblical Perspective* [Philadelphia: Westminster, 1973], Chapter Two, "Aspective yet Holistic.") It is against this background that we are to understand the difference between Paul's doctrine of resurrection and the pagan idea of immortality of soul. For Paul it was a horrible thought that one might be "found naked," an unclothed soul or disembodied spirit (2 Cor 5:3).

Paul links our hope of full redemption in resurrection with the hope of all creation (v. 19). This is a rare passage in Scripture, but here Paul clearly sees that the creation itself will participate in a "redemption" related to ours in resurrection. He does not see the created world as worthless, meaningless, or doomed to pass away. Paul was more than an "environmentalist," but he lays a foundation for environmental responsibility. Just as in 7:7–25 Paul described the tensions and frustrations of persons, here he indicates that the creation itself "groans and is in travail" (v. 22). For creation as for us, there is hope. Travail looks to deliverance and birth. Creation for the present seems subjected to "futility," but for it there is "hope" (v. 20). It will be liberated from the servitude of corruption into the freedom of the children of God (v. 21). The destiny of creation is bound up with the destiny of the children of God, and both await a fuller redemption (vv. 19, 21). For us this means "the redemption of the body" (v. 23). It will undergo a major transformation, but it remains body (1 Cor 15:35–58). The creation itself awaits its redeemed body. Salvation then as redemption (liberation) is seen as the full, bodily self living on in a redeemed creation.

Man's corrupted nature is clearly seen in his "rape" of physical nature. The hope for the redemption of nature corrupted by mankind's sin is first the redemption of mankind.

A sermon or sermons here could deal with various aspects of what is implied by Paul's larger idea of "redemption." It refers to the future with implications for the present. The pagan idea that we are "souls" temporarily caught in a body has produced many disastrous results. It contributes to the false "spirituality" which is otherworldly. It encourages the fallacy that we must choose between a "social gospel" and "soul winning." It has contributed to our ecological crisis, for to view the material world as evil or as of little or no worth opens the way to its destruction through pollution and depletion. Resurrection implies a holistic understanding of a person, with implications for the redemption of the self in its various aspects now and ultimately the body itself.

In preaching you might show the distinctiveness of the view appearing here. There is the pessimistic view that the universe will burn itself out, with no ultimate hope. There is the cyclic view, as among the ancient Stoics and in some Eastern religions, which sees periodic recycling of the universe, as from one cosmic flame to its breakup into its sparks and then reabsorption into a single flame. Reincarnation of souls is a variation of this. Another view is that pure spirit will ultimately be freed from matter, soul from body. Another view is that creation and we will continue into eternity but with no basic change, like the primitive idea of "a happy hunting ground" or the Egyptian idea of resuming life beyond death much as here, as provisions in their ancient tombs reflect. Paul's view is different. It is that of a redeemed creation and humanity, bodily but freed from frustration, decay, and death. He does not go beyond this, but he holds it out as a "hope" which should sustain us now through whatever sufferings are ours as we await our "glory" (vv. 24 – 25).

Preaching here can deal with at least two major ideas: salvation as holistic and ecology as a theological issue. God made us in the totality of our being and all of selfhood, including the body, is God's concern in salvation. What we do now in our bodily, historical existence is important to a proper understanding of salvation. What we do to or with the material world or universe is a moral/religious issue, not just economic or political. God wants to redeem us in our total being and also redeem his whole creation. Sermon topics may include "Toward a Christian View of the Body" and "Toward a Christian View of the Material."

For Whom God Works in All Things for Good (8:26–30)

Few texts are so cherished and quoted as v. 28. Few are so misunderstood and abused. From it comes the glib idea that everything is going to work out all right. From it comes the atrocious idea that God wills everything that happens or that everything that happens is good. Some get the idea that God will unconditionally take care of them. There are ideas about the promised "good" which can only disappoint. This is a truly great text, but it must be understood in its wholeness and in its context. This is a text to preach, but with a feel for its intention.

The unit begins with a return to the recognition that alone we are not equal to the demands of life. We need help. Sometimes we don't even know how to ask for help, possibly because we do not understand ourselves, our needs, or longings. Paul assures us that the Spirit "takes hold along with our weakness" (v. 26). The Spirit does not displace us; that would be to negate us as dispensable. The Spirit does not abandon us to ourselves. The Greek verb beautifully pictures the help given by two prepositions which it incorporates: *syn*="with" and *anti*="over against." It is as though the Spirit carries the load with us, our weakness on one end of the stick and the Spirit's strength on the other. This is true help with fullest respect for the dignity and personhood of the one helped. It is against this background picture that v. 28 follows. These ideas may be gathered up in a sermon entitled, "The One Who Knows the Question We Are Struggling to Ask" or even "Two Can Tote Better Than One." Another sermon may be entitled, "The Nature of Help." How can one be helped without losing one's personhood (freedom, dignity, responsibility, etc.)?

"God" is the active agent who works in all things in the direction of "good." Most manuscripts lack *ho theos*=God; and the Greek for "all things" is neuter gender, so that grammatically it can be subject or object. Consequently v. 28 has been rendered, "All things work together . . . ." Even without *ho theos* this is not likely Paul's intention. Some highly significant manuscripts have "God" as explicitly the subject. Either these old manuscripts retain the original or they remove ambiguity by correctly interpreting Paul's intention. There is a world of difference between the glib faith that things work out and the faith which sees God at work in all things with a view to bringing about what is good. Things do not work out; they usually fall apart. Only where there is someone responsibly at work is there ground for hope that out of a given situation good may come.

The promise is not unconditional; it is for those who love God and who are "the called according to his purpose." The latter phrase is difficult. Paul sees God as having the initiative in revelation and redemption; he calls and we are to respond. Paul never speaks of the "uncalled." The opposite of the called are not uncalled but the disobedient. He reserves the term "called" for those who have responded to God's calling. Calling is not coercive, and we can talk back to God (10:21). Paul's meaning here is that God works for good in the lives of those open to him. To return to an earlier analogy; God is not a mechanic fixing motors. At the deepest or highest levels of human need, only those open to help can receive it. God does not violate our humanity when he helps us. He can give sunshine and rain to the just and the unjust (Matt 5:45), but his highest gifts can be given only to those willing to receive them.

There remains the question of the "good" toward which God works in everything. Nothing in Paul's experience or writing encourages the idea that the good is to be understood as material gains, health, position, etc. Paul suffered hardship of every kind: shipwreck, jail, whippings in the synagogue, scourging by the Romans, character assassination, etc. (see 2 Cor 11:16–33; Gal 4:13–14). Followers of Jesus are warned that they may lose all in following him. Never are they promised exemption from temptation, privation, persecution, or even death. The "Good" must be of another kind. The good is being made into the likeness of Jesus Christ (vv. 29–30).

"Whom he foreknew" (v. 29). Foreknowledge here means that God knew us before we knew him (see Gal 4:9). Knowing us first, he also foresaw precisely what he purposed to bring about for us, that we be "conformed to the image of his son." "Foreordained" sometimes translates Paul's second verb in v. 29, but "marked out before" comes closer to it. Whom God foreknew he marked out or designed to be like Jesus. He called them to himself, justified or rightwized them (standing and quality of life), and "glorified" them. The last term seems to pick up the idea of "the glory" of which man fell short (3:23) and which is restored in redemption. In other words, God knows from the outset what he wants to bring about in us. Only our unwillingness to respond to his call can defeat his purpose.

I have found that in preaching on Rom 8:28–30, it is most effective simply to move through the passage much as we have done in the above paragraphs. Show what are the mistaken ideas often drawn from this passage. Give most attention to the positive ideas—God's deliberate purpose to bring about in us a likeness to Jesus and his power to do just that, whatever the circumstances of our lives, if we will but entrust ourselves to him.

If a homiletical frame is sought for these exegetical ideas, it may be something like this: "The Grounds of Christian Optimism." (1) It is not found in the nature of things. This is a Pollyana view of life. It is senseless and contrary to experience and Scripture. (2) It is not found in the deterministic view of life—call it fate, biological determinism, or theological determinism. (3) It is found in the relational view of life—one's relationship with God—a God who loves, has a purpose for us, and who provides strength for us.

If God Be for Us (8:31–39)

Suppose God were against us? Suppose he were indifferent to us? Under either of these conditions our case would be hopeless. Paul has no doubt about it; God is for us. He has just taken the position that God works in all things for good to those who love him and respond to his calling. This is the mighty plus which makes the difference between chapters 7 and 8. In what follows there is not a hint that for God's children there shall be less temptation, trials, hostility, privation, persecution, or physical death. In fact, he portrays the overcoming presence of God in our lives in the very face of all these adverse things. We remain in the same old world with the same old problems, but the outcome is assuredly different. The difference is that between "I myself" and "in Christ." The difference is that between "flesh" (without God) and "spirit" (with God). The difference is that which God makes. The text is itself a sermon topic: "If God Be For Us."

"Who will call out against God's called out?"(v. 33). There is a play on Greek words here, reflected in our translation. If God acquits, who dare condemn? Let none other do it. Don't do it to yourself. It is wrong for us to refuse to forgive ourselves when God has forgiven us, just as it is wrong for others to condemn where God has acquitted. This is a much-needed message for many people. Many punish themselves long after confessed sin should be forgotten. We cannot forgive, self or others, simply by forgetting; but the point of forgiveness is the point at which the forgetting is to begin. The only justification for remembering confessed sin is that we may be able to avoid its recurrence or repair its damages.

Simply to live in the memory of it is wrong and unnecessary. What a sermon in v. 33!

"Who shall separate us?" (v. 35). Paul sees life as filled with demands and hostile forces on every hand. This has been his experience and this is his expectation for the journey ahead to Jerusalem and wherever. He is not daunted by this, for he counts on resources more than sufficient for every demand. In fact, we are "more than conquerors through the one loving us" (v. 37). Conquerors over what or in what sense? Paul puts no limit on it, but the one point at which he is explicit is that of the love of God. No force or factor, however strong or hostile, can cut us off from God's love. Belonging to God and the family of God is to him the essence of salvation. All other good flows from that relationship, and Paul sees it as unbreakable. That is his confidence. If God be for us (v. 31) we are secure though there be against us suffering, anguish, persecution, famine, nakedness, peril, sword, death, life, or any creature earthly or heavenly.

What does Paul mean by "more than conquerors?" Presumably he means that it is not mere survival (rolling with the punches) nor a "cliff hanger." It is not a bare victory. What is for us in the love of God is more than a match for all that can be against us. For "I myself" it is "wretched man I am." For one "in Christ," it is "more than a conqueror."

Jew and Gentile
Under God
(Romans 9–11)

In these three chapters appear some of the most difficult statements in the letters of Paul. Isolated, some verses defy any apparent interpretation which does not leave them in conflict with positions taken by Paul elsewhere. From chapter 9 a thoroughgoing divine determinism seems to appear, especially if the analogy of the potter and the clay is pressed (vv. 19–21). If we really are but clay in a potter's hands, it would seem that all warnings, pleas, and Paul's own anguished writing and journeys are redundant. If 11:26 is isolated and given its most apparent meaning, then there need be "no sweat" about Israel, for "thus all Israel shall be saved." I cannot believe that these simple interpretations do justice to Paul or to reality as we confront it.

Taken as a whole and in the larger context of Romans, chapters 9–11 do make sense and are highly instructive for us as for their first readers. Rom 9 says one thing chiefly: Israel can be lost and God yet be found righteous. Chapter 10 narrows the explanations down to one: God spread out his hands to a people who disobeyed him. Chapter 11 says two things: Gentiles, now in a favored position, can be lost; and Israel, now in an unfavorable position, can be saved. Paul thus vindicates God as righteous in both judgment and redemption, with respect to both Jew and Gentile. He also justifies his continuing concern for Israel, for they can be saved. As apostle to the Gentiles, he warns them that presumption on privilege will be as disastrous for them as for his own beloved people.

God's Freedom in the Election of Israel (9:1–29)

Paul builds here on the recognition of Israel as in a real way the chosen people of God. Against this background, he maintains that Israel can be lost and that this does not imply that God has failed to keep his covenant with Israel. He rejects the idea that God is bound to Israel by previous commitment in such a way that he must always recognize Israel as his people. Israel can be lost and God not be found unfaithful. God remains free, never subject to being "called upon the carpet" by anyone. So incensed is Paul by any suggestion that God may be found unfair that he engages in a near "overkill" in vindicating God as really answerable to nobody.

Paul was not a systematizer, and he leaves himself open to logical conclusions from which he himself backs off. He teaches election and to a point seems to see it as thoroughgoing divine determination of human destiny, but he backs off from this, especially at v. 22b. He has it that God is free to do as he pleases, but he then shows that God pleases to extend his mercy to people who really do not deserve it. God chooses people but does not coerce them into becoming his people. He continues to deal patiently with them, even when they are negative or rebellious.

Predestination is a belief widely held today in both secular and religious forms, and preaching needs to cope with those ideas. Some hold that all of us are genetically and/or socially determined, that no one is really free. They teach that our basic character and direction are fixed for us by the genes we inherit and/or by how home and society have conditioned us. This is a secular doctrine of fate. Religiously, some hold that God himself determines fate, electing some to salvation and some to damnation, leaving us no real choice. Some go even farther, seeing everything that happens as the will of God. These extreme ideas are misleading, and they do not do justice to Paul or to reality. Election is God's initiative in seeking us before we seek him. From Genesis to Revelation, including Romans, it is clear that we can say "No" to God (10:21). God does not fix fate. Genetic heritage does have much to do with our options, but anyone able to read these lines or listen to a sermon has significant options. Society does go far to shape us in our emotions, values, and directions; but there is something deep within us which can fight back against genetic and social heritage just as it has the awesome power of saying "yes" or "no" even to God.

Paul's Grief for His Own People (9:1–5)

In this deeply-moving passage, Paul pours out his heart for his own people, Israel. If he did not see many of them as really lost, these tears are a mockery. Obviously, from his words and actions, Paul did see his kin folks as lost. If he did not believe that Israel could be saved, the words are pointless. He writes as one seeing his people as hanging in the balances, and what he does and what they do have something to do with the outcome.

The pathos for Paul is heightened as he contrasts their present condition with their rich heritage: as Israelites theirs is the richest heritage of all (vv. 4– 5). Here is a sermon. No heritage, however rich, guarantees our fate. An Abraham Lincoln can come out of seemingly nowhere, and one born to privilege may "blow it." A sermon topic might be "Roots," showing not only what one's heritage may do for one, good or bad, but also that our roots do not by themselves determine us, for good or bad.

God Vindicated in All His Dealings (9:6–18)

God's choice of Isaac over Ishmael and Jacob over Esau is the background to Paul's vindication of God, as remaining both free and righteous in all his relationships. His first point is that becoming a child of God is not through "flesh" (v. 8), i.e., not a human achievement, but through God's own initiative. It is by "election" and not human works (v. 11). The choice of Jacob over Esau, twins from the same womb, is Paul's prime example of the working of God's purposes through his free choice and not through human merit. Paul pressed his point and in an "overkill" left himself wide open to the very charge an opponent would make—How, then, can anyone be blamed for what God himself has determined (v. 19)? Paul faced that question only after he had pressed to the limit his claim that God is free to do as he chooses.

"Jacob I loved and Esau I hated" (v. 13). At face value this is impossible to reconcile with human freedom or divine justice. Did God literally hate Esau? Did God actually mark out poor Esau for his hatred before Esau was born? If this is what Paul really means, only special pleading can maintain God's justice or any case for human freedom. To hold one guilty without options is injustice compounded. Paul's logic was driving him into that corner, but he backed off from it, beginning in v. 22b. Possibly he uses "hate" only in the sense of "reject," but even so it is little relieved. V. 15 drives on to what seems to be absolute determinism: "I will have mercy on whom I have mercy." If purely arbitrary, all human effort is meaningless, including Paul's letter and the trips he contemplates. Somewhere in it all, Paul must not hold to real determinism. If he means that it is God's right alone to determine (judge) who is in position for mercy and who not, the point is tenable in context. The example of Pharaoh (vv. 16–18) poses the same problems. If God used Pharaoh simply as a tool, manipulating him to suit his purpose, it is impossible to see how Pharaoh could bear any moral responsibility for his action. Paul will avoid this conclusion, even though he started down a road which compels it.

Why does Paul go so far with his case for the freedom of God? Apparently it is to answer the claim made by those with whom he once stood that God was bound by covenant to save Israel. Paul's pattern is to attend to one point at a time, with little regard for implications in directions he does not favor. Having made his point, often with an "overkill," he then faced the sometimes awkward implications of what he had just written. His point in vv. 6–18 is that God is sovereign and free, and that he alone determines his course. Logic requires other conclusions which Paul simply rejects or ignores.

Patience with Vessels Suited to Destruction (9:19–29)

At v. 19 Paul begins to face the question which follows logically from his argument in vv. 6–18: Why blame anyone for what God determines? The questioner is right. One cannot have it both ways, divine determination and human freedom or responsibility. Paul's initial answer to the objector could hardly satisfy his question. In vv. 20–21 Paul simply tells the questioner that he has no right to question. Of course, it belongs to the essence of personhood to question. To say that God is to be trusted and not doubted is one thing; to say that we have no right to ask about our own rights and responsibilities is another thing. Paul reaches the brink of the chasm of absolute determinism in his analogy of the potter and the clay. If we are nothing more than clay, then we have neither rights nor responsibilities. Made in the image of God, man is more than clay or a clay pot.

Paul leaves himself one narrow door of escape by stopping short of saying that God actually treats us like passive clay. He asserts that God has the power or authority *(exousia)* to do so, but he does not go the further step in saying that this is what God actually does.

"Endured with much patience" (v. 22). Even this transitional verse begins as though it would drive on relentlessly toward divine determination, manipulating people like clay: "If God willing to show forth the wrath and to make known his power!" Already we have seen from 1:18–32 that by "wrath" Paul means the outworking of sin as God gives one over to his own choosing when he refuses to have God in his knowledge (not divine determinism). Even here, v. 22 seems to be preoccupied with the negative side, man's getting what he deserves. But suddenly the verse takes a new direction. Having made his point that God is free to do as he pleases, Paul now holds that God pleases to be patient with people who already are in a condition suited for destruction. He does not say that God molded them like clay into such vessels. Already he has established the fact of human choice leading to the wrath. People are responsible for becoming "vessels of wrath suited unto destruction." If God did nothing, the destruction would follow. Such people would self-destruct. God neither determines their fates nor abandons them to their self-chosen fates. He chooses rather to deal patiently with them, opening up to them new possibilities for their existence. God uses his sovereignty redemptively. Vessels of wrath suited to destruction can become vessels of mercy "prepared beforehand for glory" (v. 23).

"I will call 'Not My People' 'My People'" (v. 25). From Hosea, Paul draws the beautiful model of God's redeeming love, changing Lo Ami into Ami (Hebrew for "Not My People" and "My People"). In poetic parallelism "Not Loved" becomes "Loved." This is the gospel! Preach it! One does not have to continue in a fixed fate. There can be a mighty reversal. God can call "Being" out of "non-Being" (4:17). He can bring Isaac from a barren womb (4:19) and bring Jesus alive from the tomb (4:24). Those who were not his people can become his people: "It shall be in the place where it was said to them, 'You are not my people, there they shall be called the sons of the living God'" (v. 26).

We would be more comfortable with Paul had he not gone so far in presenting God's freedom as though it were arbitrary power employed with no regard to the rights of mankind even to ask "Why?" In fairness to Paul, we must understand him in terms of his own way of putting things, and especially must we hear him out. When we do, as here, the apparent divine determinism gives way to God's freedom used patiently with a view to redemption. Whatever Paul claims for God as his sovereign right or freedom, he clearly sees mankind's fate as hanging in the balances, with God keeping open options for "wrath" or "mercy." This agrees with Paul's agonizing concerns as reflected in the very fact that he engages in a ministry of writing and missionary travel.

Preaching should make clear the difference between determinism and such exercise of divine sovereignty and freedom as Paul develops here. Isolated proof-texts can go either way. Seen holistically, Romans avoids any idea that God manipulates us like clay. Were we just clay, not only would we have no right to ask "Why?" but Paul's very letter would be pointless. The letter does in fact take most seriously our "Why?" A sermon here could show how we remain free and responsible in the presence of God's dealing with us in both judgment and redemption. God's sovereignty does not rob us of freedom of choice nor free us from freedom or responsibility of choice.

The One Reason for the Plight of Israel
(9:30–10:21)

This unit is less problematic than the preceding one, with some elusiveness but clear enough in the main. In brief, Paul moves through a long series of possible explanations for Israel's plight, narrowing them down to one: "To Israel he says, 'All the day long I stretched out my hands to a people disobedient and obstinate' " (10:21). In 10:2 it is a misinformed zeal in which they rely upon themselves and not God that accounts for it. It is not due to any neglect on God's part, for there is an accessible Christ (10:6–8); salvation is theirs on attainable terms, by simply calling upon the Lord (10:9–13); the saving word has been proclaimed throughout the world (10:14–18); even the "no nations" have found God through this word (10:19–20). Only one explanation remains: Israel rejected God's overture (10:21).

In preaching from this passage, one might liken it to a long chain in which is one weak or missing link. From God's provision to mankind's reception of salvation there are many "links" or steps: the fact of a savior; the accessibility of the savior; conditions that are attainable (hearing, faith, understanding). All these conditions are satisfied. There is the Christ, and he is as near as the word in one's mouth. One needs but to call upon him. The word has been preached and it has been heard and understood by nations despised by Israel. Only Israel's presumption of her own merits blinded her to her only hope, simply in faith to receive God's offered gift. God willed it, but they did not. God spoke; they talked back.

In preaching today, utmost care should be taken not to reflect adversely upon Jews generally or Jews today. Paul was a Jew, and he was pleading for and with his own dear people. In no sense was he anti-Jewish, and nothing here warrants our being anti-Jewish. The enduring point is that privilege tends to make us presumptuous. We presume upon privilege. The advantaged tend to let their advantage obscure their need for help beyond themselves. Wealth, position, personal gifts, and the like tend to make us feel self-sufficient. Paul found this in his own people. We may well find it in ourselves and in our people. One might entitle a sermon: "Presuming Upon Privilege." This presumption may include our consciously or unconsciously putting God in a theological box. It may be the presumption of excluding others from privilege claimed for ourselves. It may be the presumption by which we unwittingly exclude ourselves as Paul saw Israel as having done and the Gentiles as equally endangered. Any of us can blow our opportunity by presuming upon privilege.

The Stone Over Which Israel Stumbled (9:30–10:4)

Israel stumbled over "a stone of stumbling, a rock of offence" (9:33). Paul is not explicit, but his reference may be to Christ, with salvation by grace through faith in mind. Probably Christ himself is the "stone of stumbling." In a real sense, they stumbled over grace, for human pride resents the idea of dependence upon grace. We as Paul's people prefer to see ourselves as deserving of the best which comes to us. We likewise like to blame someone else for all that is adverse in life for us. Preaching today needs to help people see that salvation with movement toward true righteousness begins at that point where we are willing to acknowledge our sins and our needs and look to God in faith, confident that he can bring about in us the righteousness which eludes our own zeal. Paul is surely right; those who trust him will not be disappointed (v. 33).

"A zeal for God they have, but not according to knowledge" (10:2). A suggested sermon topic is "Zeal Is Not Enough." Paul saw his people as lost. The anguish of 9:1– 5 reappears here. Paul's "prayer to God" for Israel would be pointless if he really believed that God completely determines human fate, if he believed that Israel was already saved, or if he believed that there was no hope for Israel. The prayer voiced in 10:1 implies that he did see Israel as hanging in the balances and that his entreaties and their response had meaning. Isolated verses in Romans which seem to imply the contrary are overcome by the thrust of this passage and the prevailing thrusts of the letter as a whole. Paul is not beating a dead horse. He is pleading for decisions which are authentically that. Paul is repetitious here, which itself accents his concern that his people exercise options which are live and real.

"The end of the law" (10:4). By "end" Paul means goal. Christ is the fulfillment of what the law intends. In particular, the righteousness which the law demands but cannot accomplish is a reality in Christ. He embodies that righteousness, and he is able to bring it about in the one trusting him. This is more than "forensic" (legal) or bookkeeping righteousness. It is not make-believe righteousness. It is new standing and new quality of existence. A sermon may be developed here on the intriguing title, "The End of the Law." Of course, the ambiguous term "end" would need to be clarified. Legalist fears of moral laxity and libertine euphoria of license to do as one pleases both need to be answered. The nature of and means to righteousness call for clarification in sermon. Righteousness is uprightness in life, and we catch it from exposure to God.

How So Great a Salvation Is Missed (10:5–21)

Against the background of a "doing" kind of righteousness as in the law of Moses (v. 5), Paul gives a depth analysis of how "the righteousness out of faith" is possible (6– 20). In a single verse (21), he declares the one ingredient lacking in Israel, the obedient faith which alone can receive God's free offer of salvation.

"Do not say, Who shall ascend . . . descend . . .?" (vv. 6 – 7). Paul liked to clothe his thought in Scripture (our OT), and he almost talks in riddles at times, as here. In context his intention seems to be clear enough. He is declaring that Jesus Christ is alive and accessible. He is not a distant Lord, inaccessible in Heaven. No search party needs to be sent above to look for him, "to bring him down." Neither is he a dead prophet, down in "the abyss" and requiring that someone go down there and bring him up. This is the first ingredient in what Paul sees as necessary to salvation: a living and accessible savior. Jesus Christ is such a one. He is alive and here. A sermon here may point out that deism is a belief in God, but in one who is remote from his world. Pantheism is the equation of all that is with God. Biblical faith (Theism) sees God as distinct from his creation but always related directly to it. God works within history and in his world, sustaining it, judging it, commanding it, saving it, and bringing it forward toward its goal (this is what eschatology means). Jesus Christ is God in his deepest involvement in his world.

"Near you is the word" (v. 8). Shifting from the living presence to Christ, Paul turns to "the word" (rhema). This "word" is the proclaimed word and the word which calls to saving faith. The term logos is often employed for this "word," but here rhema seems to carry the same force. The preached word must become the heard word (Paul returns to this in vv. 11 – 18). This is a second ingredient necessary if salvation by faith is possible. This "word" is accessible, just as the Living Christ is accessible. It is as near as the word in the mouth and in the heart. God is able to speak to us, and we are able to hear and answer him. This is how salvation begins. It is not by keeping this law or that one; it is by hearing God and answering him. The word has been preached, and it can be heard: received in the heart and confessed with the mouth.

"With the heart . . . with the mouth" (vv. 9 – 13). Confession is more than verbalizing; a tape-recorder can recite anything we record on it without knowing what it is doing. Salvation is not gained simply by creedal confession. Meaningful confession must correspond to what is in the heart. One believes "with the heart." The term "heart" refers to the whole inner structure of feeling, thought, and will. It is trust, an openness to God to receive what he offers and yield what he requires. This is saving faith. It is first faith in the heart and then confession with the mouth. Through his word God calls out to us, and in faith we call back to him. This option is open to "Jew and Greek." Salvation is available on these simple terms to "whoever may call upon the name of the Lord" (v. 13). The "name" stands for the person. Salvation takes place where God and we come into direct relationship with one another, possible only where faith meets faith, where his entrusting himself to us awakens us to trust in him.

"How shall they call upon him?" (vv. 14–15). Unless one trusts God, one will not call upon him. To trust him, one first must hear him. To hear him requires that there be some channel through which he may speak and we may hear. Such a channel is found in preaching. Paul declares that all these conditions have been met, for there is such preaching as makes it possible for one to hear God, trust God, and call upon God. This is quite a compliment to preaching! It likewise is a frightening demand upon preaching. Does our preaching meet this test?

"Who has trusted our hearing/report *(akoe)?* (vv. 16–17). Paul makes a play on the Greek term *akoe,* letting it serve for both faith's hearing of the word of God and the preacher's proclaiming of the word. The word must be heard before it can be preached. It is the "heard word" which stands behind authentic preaching. The heard word becomes the preached word, and thus it may again be heard by anyone with faith, the openness of trust. By preaching Paul does not mean just any kind of mouthing of words such as plagues the air waves today. Much passes for preaching where the Word of God has not been heard and thus is not what is proclaimed. Paul speaks of a beautiful "chain-reaction" as the preacher's *akoe* is the word which he first hears and then proclaims and which in the heart of the believer is heard again and in his mouth confessed again.

May Israel plead that she did not hear? (vv. 18–20). If not, it is not because there was no opportunity. The "utterance" went out into all the earth, and the "words" unto the ends of the inhabited world (v. 18). Were the words past understanding? This does not follow, for less advantaged ones heard and responded (vv. 19–20). Moses warned that "no nations" (nobodies) and people "without understanding" (as seen by the advantaged) would respond in such a way as to move Israel to jealousy. Isaiah boldly declared that God would be found by those not seeking him, meaning the Gentiles. Surely then, Israel is without excuse. Sermons today may follow Paul, except that where he chided his own people, we may chide our own advantaged people.

"A people disobedient and contrary" (v. 21). This is it. Only one ingredient is lacking, the willingness to trust God. God talked and favored people talked back ("gainsaying" in KJV is a good rendering). If Israel is lost, this and this only accounts for it. God does not fail us, but we may fail him. This is "The Missing Link." Here is a sermon topic for today.

Rejection of Israel Not Total Nor Final (11:1–36)

Moderation did not come easy to Paul. In chapter 9 he wrote with such intense passion in vindicating God's right to full freedom that he almost did an overkill, stopping just short of representing God as arbitrary in dealing with people. In fact, he went so far that logic compelled what he himself had to draw back from. In chapter 11 Paul is just as intense, this time in his case for Israel. In chapter 9, Israel can be lost. In chapter 11 Paul clings to his confidence in Israel's future, building up to the baffling claim: "Thus all Israel shall be saved" (v. 26). The chapter has four movements: rejection of Israel has never been total, for there is the saved remnant (vv. 1– 10); Israel's temporary stumbling is a factor in the salvation of the Gentiles, who themselves may be rejected should they fail in faith (vv. 11 – 24); the final restoration of Israel (vv. 25 – 32); and a doxology confessing that God's ways are beyond our understanding (vv. 33 – 36).

The problems of this chapter do not yield to any fully satisfactory solution. Taken literally or at face value, unrelieved tension remains especially between v. 26 and much else which Paul has written. Without resort to special pleading, the interpreter must either find Paul in hopeless conflict with himself or else seek the underlying thrusts of his letter, simply recognizing that Paul was not a systematizer, tying up all loose ends in perfect coherence. Another way of putting it is that Paul must be heard holistically, and his interpreter must bear much of the burden of modifying one of his statements by another. If Paul really believed that literally all Israel would be

saved, it is not apparent why he agonized over Israel as he did
or why he could speak in terms of a limited number to be
saved (11:14; see 9:6). Further, Paul's vision that the Gentile
mission and Israel's ultimate salvation are accelerated by
both Israel's stumbling and Israel's return to faith is hardly
compelling to the modern mind. I would not try to build a sermon upon this. However, there is an exciting basis for preaching as one senses Paul's spirit, with its fierce loyalty to his own
people. That he could risk all for his mission to the Gentiles
and yet maintain such deep devotion to his own people is a
model instructive for preaching today.

Rejection of Israel Not Total (11:1–10)

Did God reject Israel? Paul rejects this idea. One is not
saved by being an Israelite (chap. 9) and one is not lost by being an Israelite (chap. 11). Paul is an Israelite and proud of it.
Even in the time of Elijah when Baal worship was strong,
there were seven thousand in Israel who had not bowed the
knee to Baal. Paul is consistent in holding that salvation does
not stand in a one-to-one relationship with ethnic identity. We
are not saved *en bloc* but individually, although in salvation
we are saved into a new "block," the church the body of Christ
(12:5).

"A remnant according to the election of grace" (v. 5). Salvation is God's gift out of his grace and not a reward for keeping the law of Moses or for any human merit. Further,
salvation cannot be both by God's grace and human works, for
one precludes the other. To this point Paul is perfectly clear,
and "Election" can be preached clearly today. Election is
God's initiative in opening up new ground upon which sinners
may stand. It is his knowing us before we know him and his
calling us before we answer. It is his achievement and not
ours. Only if "election" is seen as arbitrary, coercive, or deter-
minative does it become problematic. If election overrides or
ignores human freedom, it is only by special pleading that it
can be defended as just on God's part or salutary for mankind.
If human freedom is set aside, what follows is destruction and
not salvation. Paul leaves himself open to this understanding
of election, but he writes much to prohibit this deterministic
understanding of election.

"The election obtained it" (v. 7). There is no problem in

the claim that Israel failed to obtain the salvation which she sought by works of the law or that it was through election that salvation did follow. If vv. 8–10 compel that election be understood as divine determination of human attitudes or action, it is not apparent how this can be reconciled with justice or Paul's stance elsewhere. There is an old argument which tries to defend election as selective, coercive, and just. It argues that none merit salvation, so any salvation is gift. Further, it is assumed as established that God saves some but not all. Now comes the "logic." If God has the right to save some but not all, he has the right to choose to save some but not all. This simply does not follow. It is a *non sequitur*. You have the right to enter a burning house and rescue everyone in it as far as you can. It does not have to be "all or none." But it would be an entirely different matter to choose to rescue some but choose not to rescue others. If God chooses that some be lost and only some be saved, there is no way this can be vindicated as right. Is this Paul's position? I do not believe that it is, even though he leaves himself open to this conclusion. Where do we find "the bottom line" in Paul's theology of salvation? It is not in isolated texts but in the wholeness of his writings and in his missionary action.

"The rest were hardened" (v. 7). The hardening came as a result of divine action, but that does not mean that God willed the hardening. When God speaks one does not remain the same. One is either bettered or worsened. To resist God is to become hardened. It may be said that God hardens our hearts, but this is true only in a resultant sense and not in terms of God's purpose. Love always runs the risk of hardening the other, whether expressed by God or by us toward one another. A loving parent may awaken only a negative response in a child, in effect hardening the child although this is the opposite of the intention.

"God gave them a spirit of stupor" (v. 8). If God purposed that Israel be in a stupor, blind, and deaf, that is irreconcilable with divine justice or human freedom. Isolated, this verse may so teach. In context it seems that Paul's meaning must be understood as a result of divine action and not intention. We have seen in 1:18–32 that God gave people over to their own stubbornness, but this was against the background of divine overtures designed for a better result. In 10:21 Paul is explicit

that Israel's plight was due to resistance to God's overture.
Grace is not irresistible. Jesus wept over Jerusalem: "I would
... but you would not"(Matt 23:37). Stupor, blind eyes, and
deaf ears result from refusal to see, hear, and respond. A sermon here may be developed under the theme: "Blinded by the
Light." Light may result in sight, but it likewise may blind
one. Sound may be heard, yet it may deafen the ears. In a sermon, of course, the difference may be shown to be bound up
with our response. To close our eyes to the light does not put
out the light; it puts out our sight. What happened to Paul's
kin may happen to us.

"Let their table become a snare and a trap" (v. 9). It is not
apparent what Paul intended in much of this quotation from
"David." Probably he was attracted to the passage because of
its line about eyes darkened so as not to see (v. 10). This rein-
forces v. 8; and probably v. 9 is not to be pressed, it simply belonging to the passage quoted for the sake of v. 10. If v. 9 is to
be pressed, the point may be the peril of presuming on privilege. Israel misread favor (the table God spread for her?) as
something she deserved, leading her to think of righteousness
as her own achievement. In a sermon today on "The Peril of
Presuming on Privilege" we might remind ourselves of the
danger of misconstruing our advantages as signs of our merit.
There is a theology which interprets favorable position
(health, wealth, power) as God's blessings upon our faith or
piety. To some, health or wealth implies human goodness or
piety; illness or adversity implies sin or failure (for example,
Job's friends). "Faith healers" are guilty of this fallacy, but the
fallacy crops up in more camps than this one.

How Israel Affects the Gentile Mission (11:11–24)

Paul's optimism for the conversion of Jews and Gentiles
was seemingly unbounded as he wrote this chapter. Jewish
defection was only temporary, and it opened the door to a
more direct Gentile mission. When synagogue doors closed to
the missionaries, they went more directly to the Gentiles (Acts
13:46). Next, the conversion of the Gentiles would move the
Jews to jealousy as they saw these aliens entering into their
heritage, and this would bring about the conversion of the
Jews. Somehow both the defection of the Jews and their conversion effects the same result, the winning of the Gentiles.

Paul's vision still awaits fulfillment. If chapter 11 be taken as history written in advance it is most difficult to sustain. If Paul be permitted to be a Jew who dearly loves his own people even as he is driven by a strong sense of mission to the Gentiles the chapter makes sense as it reflects his heart throb. Love does not give up on its own. We do not fault the mother who yet believes in her child when all others see reality otherwise. Paul cares enough for Jew and Gentile to commit himself fully to all the risks of a mission to Spain by way of Jerusalem and Rome. More than love and courage motivate him; he really believes that the gospel will prevail over both Jew and Gentile, winning both to a fellowship in Christ which overcomes historic alienation. He is sustained by hope.

There is room here for a sermon on "Sustained by Hope" or "Love Does Not Give Up on Its Own." Deal with the human situation today in which many parents and others see their loved ones apparently lost yet cling to the hope for a better outcome. Show the need for the realism that sees that there are no "fail-safe" nations (Israel or others) or people. We can fail. On the other hand, show that, like Paul, it is a right thing to cling to hope and that true love does not give up.

Chapter 11 has been used for unrealistic predictions of a wholesale return of the Jews to the Holy Land with a returning Messiah at last establishing there the kingdom of God. Such preaching awakens expectations doomed to disappointment. Fanciful scenarios can be fashioned in sensational sermons, but this is religious show business which has little touch with reality. It overlooks Paul's own solid position that "in Christ there is not any Jew and Greek, bond and free, male and female" (Gal 3:28). It revives claims for ethnic and geographical significance   ade obsolete in Christ, to say nothing of confusing the kingdom of God with the very kind of messianism Jesus rejected (see Mk 8:31; 10:45; 13:22; Acts 1:6–7). We need no such sermons from Rom 11.

"To move them to jealousy" (v. 11). Isolated and taken at face value, Paul simply "used" the Gentiles as a means of winning Israel. Nothing is more degrading or dehumanizing than to be used. Does Paul write Gentiles and admit to them that their value is chiefly that they can be used to make Jews jealous? How significant is a "salvation" motivated by jealousy? When Paul is seen and heard in the larger context of his ministry and writings, these motives seem surely to fall far short of explaining him. Paul had a way of reaching out for every analogy or argument to establish a point, and he left himself open to some surprising postures. Paul did write the amazing paragraph in vv. 11 – 16, where he is explicit in his intention to move his people (flesh) to jealousy by his Gentile mission (v. 14), and this enters into the evidence as to how Paul thought. The plea here is that Paul be heard in other moods and other expressions as when he is willing to become *anathema* from Christ for his kin (9:3) and when he rejects a slight to the uncircumcised as not even walking in the direction of the Gospel (Gal 2:11 – 14). There is a hermeneutical principle here, a principle for biblical interpretation, essential to sound preaching. To flatten the Bible, according each verse equal authority, opens the way to any position on any subject one chooses. For example, one could from Scripture prove that it is wrong to eat catfish (Lev 11:9 – 12), even though many Bible-believing Christians participate in catfish suppers at church. From his own lines Paul can be made to look foolish, bigoted, or partial. This does no justice to Paul or Scripture. Intention behind words and larger context must be considered in biblical interpretation and preaching.

"If the first fruits be holy, also the lump" (v. 16) is an amazing analogy, along with the further one to the effect that if the root be holy so also the branches. Logically, then, the solidarity of Israel is maintained and the salvation of Abraham or Jacob assures the salvation of all Israel (as in v. 26). But this poses insoluble problems for chapter 9, where "not all out of Israel are Israel" (9:6) and where "election" is independent of parentage, even where Esau comes from the same womb as Jacob (9:10 – 11). This is further evidence that Paul can be quoted in support of opposite positions. There are prevailing currents in his thought and expression, supported by his actions, and these must be sought as in commentary or sermon we try to understand Paul. Isolated, v. 16 settles the question of Jewish salvation and makes Romans redundant. Paul's intense actions and agony require a different answer. Even the next paragraph shows this, for "branches," Jewish or Gentile, may be torn out or grafted in. The situation is "live," not fixed like a pre-recorded TV program. The abiding truth here is that "roots" do have something to do with "fruits." We can be served by our heritage. The error is to absolutize this as a principle. Don't forget that both Jacob and Esau can come from the same parents. From the same root came different fruits.

"A wild olive, contrary to nature, grafted into a good olive" (v. 24). Paul has been laughed at here, seen as a city man who did not understand horticulture. The joke is on his critics, not on Paul. This is one of Paul's better illustrations. He knows that it is contrary to nature to graft a branch from a wild olive into the stock of a cultivated olive. That is his point. For Gentiles to be in the family of God and Jews not is as surprising and contrary to Paul's past history as for a nurseryman to graft a wild olive branch into the trunk of a good olive. We get Paul's point only if we look around and see who we are—almost exclusively Gentiles! Who would have foreseen this, say around A.D. 30? Imagine a succession of Abraham, Isaac, Jacob, and Bill! Only because we have lost touch with our roots do we take it for granted that a Gentile church is normal and the conversion of a Jew is news. The church was cradled in Judaism, but by Paul's time it already was becoming more Gentile than Jewish. Paul could not envision a church without Jews.

The Restoration of Israel (11:25–32)

"And thus all Israel shall be saved" (v. 26). This much controverted verse gathers up the force of the whole paragraph with its amazing scenario of Jewish and Gentile fluctuating states and roles. Paul's practical concern is to justify his mission to Jerusalem, contending that God yet has a place in his purposes for Israel. Writing from Corinth, he is justifying to Gentiles (see v. 13, "To you the Gentiles I speak") his mission to Jerusalem (15:25 – 32) as he anticipates criticism for it. The Gentiles could ask, "Why should you as apostle to the Gentiles delay your mission to Spain and risk so much by this journey back to Jerusalem? Why not go immediately to Spain?" Paul is fighting desperately to hold on to his own people without jeopardizing his mission to the Gentiles. He is warning Gentile Christians that they dare not forget Israel. Paul engages in almost an oversell in a picture in which God is faithful to his covenant and uses every means to save Israel, including the changing stances of each. If we press Paul's scenario and write history from it or build systematic theology from it, we become enmeshed in insoluble problems. If we are willing to listen to this as the heart throb and pleadings of a missionary hard pressed by Jewish/Gentile tensions, the paragraph speaks meaningfully. What is of abiding value for us is the recognition that God cares for both Jew and Gentile and so must we. Salvation remains an open option for both. This is what we may properly preach from this passage.

The adverb "thus" is a key word in v. 26. It is not "then" but "thus" all Israel will be saved: a Deliverer comes out of Zion and turns ungodliness from Jacob; God keeps his covenant with Israel by dealing with his sins (v. 27); Jew and Gentile are brought under the same judgment, so that both may come under the same mercy (v. 32). Each must hear God's "No" before that one may hear God's "Yes." The promised salvation for Israel is not arbitrary or coercive; it is moral and right. It is deliverance from sins. Paul's purpose here, however, is not to describe the nature of salvation so much as to vindicate his mission to Jerusalem and show its correlation with his mission to the Gentiles.

How Inscrutable Are God's Ways (11:33–36)

Paul realized that his scenario was becoming difficult, so he broke it off. He had introduced it as a "mystery" (v. 25), and he left it as such: "Oh the depth of the wealth and wisdom and knowledge of God!" God's judgments are unfathomable and his ways past tracing out. We can see God's "tracks," but we cannot trace out his trail. Paul means that God deals with Israel and with Gentiles, both in their defections and obedience, in ways beyond our understanding. Despite the mystery, Paul remains confident that God has the good of Jew and Gentile at heart and that he will carry through in his commitment to the salvation of both. This is Paul's warrant for his mission to Spain by way of Jerusalem.

Preaching here had best avoid any attempt to predict history or work out elaborate eschatological scenarios. There are rich and relevant preaching themes here: the faithfulness of God to his commitments, the involvement of God in history, the impartiality of God, the role of judgment in salvation, sins and the human predicament, the residue of mystery beyond all human understanding.

Righteousness in the Workaday World
(Romans 12:1–15:6)

The tone of the letter changes perceptibly here. It is an over-simplification, however, to say that chapters 1–11 are theological and chapters 12–16 practical. The whole letter is practical, in that its basic concern is to justify both Paul's Jewish and Gentile missions, in particular his mission to Spain by way of Jerusalem and Rome. To this point he has given a theological foundation for a mission inclusive of Jew and Gentile. Chapters 12–16 are more overtly practical and less apparently theological, but they are both. Theology underlies all the practical concerns of these chapters. Paul is not interested in theology for its own sake but always relates it to the decisions and commitments of life. Likewise, his practical counsels are grounded in theology. Preaching should show that the real value in theology is not speculative but practical. Doctrine is guidance for life.

Servanthood in the Body of Christ (12:1–8)

The gospel makes moral and ethical demands upon the whole self in one's bodily existence in the everyday world. This is one's "spiritual service" (v. 1). There is a sermon here on "Spirituality Embodied." Just as Paul had to refute the libertines in chapter 6, so here he refutes the idea that "spirituality" is ghostly instead of bodily. This anticipates chapter 13, where Christian life is to be "bodily" even to the extent of paying taxes. Being "in Christ" does not mean that one is not to be responsibly in the world. Whether a problem in Rome or not, Paul did encounter this problem at Corinth, from which this letter was written. Presumably, the problem of pseudo-spirituality was general enough that Paul felt it necessary to deal with it here. Much of the letter refutes legalism; equally dangerous was its opposite threat of otherworldliness in the name of spirituality.

"The renewing of your mind" (v. 2). Paul believed in conversion as a radical turn when one makes a response of faith to God's grace. But Paul also saw salvation as dynamic, not static. "Mind" does not imply "mind-set." Mind represents the inner self of feeling, thought, and will; and this is to be under continuing renewal. Its goal is conformity to God's will. That will is not arbitrary; it is good, suited to our personhood, and perfect. We are not to be fashioned to this age (the world apart from God) but to be in an ongoing transformation as the inner self is being made more agreeable to the will of God (conformed to the image of God's Son as in 8:29). Here are two related ideas for preaching: "Service in Bodily Existence" and "Continuing Renewal Within." Christian life is to be neither ghostly nor secular.

"One body in Christ" (v. 5). Christians are neither naked souls (ghosts) nor lone rangers/rangerettes. We live and serve in bodily/historical existence, and we live and work in community, in the Church as the body of Christ. We are in the "one body" because we are "in Christ," not vice versa. One cannot be "in Christ" and remain alone or apart from others (14:7; 1 Cor 12:13). The Church is "the body of Christ," not just a body of Christians. It is Christ's continuing incarnation. This is a dangerous idea, yet it appears here. The danger is that we confuse ourselves with God, and this is idolatry. In a real sense Christ does continue to live and work in the fellowship of his people, and "body" serves as a powerful analogy for this relationship.

A body is a unity but not just a member. A morgue full of parts does not constitute a body, however many arms, legs, heads, etc. It must be holistic; so with the Church. Again, a body never consists of just one member (see 1 Cor 12:12–31 for elaboration). The church, as a body, has many members, and each has its own function (v. 4). This leaves no room for conceit. There is a play on words in v. 3. Although renewal of mind *(nous)* is proper, we are not to be "superminded" *(hyperphronein)*. Apparently, Paul had to deal with a form of "spirituality" marked by conceit. There are many sermons here on bodily service, renewal, the body of Christ, sober mindedness.

"Gifts according to grace" (v. 6). Paul's play on words here is deliberate and powerful: *charismata* (charismatic gifts) *kata charin* (according to grace). *Charisma* is the word for grace *(charis)* with a result suffix *(ma)* added. Anything we have by the grace of God is charismatic. In the secular world today charisma implies some gift of personality attractive to other people. We used to call this "it." Without being specific, one was said to have "it" or not. At least this usage retains the idea of *charis* as gift. In popular religion "charismatic" stands for some exotic or superworldly gift. Neither the secular nor popular religious idea represents NT usage. Paul included one's gift for celibacy or marriage among the charismatic gifts (1 Cor 7:7)! In the text before us (vv. 6–8) the "gifts of grace" or *charismata* include preaching (prophecy is a form of preaching), ministry *(diakonia)*, teaching, counselling, distributing money, the executive or administrative function of presiding, and mercy. The list is representative, not exhaustive. The point is that these are gifts, so not to be competitive or occasions for conceit. They are to be exercised. Possession of the gift carries with it the responsibility for its usage.

Much needed is a biblical doctrine of charisma. Why let the secular world or religious extremism obscure the clear teaching of Paul as to what is the nature of the charismatic? The whole church is charismatic. Unfortunately, not all God's children have shoes, but all God's children have charisma. Eternal life itself is "the charisma of God" (6:23). Charisma relates no more to Holy Spirit than to Father or Son. It is any gift by the grace of God. There is not only the falsely-based pride of some to be challenged, but more importantly good people who have been made to feel inferior in the presence of some boasting to be "charismatic," need to be helped here. They are entitled to a better self-image, and sound preaching on "the charisma of God" can help them.

Women are not mentioned in vv. 6–8, but there may be far-reaching implication for them in what Paul says about "the charismata according to grace." His main point is that there is a variety of gifts, but he is clear in the teaching that the possession of a gift carries with it the responsibility for its exercise. Suppose a woman has the gift of preaching, teaching, administration, or any other? The question is not whether she has the right to use the gift, but does she have the right not to? Does the church have the right to deny a woman the right to exercise a gift she has by God's grace? Gal 3:28 may be Paul's most forceful text bearing upon the rights and responsi-

bilities of woman ("in Christ there is not any male and female"), but Rom 12:6– 8 may be as significant.

Love Issuing in Goodness (12:9–21)

Every verse in this passage is loaded with insight and relevance to Christian living. There is an important sermon in almost each verse. In brief, Paul contends that genuine love
should be reflected in our cleaving to the good and loathing
the evil, in affection like that within a family, in hospitality, in
sharing *(koinonia)* , in sensitivity to one another in joy and
sorrow, in being at peace with others, in shunning vengeance,
and in bringing good out of evil. The passage sounds much
like the Sermon on the Mount.

Two verses in this rich paragraph are especially suited to
preaching (vv. 15, 21). It probably is easier for most of us to
weep with those who weep than to rejoice with those who
rejoice. Those who weep probably need us more than do those
who rejoice, but we may stand in greater need of the grace of
rejoicing with those who rejoice than of weeping with those
who weep. Although it is all too common for us to be insensi-
tive to human need, it sometimes is easier to move us to pity
than to joy over another's good fortune. The two moods need
not be competitive, and we need to work at both capacities,
weeping and rejoicing. Anyway, there are many facets to this
subject ripe for one or more sermons.

"Conquering Evil with Good" (v. 21) likewise lends itself
to many-faceted development. Evil has its most complete victory over us when it makes us over into its image. The great
peril in war is that a nation simply outdo its enemy on its own
ground and in terms of its own evil. The same peril lurks in all
our fight with or against evil. Herman Melville in *Moby Dick*
developed this theme in a novel. Moby Dick, the white whale,
symbolized evil; and Captain Ahab was driven by the obses-
sion that he alone could and must destroy Moby Dick. He became a fiend in his fight against "evil," and he destroyed not
only himself but his crew with himself. We can be overcome
by evil in the very way we fight it. Less disastrous is to "roll
with the punches" and neither defeat evil or succumb to it. A
third outcome is to remove the evil without filling the vacuum. Paul's admonition is the creative one of bringing about
good out of a situation of evil (as in 8:28). This does not imply

that evil is of God, that God wills it, or that it is good that
there is evil. Evil is just that—evil. It is not of God. Yet against
the background of evil good can come. We can get a better
sense of value and direction as we cope with evil. We can be
awakened to a better awareness of one another. We can find
new sources of strength. Both natural "evils" like earthquake,
tornado, or flood and moral evils like war, discrimination,
and oppression can become dynamic situations out of which
are found new incentive, courage, and direction for good.
"Heaping coals of fire upon the head" of one's enemy by returning good for evil is a victory over evil for oneself, and
hopefully for the other. If just to shame him, it is another form
of evil.

Christian Citizenship (13:1–7)

The classic statement on this subject comes from Jesus:
"Give back to Caesar what belongs to Caesar and give back to
God what belongs to God" (Mk 12:13–17). Paul follows Jesus
closely here as in the preceding paragraph. Jesus did not imply that Caesar and God are peers, each with a sovereign zone.
What we receive from or owe Caesar does not compare with
what we receive from and owe God. Both Jesus and Paul did
recognize that we do receive benefactions from "Caesar" and
thus have certain debts to "Caesar." Jesus demonstrated it by
calling for a coin. The very fact that his questioners carried
Caesar's coin was evidence that they already were in business
with him. Paul was unambiguous, even to taxes (v. 7). Every
time we drive down a public road, cross a public bridge, or rely upon the protection of the police we show ourselves to be
beneficiaries of and thus debtors to government at some level.

Paul did not accord absolute sovereignty to "the authorities that be" (v. 1). He saw the authority to be "God's servant
(diakonos) unto good" (v. 4). Civil authorities themselves are
answerable to God, and the public good is the validation of
their authority. Any human totalitarianism is idolatrous and
evil. Only God has total claim upon us. Human authority over
another, whether corporate or individual, is to be that authority alone which is necessary to the discharge of responsibility.
The driver of an automobile must have the authority of the
wheel, but this does not give him authority over the passen-
gers otherwise, as for example when they stop for a meal. A

parent must have just that authority over a child necessary to meeting the responsibilities to the child—no more, no less, and no other than that precise authority. So it is with government. The basic controls are: under God and for good. Preaching should inform people as to the proper role and limits of government and sensitize them to their civic responsibilities.

Why did Paul introduce this theme into Romans? We know that at Corinth, the place of writing, there were some "pneumatics" who saw spirituality as setting one apart from the world. In 12:1–2 Paul called for "bodily" spirituality. Probably this call to responsible citizenship was directed against a Gnosticizing tendency or some kind of world-escaping "spirituality." Paul took the position that it is proper for a Christian to try to be a responsible citizen. The situation behind Rom 13 is nothing like that behind Rev 13, where the state has become beastly. In Revelation, Christians are not encouraged to fight the state with its weapons, but they are called to non-violent resistance. Dealing with different situations, Rom 13 calls for Christian engagement with the world and Rev 13 calls for Christian disengagement from the world. These motives are not contradictory; they both answer to the claim: Render to Caesar what belongs to Caesar and God what belongs to God.

Sermons explicating these principles are much needed. Preaching should help people grow in civic responsibility without falling into the trap of civil religion, confusing God and country. The need for government, not anarchy, is to be recognized. No form of government is to be identified or equated with Christianity. Though some forms of government are more open to humane principles than others, no form is fail-safe. Any form can be corrupted. No government can properly take the place of God. Final allegiance is to God.

Not to be overlooked is Paul's grounding of citizenship in "conscience" (v. 5). Christian citizenship is determined not by the moral quality of the state, often found wanting. It is determined by the moral quality of the Christian. One's disposition is to be supportive. On the other hand, conscience opens another door, not dealt with by Paul here—civil disobedience when required by conscience. Daniel, Peter, and many others belong to a long line of people who have found it necessary on occasion to obey God (as understood by conscience) rather than civil authority. The NT clearly provides for non-violent civil disobedience, where one answers to a higher claim and is prepared to suffer for it. Preaching should not leave this matter in doubt or leave it fuzzy.

Love as Fulfillment of the Law (13:8–10)

The highest claim upon us is that of love. All that is intended by laws against adultery, murder, theft, and covetousness is covered by the law of love. Love as understood here is more than a feeling, although it includes that. It is not to be confused with the self-centeredness which often is called love. Often when one says, "I love" one means "I desire" or "I want." When one "loves" chocolate pie one wants to eat it, not bring about its fulfillment or wellbeing. To love one's neighbor is to have the disposition to relate to the neighbor for that one's good. Love may be expressed by giving or withholding, determined by what seems best to serve the good of the other. Love does not ask if the other is deserving but only what will enhance. In preaching on love *(agape)* one might contrast it with the Greek *eros*, an acquisitive kind of "love." Plato in myth explained *eros* as the child of *penia* (need) and *poros* (means), hence a sense of need seeking some means of fulfillment. He described *eros* as either "heavenly" *(ouranios)* or "earthly" *(pandemos)*. It could seek fulfillment in the good and beautiful or in the sordid, but its constant was self-centeredness. What Paul means by *"agape"* is the kind of giving or serving love which became incarnate in Jesus Christ, not the world's self-serving "love."

A sermon on "The Nature of Christian Love" should show that it is not predicated on the qualities of the object but of the subject, that it is always concerned for the good of the object, that it is morally responsible, and that it is sacrificial.

Life Suited to the Day (13:11–14)

Paul apparently saw himself as living "in the last times." All early Christians did. They expected "the day" of Christ to come soon, bringing both judgment and salvation to culmination. There is no evidence that Paul expected two millennia or more of continuing history. To live in expectancy of the near return of Christ is positive; to fix a time table is unwarranted. Paul's concern was not to set a date for the return of Christ but to call his readers to a moral quality of life suited to the presence of Christ, expected at any time.

"Now is our salvation nearer than when we first believed" (v. 11). This sees salvation as a process, with a beginning and a goal. Only in the resurrection of the body and the renewal of creation does Paul see salvation as completed (see 8:18– 30).

"Light" and "darkness" are moral conceptions in Paul's usage, as generally in the Bible. We think of a "benighted person" as ignorant, but biblically such a one is evil. To be "enlightened" today is to be informed, but in the NT "light" has to do with goodness. To "walk in light" is to live morally. Note also that "strife and jealousy" are as much "darkness" as "drunkenness and bedding down" (v. 13). Good and evil to some of Paul's contemporaries (Gnostics?) were understood as spirit vs. matter. To Paul the distinction is moral. The material as such is not moral or immoral; what we do with it is good or evil. One might preach here on "Walking In Light" or "Who Are the Enlightened?"

Answering to God Rather Than to One Another (14:1–12)

Two groups within the church appear here, divided over such matters as diet and a religious calendar. Some rejected meat in favor of vegetables (v. 2) and some (the same ones?) esteemed one day above others (v. 5). Others had no scruples against meat or vegetables and esteemed all days alike. The former were seen, apparently even by Paul, as weak in faith, and the others found their freedom not in indifference but in the strength of their faith. Paul seems clearly to identify with those whose faith freed them in matters of diet and calendar. Paul's concern was to get the two groups to respect one another, refraining from judgment as belonging to God alone.

The "weak" tend to be judgmental, finding those with a freer lifestyle to be guilty of sin. The "strong" tend to despise those who permit themselves to be restricted by scruples of diet and calendar. Paul wants each to make room for the other, each to test his/her own convictions and motives, and each to recognize that ultimately it is before God that we stand or fall, not before one another.

How do we preach this today? Several points seem clear.

Good and evil are not inherent in diet and calendars but are to be found rather in attitudes, feelings, motives, etc. Good and evil come to expression in the outer life of words and deeds, but their origin is from within. The scruples of the "weak" are to be respected, but this does not mean that the "strong" are to be indifferent to them. Some scruples, like racism or sexism, hurt innocent people. These scruples must be overcome. There is a richer life for those burdened by scruples, however sincere; and love's duty to the weak includes a creative relationship intended to free one from hangups with lesser matters and to awaken them to the issues that are more important. All of us need constantly to test our motives and values. We need to refrain from playing God, as though we were called to judge or despise one another. It is proper and possible for us to accept one another with respect and in that context examine the whole issue of right and wrong. What about a sermon here on "How to Get Along with People Who Bug Us."

Building Up and Not Tearing Down (14:13–23)

Paul is at his best here. This paragraph continues the discussion begun in v. 1. Paul is thorough, clear, and profound. This passage bears directly upon our existence. Paul does not hedge as to his own position; he personally rejects the idea that some foods are "clean" and some not. He is not dealing with matters of sanitation, nutrition, or health but with the nature of good and evil. Of course it is wrong to eat what harms the body, but we are not all helped or hurt by the same diet. We have different body chemistry or allergies. If one is allergic to cornbread, it is wrong for him to eat it. If it nourishes the body, it is right to eat it. As such, foods are neither good or evil, clean or unclean, kosher or non-kosher. How they affect us, how our habits affect other people, and whether our lifestyle is governed by conviction or indifference—these are moral issues.

"Common" and "clean/unclean" were religious terms in Paul's time. On arbitrary grounds a food could be declared acceptable or not, determined by religion and not by nature. Paul stands with Jesus in approaching good and evil from an entirely different perspective (cf. Mk 7:1–23). However, he holds that love is willing to relinquish personal rights where so doing avoids causing another to stumble or where it may be a factor in building up rather than tearing down the other. A sermon may be built on the theme, "Right Rather than Rights." Of course, care has to be exercised here. It is one thing for me to give up my rights but another to give away the rights of someone else, even as a concession to the weak. Paul refused to give in to scruples of the circumcised against eating with uncircumcised people (Gal 2:11-14). It does not follow that it is always right or salutary to give in.

Does what we think or feel make a thing right or wrong? Paul holds that it may. If I think it wrong to eat or do this or that, it is wrong for me. The wrong is in my willingness to do what I think is wrong. It is morally wrong to do what one thinks is wrong, however innocent the thing may be in itself. If we start down the road of "I think it's wrong but I'll do it anyway" there is no end to that road. If a quarter drops out of my pocket unknown to me and I pick it up and put it back in the pocket from which it fell, thinking that it is yours, I have stolen a quarter. Paul is right here: "What is not of faith is sin" (v. 23). He is right in saying, "All things are clean, but evil to the one eating by failing [his conscience])" (v. 20; see v. 14). It is important to respect conscience in ourselves and others; it is a duty to inform conscience in ourselves and others.

Where there are scruples over such things as diet and days they must be dealt with realistically, responsibly, and creatively. Ideally, these become non-issues in mature faith. The kingdom of God is not a matter of eating and drinking (pro or con) but of "righteousness and peace and joy" (v. 17). The immediate concern of the paragraph is mutual respect, especially that the strong be willing to relinquish personal privileges where others may be helped. This of itself is not enough. We have not yet arrived so long as we are hung up here. Most of the world is hungry. It is a sin for the church to spin its wheels over scruples while a world starves. There are such threats as pollution, war, disease, and lack of even basic freedoms. The church dare not exhaust itself over its intramural battles over things which in themselves are non-issues. If preaching can sort out the issues, assess them, and guide us toward righteousness, peace, and joy it will have justified its right to be.

The Mind of Christ in Concern for Others (15:1–6)

This paragraph has much in common with Phil 2:4–11. Each passage appeals to "the mind" of Christ, mind referring to attitude or disposition. Both passages have to do with Christians getting along with one another. In each passage Paul wants the "mind" which necessarily belongs to being in Christ to be activated in Christians' relationship with one another. In Romans the problem has to do with the strong and the weak in faith. Christ relinquished his high privilege and rights as he took the humble role of a servant and gave himself even unto death (Phil 2:5–11). Paul appeals to himself and those like himself as "the strong ones" to put aside personal advantage and give priority to the weak.

Mission to Jews and Gentiles
(Romans 15:7–33)

The letter proper closes with an impassioned plea for the very unity of Jew and Gentile which occasioned the letter and determined its character. Most of the letter was written to explain and vindicate Paul's dual commitment, to the Gentiles and the Jews. He sees himself and apparently was known as "priestly servant of Christ Jesus unto the Gentiles"(v.16). The letter is addressed primarily to Gentiles (1:13; 11:13). Paul had longed for years to visit Rome (v. 23), and he was firmly committed to Spain (v. 24) as his mission beyond everything from Jerusalem to Illyricum (modern Yougoslavia)(v. 19). But for the present everything must give way to an urgent mission to Jerusalem! (v. 25). Why? Gentiles would doubtless ask why. There is not a hint that anyone in Jerusalem, Jews or Christians, wanted Paul to visity them and much to indicate that they did not (v. 31). From Acts 21 we learn what happened when he reached Jerusalem—he was received with apprehension by James and other Christians and was thrown out of temple by some Jews and arrested by the Romans. Both Romans and Acts agree that it was anticipated by Paul and his friends that a visit by him to Jerusalem was a high risk. Why was Paul so determined to go? Did he make a mistake? Paul went because of an inner compulsion so strong that it overrode all fears, warnings, and the longing to be on his way to Spain by way of Rome. This is what Romans is all about: the apostle to the Gentiles could not divorce his commitment to his fellow-Jews from his commitment to the Gentiles. He would not because God did not, because Christ did not.

Christ's Ministry to Jews and Gentiles (15:7–13)

As in 14:1 Paul pled with "the strong" to "take to yourselves" the weak, so in 15:7 he pleads with all his readers: "Take one another to yourselves, just as Christ took you/us (mss. differ) to himself." The letter and the journey just ahead for Paul were concerned with just this, with special reference to Jews and Gentiles accepting one another, especially Jewish Christians and Gentile Christians. A split church was to him an anomaly. Rejection of Jew or Gentile was incompatible with his commitment as it was for Christ's.

V. 8 is foundational for the concern of Paul in Romans. Christ became a servant *(diakonos!)* of "the circumcision" in behalf of the truth of God, both confirming God's promises to "the fathers" and enabling the Gentiles to glorify God. Christ's mission was to both Jew and Gentile, and this was one mission, not two. Concern for Jew and Gentile was anticipated in the promises to "the fathers," in particular to Abraham, to whom were promised the nations (Gen 12:3; 18:18). The promises of God fulfilled in Christ's servanthood to all people is the solid foundation upon which Paul vindicated his embracing Jerusalem and Spain in one great mission.

A sermon here may be found in terms of God's purpose from the beginning to unite all people under one rule and to offer all the same hope (v. 12). The age-old problem of exclusion takes many patterns, but against all such must be the call, "Take one another to yourselves." In this is the fulfillment of hope, joy, peace (v. 13).

Paul's Ministry to Gentiles and Jews (15:14–21)

Paul's ministry is modeled upon that of Christ, to Jew and Gentile. Paul addresses the Romans as ones filled with goodness, knowledge, and power. Paul has not forgotten 1:18–3:20 with its devastating picture of the universality and radicality of human sin. Neither has he forgotten 3:21–8:39, with the picture there of what God can do in salvation. Paul is not afraid to recognize goodness in people. It is highly dangerous for one to think too much about one's own goodness, although a good self-image is highly important. One can be realistic about evil all around us and yet see goodness in people. Nature is not all "red in tooth and claw," for there is also in it the disposition to sacrifice for some other. Not all survival is that of the fittest; much that is weak survives because the strong give themselves up for the sake of others (cf. the parent bird protecting the young). There is goodness in human nature alongside the bad. Preaching needs to give a balanced view of human good and evil.

Jerusalem and Then Spain by Way of Rome
(15:22–33)

This concluding paragraph to the main body of Romans has been before us throughout our study, for it more than any other puts Romans in focus. This is not a postscript. Here Paul opens his heart and speaks directly about his immediate as well as long-range concerns, dreams, hopes, and even apprehensions.

"As I go to Spain" (v. 24). For years Paul has longed to visit Rome on his way to Spain. He feels that his work from Jerusalem to the borders of Illyricum has been completed, and he wants to push on into unexplored territory. He addresses the Romans as peers, with the prospect of mutual enrichment in their relationship (1:8–15). He wants their friendship, understanding, and backing in a mission which will take him both to Jerusalem and Spain. Apparently Paul had no assurance that the Romans were ready to receive him. We have nothing directly from them as to their feeling toward Paul. Without debasement to his own dignity, Paul is extremely tactful in cultivating this strategic church in Rome.

"But now I go to Jerusalem" (v. 25). The editors of the United Bible Societies' Greek New Testament show real insight in placing a long dash between vv. 24 and 25. Paul never finished the sentence in v. 24. It just breaks off. Yearning to go to Spain with Rome's help—he must go to Jerusalem. He must go "ministering to the saints." Explicit is "a certain *koinonia*" which Macedonia and Achaia (Greece) have made "for the poor among the saints in Jerusalem." Only in 1 Cor 16:1 does Paul refer to "the collection" by that term. Elsewhere he speaks of it in the higher dimensions of grace, *koinonia* (the common life in Christ, the shared life of Christians), fruit, ministry *(diakonia)*, self-giving, etc. (2 Cor 8–9). There were material needs in Jerusalem, and Paul gave major attention for some years to raising money from churches in various Roman provinces for the poor among the saints in Jerusalem. Hunger itself is a spiritual problem for Christian conscience.

But Paul was concerned for more than this. He hoped through this medium also to help Gentile and Jewish Christians to rediscover one another and accept one another. Once the money was collected, a committee could take it to Jerusalem if all at stake was transporting the money. But from the first Paul had seen that something more might be so sensitive that his personal involvement all the way to Jerusalem might be necessary (1 Cor 16:3–4). During the winter months in Corinth Paul came to the firm conviction that he must personally deliver the offering of the Gentiles to the Jewish saints at Jerusalem. He wrote Romans instead of going there, and he wrote to explain and justify his course of action as well as to enlist support in the intention behind his whole mission, inclusive of Jew and Gentile.

"They were pleased, and they are their debtors" (v. 27). Paul stressed two basic motives in giving: desire and duty. The Gentile churches "were pleased" to do this. Something in them responded to a situation of need, and they wanted to give. But Paul did not hedge on the aspect of duty. The Macedonians and Achaians owed it to the saints in Jerusalem. Their rich heritage in Christ came from these people. The *koinonia* included the sharing of "spiritual things" as well as material things. Even so, Paul did not see the gift of money as just material or carnal. He saw it as a "priestly ministry." He further calls it "this fruit." This offering was fruit which had ripened out of what in Christ they were becoming. It was a part of themselves which they were giving, not just money. There are rich themes for preaching throughout this paragraph, with the multi-relationships implied between person and person and even person and things.

"I beg you" (v. 30). High hopes and deep fears were mingled as Paul reached out to the Romans for their help. His confidence as to the awaited "fulfillment" is real, but so are his apprehensions that after all he may be rejected in Jerusalem. He implores them "to agonize" with him in their prayers to God for him. He is agonizing for two things: that he be delivered from the disobedient ones in Judea and that his "ministry" *(diakonia)* become acceptable to the saints. He had suffered much already at the hands of his own dear people, including beatings in synagogues (2 Cor 11:24), and he knew that his very life would be in danger in Judea. There was more. He had no assurance that he or the offering would be accepted by the saints in Jerusalem. Why? They knew Paul as the apostle to the Gentiles and many saw him as disloyal to their traditions and way of life. He was a Gentile lover. Paul knew that hungry people might reject money from Gentile hands.

This is why Paul must go to Jerusalem. This is why he wrote Romans. The missionary must put a pastoral priority ahead of the most exciting missionary journey he had ever dreamed of. A mission to Spain with a reconciling gospel would be undercut should he leave behind a split church. A split church is an anomaly. So it is today; it ever must be Jerusalem before Spain. In preaching here it should be easy to draw parallels. Sermons can show how what goes on or does not go on among us in local churches and/or in the larger church directly affects missions and evangelism or any outreach of the church.

In preaching from this closing paragraph, as from any of Romans, we should make it clear that it was one thing for Paul to write so freely about Jews in his time, both positively and negatively, but it is not that simple for us who are not Jews. Paul was a Jew and he was pro-Jewish, with a loyalty and love compelling him to write as he did. Preaching today dare not falsify history, yet it must guard against so dealing with the past as to encourage or condone anti-Semitism today. We can be honest with Paul and his situation and at the same time deal with our own present. Prejudice is universal, all of us being vulnerable to it. Likewise, any of us may properly be challenged to a higher quality of life where we discover our truest selves in discovering the other across chasms which may be as wide as those between Jew and Gentile in Paul's situation.

Personal Greetings
and Doxology
(Romans 16:1–27)

Whether a separate letter or a postscript original to Romans, these verses are highly significant. They take on new force now that the whole issue of woman is under reassessment in both church and world. Women are prominent in this passage, with no hint of subordination or denigration. They belong to the esteemed circle of those ministering to and with Paul. The paragraph is highly instructive for us as the primacy of the personal comes through with such clarity and force. People do matter. Warm personal relationships, esteem, affection, and mutual dependence are primary, not incidental, within the community of those under redemption. Add to that the far-reaching implications for women as belonging equally with men to this community of persons, and we have here far more than a postscript. Reflected here—existentially!—is the very *koinonia* for which Paul risked his life in going to Jerusalem and for which he wrote Romans.

"Phoebe . . . a deacon of the church in Cenchreae" (v. 1). The NT has no word "deaconess." *Diakonos* is the word for "deacon" in the sense of an order or office in Phil 1:1 and 1 Tim 3:8–13. Generally in the NT the term designates any servant or minister, with no implication of an office. Christ is *diakonos* (15:8), Paul sees himself along with Apollos as *diakonos* (1 Cor 3:5). Every follower of Christ is called to be *diakonos* (Mt 20:26). The ruler is God's *diakonos* (13:4). The men sent to draw water at Cana are "deacons" (John 2:5, 9).

In what sense, then, was Phoebe a "deacon." There is no way to know. She may have been a deacon in the sense of a special office or order. This can neither be demonstrated nor disproved. What is significant is that Paul could call her *diakonos* without apology or qualification. It may have been that as late as Romans the office of deacon was not yet firmed up. *Diakonos* may yet have implied no more than servanthood. If so, the diaconate as a recognized order is a late development. Is it proper to ordain women as deacons today? A better question has to do with ordaining anyone as deacon or otherwise. There is no solid case for ordination in the NT. It appears that if anyone is to be ordained as deacon or minister, women like Phoebe are as eligible as men. The whole question of ordination is obscure in the NT, with no indication that the ministry of the word of God required ordination. This probably grew as the church gradually evolved structures.

"Priscilla and Aquila" (v. 3). There may have been many husband and wife teams in some form of early Christian ministry, these two being among the most prominent. There were house churches, and husband and wife may have co-hosted or co-sponsored these churches. Priscilla is nowhere subordinated to Aquila; she is named first more often than he (Acts 18:2, 18, 26; Rom 16:3; 1 Cor 16:19; 2 Tim 4:19). Luke finds no problem in reporting that Priscilla and Aquila instructed Apollos more accurately in the way of God (Acts 18:26). The church moved more negatively toward women, but for most of the NT there seems to be no problem with women instructing men. Paul seems here to recognize Priscilla in the fullest colleagueship with himself and other servants/ministers of the gospel.

"Andronicus and Junias/Julia(?)" (v. 7). Manuscripts differ here, with no certainty as to whether Andronicus is linked with a man or a woman. The earliest extant manuscript of Romans (early third century) and other early witnesses have "Julia." If this is original, we have here another likely example of a husband and wife team. "Junias" prevailed in later traditions, understood as masculine; but this may simply reflect the male bias in the later church. Apart from the textual variant, there is an ambiguity in the syntax of "notable among the apostles." Does this mean only that the apostles esteemed them or that these two were apostles? The latter is possible if not probable. There is at least the possibility that Paul knew a woman (Julia) as an apostle. This cannot be pressed, and the colleagueship of women with men in ministry is secure in context apart from this possibility. Many sermons have been preached upon isolated texts in support of subordinating or even silencing women in church, but this chapter represents far more than a proof text in the opposite direction. It is solid evidence of the prominence of women alongside men in the pioneer work of the church (cf. Mk 15:40–41; 16:1–8).

"I Tertius" (v. 22). This verse not only enlightens us as to Paul's dependence upon scribal help, but it is a delightful protest against anonymity. Tertius has done the manual work at least (he may have been more than scribe) for Paul, and there has been a roll call of respected workers. But Tertius is somebody, too! He speaks up for himself, refusing to remain anonymous. Ample case has been made for self-denial, modesty, and all of that. Without in the least detracting from the self-denial which belongs essentially to the Christian calling, there is room for a balancing claim such as Tertius makes. A sermon could well be preached on "I Tertius." There is a self-love and self-respect which is wholesome and proper.

What about a sermon on "A Voice From the Silent Majority"? (1) All need to be noticed. One of the worst things we do to people is to ignore them. Even Paul in mentioning others may have taken Tertius for granted, forgetting the man at his side. (2) The silent ones often make contributions which need to be recognized. Paul needed Tertius. Our churches are filled with such "boiler room" persons. (3) Tertius offers an example to be followed, willingness to serve yet healthy respect for his own identity.

The beautiful doxology in 16:25–27 "floats" among the manuscripts, appearing variously: appearing here alone, here and following 14:23, after 14:23 alone, after 15:33, or nowhere. Whatever its origin, it points us to God whom we are to worship and calls us to the faith which obeys. A sermon here may show our proper linkage with the ages and with all nations in the worship of God grounded upon a faith which obeys him.

Bibliography

Tough reading but unsurpassed on the sin of man and the grace of God is Karl Barth's *The Epistle to the Romans* (New York: Oxford University Press, 1933). Emil Brunner's *The Letter to the Romans* (Philadelphia: Westminster Press, 1959) is very readable and sparkles with insight and expression. C. H. Dodd's *The Epistle of Paul to the Romans* (New York: Harper and Brothers, 1932) is a major contribution to the study, especially in uncovering the main theme of God's righteousness and interpreting "the wrath of God." C. K. Barrett's *A Commentary on the Epistle to the Romans* (New York: Harper and Brothers, 1957) is balanced and serviceable. Ernest Best's *The Letter of Paul to the Romans* (New York: Cambridge University Press, 1967) is brief but competent. He properly sets the letter with reference to Paul's last recorded mission to Jerusalem. For careful and detailed examination of the Greek text, William Sanday and A. C. Headlam's *The Epistle to the Romans* (New York: Charles Scribner's Sons, 1911) has been a classic. Currently rewritten by C. E. B. Cranfield, the level of research is maintained, but perspectives and conclusions are frequently subject to question.